DARK WATER FOUNTAIN

Navigating Cultural Chaos

DARYL FONTANA

Cover and book design by Asya Blue Design.
Photo credit Christopher Ian Bennett
Editor Laura Gean Stephenson

ISBN 978-1-7780174-0-7 Paperback
ISBN 978-1-7780174-2-1 Ebook
ISBN 978-1-7780174-1-4 Hard Cover

*I would like to dedicate this book to
Joseph Campbell, George Lucas, and all the young
aspiring Jedi from around the world.*

TABLE OF CONTENTS

INTRODUCTION

Writing this book did not come easy for me. I was a decent communicator and a lover of books, but I had no formal training other than two years of post-secondary education and the requirement that came with it to submit legible papers. Still, I was driven by a force so strong, I was compelled to become a writer, a purveyor of stories.

That force had grown out of a multitude of drivers: First and foremost, I wanted to satiate my desire for redemption and heal what felt like a fragmented mind. I had, at times, felt trapped inside myself and saw no way of escaping unless I dumped the load I was carrying. My hope is that if I confront my fears and add a voice via self-expressive storytelling, I might be able to narrow the divide between myself and the world of shadows I grew up loathing, with the ultimate desire to eliminate the dualism that exists between human and God.

For years I kept hidden what mattered most to me because I understood the repercussions that come with speaking truth, but I was acutely aware that keeping silent only exacerbated the internal conflicts I was dealing with.

Heart and mind were trapped in a vice that constantly applied equal amounts of pressure. My heart screamed to act on world issues, but my mind tempered those feelings with patience, what often felt like cowardice.

I justified my stratagem, content with biding my time until I was confident enough to speak out and deal with any prejudice I might encounter, believing there would be no backing down once I started the open rhetoric. Unfortunately, having my name and face plastered on the pages of national newspapers and getting coverage on TV news networks was attention that came years earlier and for reasons I did not anticipate. It took a decade before I was willing to reveal my story, playing a game that irked me, yet understanding its necessity, for it secured my safe passage.

Why now?

I gave myself twenty-five years to complete the most important goal of my life, waiting until my youngest child had reached his eighteenth birthday, concluding my primary responsibility in laying a solid foundation by training, empowering, and teaching my children to think for themselves. During this twenty-five year period of trials and tribulations, I asked for, and received, the important, though bone-crushingly painful at times, lessons and experiences I believed were needed to make me into the person I am today.

It took me five years to write this book. There was a lot to process, and it was at times cathartic. There was also a lot to plan for, as I not only had to work on creating the book but also had to anticipate potential fallout following its release and how I'm going to deal with that.

I contemplated how best to connect with the largest audience possible. I was aware that in telling this story, I could bring unwanted attention to people who prefer to remain anonymous. If I were to tell this story precisely as it unfolded, there would surely be a backlash that would prove costly to both myself and others. For that reason, I decided to weave fictional names of people and places into what is otherwise a real-life story. I am comforted knowing that I can be authentic and relay my tale without putting a target on the backs of others.

I apologize to anyone I have hurt over the years. I didn't set out to hurt anyone, and my reluctance to conform has cost me dearly. I hope this book will provide insight into some of the questionable decisions I made, though I do not offer them as an excuse. If I'm fortunate, I will be welcomed back to sit at your table.

Long ago, I accepted the belief that we all have value, that every soul that inhabits a body is a part of my family. My experiences, the evolution of my perceived reality, what has become my understanding of our collective history and how it shaped me is the same spiritual journey we are all on. I would like more of us to come together so we may contribute more fully, with intent, to affect meaningful change, as a new age dawns.

CHAPTER 1

FALLEN ANGEL

"Sometimes, it is necessary to do the wrong things for the right reasons. The important thing is to be sure that our reasons are right and that we admit the wrong. That we do not lie to ourselves and convince ourselves that what we do is right."

— *Gregory David Roberts*

April 26th, 2010 — 10:30 am

We are all exhausted, lying against the snow-packed bank on the mountain's summit that took us twelve hours to reach. No one utters a single word, as our mental capacity to engage had been challenged perhaps even more than our physical capacity. I have always taken pride in my ability to push through pain, but the feeling of euphoria that accompanied my past feats of mental-physical endurance escapes me. My watch says 10:30 am, still a couple of hours to go before we hit the rendezvous point. At least from this point on we will be travelling down instead of up.

My body beaten, I unclip the chest strap of my backpack before loosening the shoulder straps, welcoming the transfer of the load from my body to the frozen bank at my back. My shoulders roll forward, allowing my breath to slow; my concentration drifts for the first time in over twenty-four hours. Crisp air fills my lungs, the April chill expected at our elevation of 2500 metres, as I straddle the 49th parallel, which divides Canada from its neighbour, the US of A. This boundary line cuts through the heavily forested Cascade Mountain Range, including the little-known Liumchen Ecological Reserve and Mount Baker-Snoqualmie National Forest, with peaks that wear their snow until mid-July. We had trekked across well-worn animal trails surrounded by mountainous slopes of Douglas fir, hemlock, and red cedar, sharply aware that we shared the slopes with hungry black bears just emerging from hibernation.

We sit precisely on top of the imaginary line that separates the United States and Canada. Twenty feet south is hostile territory, the capital lands belonging to a behemoth of an empire. I'm consciously noting the symbolism of my defiance while entering the point of no return. It isn't too late to turn around and go back the way we came, although I know I would be on my own if I did so.

The covert operation that had us climb throughout the entire night and into the late morning was botched from the start, but I'm now too far gone to care. It wasn't the hike that did me in, though it exacerbated what I was already feeling mentally. For the previous two to three years, stress had been taking an increasing toll on my capacity for clear, focused thought. I felt my mind had been fried and wondered if I would ever be able to heal it, imagining the synapses in my brain as billions of tiny light bulbs on overload, burning out in bursts of a few hundred million in a shot. There was an all-out meltdown taking place, and I had no idea how to stop it.

There are two more hours to go before we would be in a warm vehicle with food and beverages, three hours to a hot shower and a comfortable bed, and twenty-four hours before I would be back home in the arms of my family. And soon I will be rid of the guy lying on my left.

It isn't every day you agree to go backpacking with somebody you don't like. But beggars can't be choosers, and two weeks earlier I had been down on my knees praying for divine intervention. Begging and praying are often the same when both are performed with absolute conviction, deep emotion, and the desire to change the direction in which one is heading, no matter the cost.

I shifted my attention to the two guys lying against the bank on my right, Chris and Sinisa. Their eyes were closed; their lungs were pulling in and exhaling deep, slow breaths. We were all hurting, but Sinisa was the worst for wear. His long black hair had fallen forward and hid his white, gaunt face. He hadn't uttered a word since we stopped ten minutes earlier.

I've had many adventures, workouts, and crazy training drills that would tax a few of the best modern-day warriors, but this excursion is ranking as one of the most difficult. The Iron Man triathlon I had done a year and a half earlier was in the same ballpark. But I had adequately prepared for the 3.8 km swim, 180 km bike ride, and 42.2 km marathon, whereas this event has been a shit-show from the start.

The pain I feel now is the same as I felt at the 10-hour mark of that race. My body had long passed the point of fatigue. I completed the last ten kilometres of the run focused on finishing ten-metres at a time. I remember looking into the eyes of a fellow competitor. He had stopped on the side of the road just a few metres ahead. Initially, I had no idea why he had stopped — perhaps he was injured or sick — but as I ran past him, I saw the void look in his eyes, the same look that Chris and Sinisa now had in theirs. The pupils are much darker, almost black, and have a depth that seems to go on forever. The conscious mind of the tortured individual retreats so far inside themselves they appear to be on the edge of death. And, in the case of these two unfortunate souls carrying half the load, the thought of death, though not welcome, probably held a promise of relief. They were lucky I brought extra supplies, as they ran low on water near the halfway mark. Neither brought electrolytes, and Sinisa brought little to no food.

I feel bad for these two mules who, like me, had been roped into doing something that went against their better judgment, having been manipulated and deceived with the promise of some quick cash for a job that should have been half the work. Helping them now was non-negotiable, for the guy responsible for their health and safety had abandoned his duties long before the trip ever began.

Rick, the guy responsible, sits on my left. He's mumbling.

"Are you talking to yourself, or you talking to us?" I ask. By this point, we all want to throw Rick off the mountain. As the hours passed, he became increasingly belligerent, cursing Sinisa, who was taking the brunt of his outbursts, for slowing the group down. Rick — our "team leader" — the chief manipulator who brought the three of us together, was driven by his own demons, and we were following him to Hell.

I shouldn't be too hard on the guy. His torments, his irrational behaviour, and his intense drive to push ahead when everything around him is pushing back is a mirror image of what I've been experiencing myself. He's an emotionally charged individual who can no longer contain his raw, instinctive momentum. I can relate to that.

I had first connected with Rick one week earlier, at a meeting arranged by a mutual "friend." Fredo assured me Rick was the real deal when it came to getting the job done, though he was a little high-strung, almost manic. "He's a bit of a cracker."

I was surprised when I got the call from Fredo. I crossed paths with him briefly a year before, at least six years since the last time I had seen him. We'd had some good times together. When I lived in Vancouver a decade earlier, I would occasionally venture out with him to take in the nightlife. He seemed to know every doorman at every club who would slip us in a side door to bypass the line.

A couple of weeks before Fredo reached out to me, my wife, Candace, had managed to swing an unreal deal for our family on tickets to an all-inclusive resort in Puerto Vallarta, Mexico. We needed time away together, as the past five years had flown by, with Candace and I both living at an insanely fast pace. The seventy-plus weekly hours managing my business, The Playground Health Centre was capped off with shuttling our kids between their multiple sports. I coached their soccer teams and volunteered for numerous organizations, including Search and Rescue. Candace, who was the president of our local Chamber of Commerce, had a similar schedule.

This vacation was a very much-needed break, but I needed much more than a brief interlude on a sandy beach. I was fried! I was no longer walking my talk. I was failing to keep up with the daily rituals that had served me so well for so long. I was way past the point of showing cracks in my armour; I was hemorrhaging.

And yet, knowing perfectly well I needed some downtime, I had said to Candace, "I should stay behind. We're low on funds, and the business is suffering."

"If we don't get some rest, we'll never make it through this. We need to recharge," she pointed out.

"Taking a week and sleeping it away would probably be the best thing for me."

"You might as well sleep it away on the beach in Mexico," she said.

CHAPTER 2

THE OFFER

*"The man who promises everything is sure to fulfil nothing, and every-
one who promises too much is in danger of using evil means in order
to carry out his promises, and is already on the road to perdition."*
— *Carl Jung*

February 26ᵗʰ, 2010

O ur flight was scheduled to depart Vancouver on the morning of
February 27th, so we needed to get to the city the night before,
as the ferries from Vancouver Island didn't leave early enough to
get us there on time. We arranged to stay the night with friends before
heading to the airport the following morning, giving us the opportunity
to check out the hype we'd been hearing regarding the Winter Olympics.
Fredo messaged me the day before we were due to leave for the city.

"Just shoot me a text when you're downtown, and I'll come find you," he said.

"I can't promise, but I'll see what I can do."

All the hoopla and excitement around the Olympic festivities had not been exaggerated. The streets were jam-packed with thousands of people, drinking spirits and smoking BC's finest herb. The word "electrifying" was what most people used to describe the feeling in those city streets at that time. Every corner had some form of high-quality entertainment, including many of the world's top street performers and giant video screens that replayed the highlights from the day's events. Sadly, I was not fully appreciative, as my mind was thinking of ways to keep our business afloat. As we made our way to the site of the Olympic torch, outside of the Vancouver Convention Centre, Fredo called

"Heyyyy, buuuuddddy! Are you over here yet?" He would often stretch out his hello, believing it to be more endearing,

"Yeah, we've been walking the streets for the past hour and a half. Where have you been? I messaged you as soon as we got here."

"Sorry, buddy, I was entertaining some friends and didn't get the message till now."

"Always the player," I quipped.

He lived the high life, drove fast cars, always had one or two beautiful women with him, and paid more attention to his grooming and wardrobe than any other guy I knew. I said, "We're heading back to our vehicles now. We need to get some shut-eye before we fly out in the morning."

"Where are you right now?" he asked. After I told him, he responded, "I'm five minutes from you. Hold tight, and I'll come to you?"

"I have my entire family and friends with me, bro. We'll probably have to connect when I get back, sorry."

"C'mon, buddy, I'm on my way now. I need to speak with you about something. It's important."

With the slight twisting of my arm, added to the prospect that the Universe could be providing me with the window of opportunity I was looking for, I agreed. "Ok! I'll meet you on the corner of Thurlow and

Burrard in five minutes." I ended the call and lowered my youngest son down from my shoulders, saying to him, "Make sure you hold your mom's hand." Candace gave me an inquisitive look, and I reassured her with a smile, saying, "I'll catch up with you guys right away."

The wheels in my head were turning, and I began imagining some magical offer that was going to take away my worries. Those wheels were spinning desperate dreams of salvation. From that point on, I continued to build momentum on what felt like a runaway train, with me chained to the front of it.

Five minutes came and went with no sign of Fredo. I was tired and in no mood to keep my friends and family waiting. I was not surprised that he was taking so long, as he was always on Fredo-time. However, we were in downtown Vancouver during the Olympics; perhaps I should cut him some slack. *I was always cutting someone slack.*

Just as I was about to turn and walk away, I saw a brand-new Audi A8 coupe pull up with its hazard lights on. The driver's door opened, and Fredo got out and started walking over to me.

"Buddy, where have you been?" he mockingly asked.

I had never considered Fredo one of my close friends, but he was someone I allowed to see a side of me few others had seen. As he approached, our eyes did the initial greeting, both of us trying to gauge how welcoming the other would be. We shook hands and gave the obligatory bro-hug.

He stepped back, smiling, "Where's the family?"

"Sorry, but they couldn't wait. Kids are fading fast, so they're making their way back to the vehicles."

We talked about the highs and lows of the past seven years. I explained I was caught in the grind, had never been so beaten up and worn down. "I'm not seeing the light at the end of the tunnel."

"I thought you were looking a little older," he teased.

"Thanks, you have no idea."

"You chose the Island life, buddy," he said.

"Yes, I did," I muttered, rolling my eyes.

Fredo went into full business mode. "I might be able to help put some cash in your pocket, quick."

"What is it?" I asked, not trying to conceal my skepticism.

"I need to confirm a couple of things with my partner first, and then I can run through the details with you."

"What does it involve?" My patience was wearing thin.

"Marijuana, bro, what else?" he said, as if surprised by my question.

I told him I had to get going, but if we didn't connect upon my return the following week, I would call him soon after.

"Make sure you do that," he said. We parted, and I ran to catch the group while thinking of all the cannabis-related things he could possibly want my help with.

I didn't call Fredo upon our return, as I had used the week in Mexico to dissuade myself from any notions of working with him, convinced my energy was best directed toward the business. However, he tracked me down six weeks later and convinced me to meet again. "I'm super-busy. If you want to see me, you're going to have to come here," I said.

Fredo flew to the Island two days later and laid out what he had in mind. He needed someone to round off his crew to backpack cannabis over the US border.

"There has to be four guys for it to work, and when you told me about your financial situation, I thought maybe this would be something you could do once or twice to pull yourself out of the hole."

I laughed. "I'm not in my twenties anymore. I have kids and a family. And don't try and tell me this has to do with my financial situation, as you had no clue how I was doing until I saw you in Vancouver seven weeks ago. This proposal is all about you needing someone to make this work."

"What does it matter? This would be a cakewalk for you. Everyone benefits."

"I'm sorry to have wasted your time, but this isn't what I had in mind," I said.

"What did you have in mind?"

"I thought maybe you were going to offer me a farm to run, something I could run from the Island while keeping my business running."

"You should never have quit the game. You're a great grower," Fredo said.

"No need to rub salt into my wounds. Believe me, it hurts."

"Just tell me you'll think about it. We're ready to go within the week."

"I'll let you know. That's the best I can give you, ok."

"You got it, buddy," he said.

Fredo texted me three more times that week, urging me to say yes. I messaged him the following week to say I was heading to Seattle for the weekend and could make a quick stop to hear more. Though I had told myself no, I was starting to justify why I should say yes.

The Black Eyed Peas were coming to Seattle, Washington, to perform at the Tacoma Dome. Their song "I Gotta Feeling" had a special place in my heart and the collective hearts of two families we had been spending a considerable amount of time with, including the recent trip to Mexico. We danced hard to this song the summer before when our families had made a weekend trip to Whistler. The parents — Marnie, her husband Trevor, J and his wife, Lori, Candace, and I — went out on Saturday night, leaving our teenage daughters in charge of looking after their younger siblings. We were together as one large group, dancing in the middle of the crowd when that song came on. It was the first time most of us had heard it. Halfway through the song, I leaned over to Marnie, who had been feeling low-spirited due to recently losing a close friend, and said, "She is smiling down on you right now, happy you are with people who love you. It was a beautiful moment and a great night.

When it was announced that the Black Eyed Peas were coming to a venue close to us, Candace, Marnie and Lori decided to organize a weekend getaway, this time without our kids. But I hadn't been doing well and felt reluctant to do this trip too. Though these trips seemed like a good idea, I didn't feel they were conducive to getting the rest I needed.

My thoughts were on the meeting. In one week, I had allowed myself to switch from a solid no to a strong maybe.

I asked Trevor, who was driving, if we could stop for a quick coffee at the Starbucks in Tsawwassen, BC, only ten minutes' drive from the ferry terminal and half an hour from the Peace Arch Border Crossing. I wasn't hiding the meeting with Fredo, but I wasn't forthcoming about it either. I should not have asked my friends to make that stop, involving themselves involuntarily in something they may not have approved of. Nevertheless, I was now committed and proceeded to move ahead with the scheduled appointment.

Fredo was late again. I had been clear with him that he had to be punctual, as I, for obvious reasons, didn't want to keep the group waiting. When he finally showed up, he had his usual, cocky smirk on his face.

"Late as usual," I chided.

"Sorry, buddy, I had a meeting that I couldn't get out of." He said it like he meant it, so I decided to save my energy and let it go. Besides, time was ticking.

"So, what is it you couldn't tell me over the phone?" I asked.

Just as he began to open his mouth to explain, I received a text from Candace: "What's taking you so long?" I texted her right back and asked her to bring everyone over to meet Fredo. The seconds were ticking away fast, and our time to talk would soon be over. I said, "You have five minutes. Go!"

"Rick is the main man. He's experienced, a bit of a cracker, but he gets the job done. He has two friends, both rookies, but they're said to be up to the challenge. One of them is committed; the other isn't sold on the idea."

"Why?"

"He doesn't trust Rick. He's known him for a long time and thinks he's a little unstable."

"Are you serious? And you're bringing this to me? Come on, I'm hurting, but I'm not dead yet," I said.

"Hey, I'm just telling you like it is. Supposedly, once you have him on the mountain, he's the man. Chris said he would consider it after meeting the fourth guy."

"And I'm the fourth guy, right?"

"I told Rick I knew someone who could do this in his sleep."

"What did you tell him exactly?"

"That you're an animal. You did the Iron Man, you know how to navigate, and I think I told him you can live in the wild."

"Do you think you may have exaggerated?"

At that moment, Candace and the group walked around the corner. Our friends looked curious about the obviously secretive meeting that had just taken place.

"I'll let you know," I said and went directly to making introductions.

Few questions were asked about who Fredo was, but it was evident that he was a high-rolling player. If his $700 sweater and $20,000 watch didn't catch their attention, then his car certainly did. We parted ways, and my group headed for the border.

The weight that had descended upon me months before now felt crushing. I was finding it difficult to breathe. The group talked away, laughing and being silly, while I closed up tighter than ever before. As soon as we crossed the Peace Arch Border, we stopped at a convenience store and picked up some beverages. I drank close to a dozen beers in the space of two and a half hours, something I hadn't done since my teens. True, they were American beer, but I'm a guy who usually caps his intake at three.

Everyone, save Candace, just thought they were getting to see a crazier, fun side of me, and they were, but it was more crazy than fun. There was a war raging inside of me, and I was fighting what felt like a losing battle, spiralling further downwards into the abyss. I wanted to tell them what Fredo had suggested, but I didn't want to detract from the good times they were having. I didn't want them to be burdened by the weight I was shouldering. This journey was my Balrog; this was my struggle.

Once we returned from Seattle, I was right back at it, working my scheduled classes and individual clients over a fourteen-hour day. The first day back, I had a three-hour window with no clients booked. I decided to drive home to try and get some sleep. Having spent the last five years sleeping only five to six hours per night and doing high-intensity training for three hours or more every day, I wasn't too surprised when I developed insomnia.

As soon as I got home, I headed straight to my bedroom and laid down on my bed. I made sure to lay on my right side so I could look out the French doors, which gave me a view of our backyard. Our home was surrounded by a large forest, inhabited by all the creatures you typically find on Vancouver Island: black bears, elk, rabbits, deer, and even cougars. This view of the trees had always provided me with peace and the ability to relax, but no longer. I took comfort in knowing that, even though I didn't feel at ease, there still existed a reality I was once a part of; a perspective that connected me to the union of nature. *I will get it back*, I assured myself.

I tried to relax, but my brain wouldn't shut off. It was mulling over the same thoughts repeatedly, picking apart decisions I had made, ruminating over things I should have paid more attention to, thinking about every possible avenue that could lift me out of despair. I felt pathetic. I felt weak. The emergency brake I desperately needed was only going to come now in the form of someone or something else stepping in. Little did I know that an intervention was indeed coming.

I lay there for half an hour without one wink of sleep. Not wanting to waste more precious time, I decided to return to work. As soon as I rose to my feet, I felt the flicking of a switch inside me, like a five-hundred-pound wet blanket being draped over my shoulders. Instantly, I crumpled to my knees. Tears began streaming down my face. I squeezed my eyes tightly, pressing my clenched fists into them, trying to hold the tears back, but it was no use.

In that moment, I prayed as I had never prayed before. I tightly cupped my hands in front of my chest and squeezed with all my strength. "Please make it stop. Please make it all stop." I pleaded to the space that existed outside of me, as much to the depths of the abyss inside. "I don't care how you do it, just, please… make it stop." I knelt there on the floor in silence, unable to move, for another ten minutes before I could compose myself.

I picked myself up and returned to work.

This episode was one of a handful of moments during this period when I nearly burst. Months earlier I had showed up for work one morning to lead the 6:00 am Boot Camp class. Halfway through my demonstration of the class exercises, I froze for what was only a few seconds but seemed like an eternity. I looked up at the twenty people who were staring back at me and said, "Excuse me," before walking out of the room to the front desk, where I found Monni, a trainer who worked for me. I asked her to run the class, then bolted home to hide beneath my bedcovers.

I knew I needed help, but I didn't know how to receive it. A one-week trip to Puerto Vallarta barely helped, drinking twelve beers in two and a half hours wasn't going to plug any holes, and backpacking marijuana was going to do what for me?

~⊙

The following Monday morning's class was geared toward hitting the whole body, emphasizing cardio. I got off to a great start, but halfway through round two, I started to feel an ache in my left testicle. It came on slowly, but within ten minutes the pain had increased significantly, to the point that it forced me to exit the class early. It was uncharacteristic of me to quit something halfway through, but I was worried that I had somehow twisted the testicle and would make it worse by continuing. So strange. I had never done something like this before.

Despite my extreme discomfort, I decided to push on with the day, which included a return trip to Vancouver. The drive to the ferry that morning nearly had me in tears, as the pain was excruciating. I came close to turning around on three separate occasions but stubbornly drove straight ahead. By the time I made it to Vancouver, I was exhausted. The pain had not subsided, and I was now soaked with perspiration. I could not sit comfortably, or, for that matter, even walk properly. "What the fuck!" I screamed while gripping the steering wheel with all my strength. "This is not the life I envisioned."

I called Fredo to let him know I was in the city and willing to meet with his associate. He called me a couple of minutes later to say it was arranged. I was to meet Rick at the Starbucks near the Olympic torch in half an hour.

The Starbucks in question was only a couple of minutes away from my location, so I had time to get there ahead of him and set myself up with ice in a doubled zip-lock bag that the barista was kind enough to provide me. I sat down on a big comfy chair with ice on my balls and a warm mocha in my hand. Ahhh, the ice provided some relief.

Sinking further into the chair with my head dropped back, I allowed my eyes to close and my mind slowly began to drift, the voice in my head asking the same nagging questions that had been tormenting me the last month: *Where did I go wrong? Where did my passion for life go?* I nodded off into a semi-conscious time-out.

When I opened my eyes, I noticed some dude approaching from my right. He was looking right at me, and I was sure this was the guy. I began to get up, gently removing the ice bag.

"Hi, you must be Daryl," he said.

I half smiled back, "How did you know?"

"When I first came in, you had your eyes closed, and I walked by you. I noticed how chiselled your legs were; figured you must be the guy."

"Reasonable and accurate assumption. Nice to meet you," I said.

"Likewise," he said as he took the chair across from me.

I didn't hesitate, looked him dead in the eye, and asked him to explain, in detail, what he was offering. For the next twenty minutes, he explained the mechanics of transporting 108 pounds of marijuana from Canada into the US by hiking it through the Cascade Mountains. It required four people to backpack twenty-seven pounds each for a non-stop fifteen-hour gruelling hike. He had two other guys lined up; one was committed, the other still sitting on the fence. I asked him to give me the low down on them both.

The first guy, Sinisa, was a refugee from Croatia who had minimal experience and had only been training for this excursion for two months. Rick assured me that even though it wouldn't be easy for him, he would be able to push through to the end. The guy sitting on the fence, Chris, a senior marketing manager for one of Canada's top communications firms, supposedly had a wealth of knowledge and experience. He had recently climbed to Everest's base camp and was a fitness enthusiast.

I asked Rick about his own experience, and he said he knew the trail well.

"It's tough. I have no problem with it, and from what I understand, neither would you."

"What would you compare it to?" I asked.

"Have you ever hiked the Grouse Grind?"

The Grind is a popular trail on Grouse Mountain in North Vancouver. The path is just shy of three kilometres long with an elevation gain of 853 metres straight up the face. My record time, when I was in my late twenties, was a little over thirty-four minutes. It became one of my best physical accomplishments when I could still bench press 315 pounds and squat 455 pounds. When my daughter, Mariah, turned three months old, I started packing her up Grouse, nestled in against my chest. At six months, I switched her to my back so she could see more of what was going on. I packed her up every week until she was about two-and-a-half years old, at which point, refusing to be carried any longer, she wanted to do it on her own. We were carrying on a family tradition, literally following in the footsteps of my great-grandfather, who, fifty years earlier, hiked the Grind every week with my mother strapped to his back. According to Mom, it was on Grouse Mountain that she was taught the language of trees, stones, and running water.

Once a week, my good friend Richard and I would wear our weight vests to the top, take the gondola down, then go up again without the vests. I was grateful to have the richness of this forested area in the backyard of one of Canada's most incredible cities.

There are few things more rewarding than the ability to set and achieve physical goals you can measure. The attainment of your projected vision of near perfection is bliss. Keeping my thoughts to myself, I stated, "I used to hike it three to four times a week."

"This is like doing six to eight Grouse Grinds with forty pounds on your back," he said.

"Are you serious!?"

"Yeah, but the good news is, this is what makes it such a safe route to take. Few people ever attempt this trail, so it's never monitored."

Until now, I had been teetering toward saying yes to joining his team, pending my meeting his two friends, but any apprehension I had immediately doubled. His over-zealousness to impress me with his past triumphs, and his attempt at reassuring me that this would be smooth sailing, didn't jibe with his almost manic behaviour. While we talked, he constantly interrupted our conversation to send or read a text message on one of his two phones.

I try not to judge people, but at the same time, it's essential to at least qualify them. Rick was a forty-year-old hairdresser who lived and worked in downtown Vancouver. He had been subsidizing his income by packing weed across the Canadian border into the US. I could tell he was fit by the shape of his body and the leanness of his face. He was shorter than me, no taller than five feet eight, and he jabbered, rarely waiting to allow me to jump in with any of the questions I had.

I told him I was noncommittal, that I would need some time to think it through. I wanted to leave and catch the next ferry home. This day was wearing me down, and it could not end soon enough.

"How about meeting the other two guys right now?" he asked.

"Why not?" I replied, stupefied that I could so easily dismiss my strong desire to get out of there. He grabbed his phone and put his thumbs into high gear, sending messages to the other two initiates, telling them where and when to meet us. Chris could not join us on such short notice, but I would meet Sinisa within the hour.

I liked Sinisa well enough, but after spending forty-five minutes with him in the Mountain Equipment Co-Op store, looking at climbing gear and discussing the job, he added weight to the reservations I already had. I asked him a few questions about his climbing experience, fitness level, and general thoughts on the operation. Through his dark eyes, he exuded an intensity I later learned came from his younger years growing up in war-torn Bosnia. Sinisa, tall and thin, had very distinct Serbian features. He was an artist-musician with long, black hair that he kept in a ponytail. He had made his way to Canada in 2005 and was now only months away from receiving his Canadian citizenship. I could appreciate the fact that the guy had pushed through some dark days, but living through the Bosnian war of the early 1990s and three months of hiking the Grouse Grind in Vancouver, even two days a week, was not going to prepare him for what lay ahead.

Meanwhile, Rick was looking at climbing bags and other accessories he would need to outfit this excursion. He was trying his best to convince me that joining the group would be a good decision, promising that if Sinisa needed help, he would take care of him, even if it meant carrying his entire load. The more he tried to persuade me, the less I wanted to go.

"Are you in?" he asked enthusiastically, with a shifty grin on his face.

"There's nothing more for me to see. It's time to go home," I shrugged.

"Come on, you're made for this!" he said.

I paused for a beat before answering. "Listen, I have no problem with cannabis, just the laws around it that govern us. I'm not morally opposed; I just don't feel comfortable doing it."

"Ok, what else do you need?" he asked.

"I need some certainty."

"...and?"

My patience was gone. "Look, you say you're ready to go now, but you don't even know what the day will be. I haven't seen a map of the area we're hiking. I haven't met this other guy, who you say is still sitting on the fence. And frankly, your second guy doesn't look up to this."

"Chris is just nervous, this isn't his thing, but if he meets you, he'll do it. I know it. And I assure you, Sinisa will be ready for this. You have my word."

Funny, looking back, I can see now how naïve I was. Over the years, I had been guilty of accepting much of what other people presented as truth, too often placing too much stock in a person's word. I needed to be clear.

"The only way this will work for me is if we leave next Sunday. I must be back in Vancouver no later than Wednesday, preferably Tuesday, depending on my meeting with Chris that day. I need a map of the area, and you need to assure me that you are fully equipped with everything you need."

"I can't guarantee our departure would be Sunday, I have…"

"Then I can't do it."

"Ok, I'll make it work, but I'll have to make some sacrifices in my personal life to do so."

"Listen, I'm not telling you what to do. I'm just telling you what I need and what my expectations are. I'll come next Sunday, fully prepared to go."

He gave me a time and place to meet, and said he would arrange for Chris to be there. I shook hands with both Rick and Sinisa, then left.

On my way back to the ferry terminal, the pain in my testicle subsided. By the time the ferry arrived at its destination, the pain was entirely gone.

CHAPTER 3

RENDEZVOUS POINT

"Can we talk of integration until there is integration of hearts and minds? Unless you have this, you only have a physical presence, and the walls between us are as high as the mountain range."
— Chief Dan George

April 26th, 2010 — 10:48 am

Rick presses himself off the bank and glances at us. "We have two more hours to go." I pride myself in having at least a basic level of respect for all human beings, but Rick was thoroughly testing my way of thinking.

Sinisa moves to my right as he angles himself forward, turning to face Rick. He works up the strength to make his mouth move, straining to make his words come out.

"How much further?" His words are barely audible over his laboured breath.

Rick points down in what I thought to be a southwest direction as he says, "Two more hours down this way, then we'll be at the pickup location."

The last sign of hope in Sinisa's eyes drains away. He's past the point of despair. He had hit bottom five hours earlier and is now sitting there, unblinking, as if waiting for an ending to Rick's last sentence that would include the words " ... by way of a snowmobile." At that moment, I hear a mosquito buzzing near my ear. But I know it is way too cold and far too early in the season.

"Do you guys hear that?" I ask. Chris and Sinisa are too far gone to focus on listening to something that easily could be the wind, but Rick straightens up, straining to hear, his right ear cocked toward our path.

"Yeah, I think I hear something too," he says.

I try to filter out the sound of the wind as we listen for a few more minutes, but nothing changes. "I don't feel good about this," I say.

"It's probably the wind," Rick says.

I look over to Chris and Sinisa for their input, which proves scant.

Chris shrugs. "Beats me, mate. I didn't hear anything."

"Sinisa?" I ask, thinking if he too heard the mechanical hum, we're heading back home.

"Let's get going. It was probably nothing," he says.

Rick stands up, "Ok, move out. We already wasted enough fucking time."

His agitation is glaringly apparent. *What a prick!* After everything he's put us through, he's still lamenting over the mutiny that was quelled the night before. I turn and face Chris and Sinisa while pushing myself onto my feet, prodding the two men softly. "We're so close. Just one foot in front of the other, and we'll be home before we know it."

By the time Sinisa is up on his feet, Rick is gone. He's made this trek many times before, and now he's tasting the finish line. I so badly wanted to beat him. How could he leave his team to fend for themselves? Why didn't he lighten some of Sinisa's load as he had promised he would? For the next two hours, I slog through the snow, continuing to encourage Sinisa to keep up with us. Like the Iron Man two years earlier, the finish line was tangible, yet the outcome was unclear. *Where did I go wrong?*

12:32 pm

The rendezvous point is nearing, the snow is now only about ten centimetres deep, making each step easier. Chris, who has kept silent for the last hour, is holding his pace, whereas Sinisa is trailing too far behind for me to see him, as he keeps stopping every fifty feet to catch his breath and rest his legs. I am anticipating having to carry his pack the last leg. The solitude and peacefulness of being far from civilization have always been a welcome pleasure whenever I escaped to the mountains. Now I longed for the noise of city life. *Wait a second.*

I stop and hear the same low, mechanical hum I heard earlier. My mind must be playing tricks on me. I had just wished for the automation and mechanics of the modern world, and now my imagination is conjuring them up to help make me feel better. I stand still. No, I'm not imagining it. I can hear something.

"Chris," I whisper, "do you hear that?"

"I don't hear anything."

"Stop walking." The hum is getting a little louder. Chris looks at me, and his eyes widen as I rouse him out of his dream world.

"I think I hear it."

I yell at him, "Move quickly to that tree line. Hurry!" The hum intensifies, sounding more like a thump-thump as it comes up the mountain, straight toward us. "It's a helicopter!" I say. "Move!"

We're in an open clearing with no cover, and the closest protection from eyes above is a thick blanket of trees thirty to forty metres ahead of us. The thump-thump is fast approaching. Are we going to make it? Ten metres to the tree line. The menacing thump-thump is now a whooshing sound. Five metres to the tree line.

The helicopter passes directly over top of where we had been exposed in the open less than five seconds before. I don't think we've been spotted, but our fresh tracks in the snow assure me the Border Patrol will be driving here fast.

"Chris, we have to get out of here! We have to head back now," I say, knowing I'm asking for the near impossible.

"I can't go back. I have nothing left."

His look of despair and hopelessness is convincing, and my brain scrambles for another solution. I consider dropping my pack and going back on my own but leaving Chris isn't an option. There is still no sign of Sinisa, and the chopper is now long gone. *Come on, brain, think!* We are utterly exhausted, but I am fired with a massive spike of adrenaline, wanting to run straight down the mountain.

"Do you think you can manage going down if we ditch the packs?" I ask him.

"I can't do it, man. Let's wait and see if our ride comes up to meet us."

"Fuck! Fuck! Fuck!" I look up, but no answers are coming down from above. "Ok, we're going to get rid of our packs and then go see if we can find Rick."

Chris mumbles an "ok" in agreement, and we begin removing our snowshoes. We detour thirty metres into the bush and down the mountain before throwing our packs over a bank. We trudge back up to the path and walk toward the meeting spot, keeping close to the tree line just in case we need to jump for cover again. *Where did I go wrong?*

CHAPTER 4

ROOTS

"As we look back and survey the terrain to determine where we've been and where we are in relationship to where we are going, we clearly see that we could not have gotten where we are without coming the way we came."

— *Stephen Covey*

The biggest influence in my life was my mother — the eldest of seven, a mother to three sons, and a wife to four husbands. I cannot aptly describe my mom without exploring the branches from whence she came. Through her father, Arthur John, she was descended from Clan Douglas, our family history I didn't come to know until I was much older. The stories passed down through her mother's line were shared with me the most. My great-great-grandparents, Bertram and Catherine Nye, moved their family from Brighton, England, in 1894, to North Vancouver. Bertram was a remittance man. Known for his drinking and foul temper, he became the magistrate for the area, the chief constable in law enforcement. Supposedly, Catherine's mother was a Black woman, but such things were not talked about during those days.

Bertram and Catherine had seven children. The two oldest boys fought in the Second Boer War and were given large land grants for their service, including 160 acres in Lynn Valley, North Vancouver, that went to my great-grandfather's older brother, Jack. Jack followed in his father's footsteps, becoming heavily involved in the community, sitting on the board for many organizations, and becoming the police commissioner. It was said he was a much kinder man than his father.

My great-grandfather George Gordon Nye was the baby of the family. I suppose it was good fortune that he was too young to fight in the Boer War with his brothers and too old to fight in The War to End All Wars. George never attained the level of public stature that his brother Jack did, but he was considered a pioneer of photography. He captured the growth of Vancouver between 1905 – 1908 in a collection of photos that was years later published in a book called *The Boom Years*.

Every family experiences a tragedy that can affect generations to come. In 1926, George's wife, Bertha, went into labour with their fourth child. There were complications with the delivery that my great-grandfather wasn't equipped to handle on his own. Due to a bad storm, the doctor was delayed getting to the house. George did everything he could to bring the full-term baby girl into the world, but both she and Bertha died before the doctor arrived.

Months later, George's son, Gordon, started working for a woman named Helen, who had recently moved to British Columbia from Ontario with her young daughter, Grace. Helen was a fierce and attractive woman, half Cree and a quarter each of Scots and Irish. When she was three years old, her father remarried, and her new stepmother sent her to a residential school because she didn't want a "half-breed" living under their roof. She returned to the family home after her stepmother decided she needed help raising Helen's younger siblings.

Gordon urged Helen to meet his father, hoping she would bring a woman's touch to their family home, something that had been missing since his mother's passing, and within months they were married. Not long after, tragedy struck the family again when seventeen-year-old Gordon recklessly drove out into a stormy night and crashed his motorcycle. He passed away four months before his baby sister, my nana, was born.

My mother spoke highly of Nana Nye and her father's mother, Nana Tru. They were educated ladies, held in high esteem in their community. They delighted in teaching my mother the ways of the world, lessons that I too would eventually benefit from.

My grandfather Arthur John Douglas exemplified in many ways what it means to be a Peter Pan Man. He was intelligent, slightly narcissistic, and refused to entirely grow up, though he was only fifteen years of age when he took his older brother Paul's identification and joined the Merchant Marines. He spent months at sea, crisscrossing the Pacific and Atlantic Oceans, visiting countries all over the world. He shared many stories, one of which was witnessing the liberation of the Netherlands in May 1945.

World War II brought tremendous suffering, impacting the lives of millions of people. My grandfather lost his only two brothers in 1943 and 1944, and had it not been for the nurses who took such good care of him following an accident in post-war Shanghai, he too may have succumbed to his injuries.

My grandfather became involved in the Seamen's Union following the war, joining the labour movement, which started a decade of great political rebellion. Many people he knew who were involved in the labour movement had gone missing, which pressured him to tone down his rhetoric and focus on building a life for his family.

My grandparents and their children moved to Vancouver Island in 1962. For my mother, a girl of thirteen accustomed to time spent in a metropolitan city that connected to the rest of the world, this move was life-changing. The family eventually settled in a town called Duncan, in the Cowichan Valley.

My father, Daryl John Fontana, was born April 15th, 1924, in Ladysmith, BC, to Joseph (Joe) and Myrtle Fontana. My grandfather Joe was a first-generation Canadian. Both his parents immigrated to the fledgling western Canadian logging and mining town of Nanaimo, BC, from Italy in 1897. I was told my grandfather was a charismatic and charming young man who got a lot of attention from young women. He was an exceptional athlete, hunter, and fisherman, and he was decorated for his service in the Canadian Army during World War I.

It didn't take long for love to strike Joe after the fiery, red-head, Myrtle Cosier, a nineteen-year-old woman from eastern Canada made her way to the rugged west coast with her family.

Myrtle and Joe were blessed with two children, my father and his older brother, Raymond (Ray), and may well have had more if not for a tragic logging accident that claimed Joe's life when my dad was a little more than two years old. I never met Grandfather Joe, but as a boy I felt he was always watching over me. Grandmother Myrtle later married a man named Robert (Bob) Boyd. Even though she came to love Bob, I believe her heart always belonged to Joe.

Bob moved his new family out of the heart of Nanaimo, half an hour south, to a coal mining community called Extension. You can't fault Bob for making this move, as it allowed him to be much closer to his work-place, where he worked as a mechanic. Still, it sadly meant that Ray and Daryl were no longer spending consistent quality time with their loving grandparents Joseph Sr. and Asunta Fontana, who were the bedrock of the family, and closely tied to a large swath of their community.

The 1930s were challenging to say the least for many people, but Dad's family rarely went without. You could be sure both Daryl and Ray were dressed suitably, as Gramma was known to fuss over their appearance — and sure their social conduct reflected that appearance. Dad came of age during the last half of World War II. Following in Ray's footsteps, who had joined two years earlier, dad joined the Royal Canadian Air Force in 1943. He was stationed in Edmonton for his basic training, then spent four months in Montreal before shipping out to England, where he served his country and the Allied forces in what he described as a life-changing experience.

He flew thirty-nine operational sorties over France and Germany with Squadron 420, nicknamed Snowy Owl, and Squadron 425, known as the

Alouette. As a gunner, his job was to protect the plane he was flying in and the Allied planes surrounding him when possible. Dad told of his good fortune, recalling only one time his aircraft took heavy fire. He had leaned forward to loosen the laces of his boot when the back of his seat, the place where he rested his head, was ripped open by shrapnel.

During the course of the war, 364,514 operational sorties were flown, one million tons of bombs were dropped, and over eight thousand aircraft were lost in action. Bomber Command aircrews suffered a high casualty rate: 45 percent of the 125,000 aircrew were killed. Flying high in the sky in the middle of the night on bombing runs, accompanied by hundreds of other Allied planes while being shelled by forces on the ground, was an experience like no other. For years, Dad kept his memories to himself. He had played a part in delivering misery and destruction to innocent victims who were trapped by the policies and politics of others, and he was painfully aware of the far worse conditions his fellow countrymen faced in the trenches.

My father was a practical man, which helped to make him a good officer. His duty to perform never once coming into question.

Following the war, Dad stayed on as a trainer with the Royal Canadian Air Force. After two more years of service, he journeyed home and escaped into the wilderness, hoping to re-establish a sense of normalcy in his life, returning to the activities that had always given him great pleasure— hunting small game on Vancouver Island and moose and caribou in the Interior. He was happiest with a fish pole in his hand or a rifle strapped across his shoulder while traversing the pristine wilderness, the "Garden of Eden," he called it, believing his generation was going to be the last to experience Paradise.

My father got his good looks and ability to make everything he did look easy from his father, Joe. Those attributes, combined with his concern about his appearance and attention to detail, instilled in him by his mother, gave him a movie star persona and a flare that suited the hotel industry, which he moved into in the years following his return from combat. I wondered whether these qualities were as much a hindrance to him as they were a benefit.

My father had difficulty bridging his desire for comfort and companionship with his desire to be free and independent, which included the many games and events he both participated in and watched. The length of his marriage to my half-sister's mother: they were married for five years, constituted the longest love relationship of his life.

As I noted earlier, my father moved into the hotel industry and managed many establishments during their prime. He was there for the inception of the Village Green Hotel, which opened in Duncan, 1970. The Village was a central hub, linking the movers and shakers from British Columbia, Washington State, and Oregon State, people who relied on my father for his discretion and provision of a safe haven. Dad enjoyed being at the centre of it all, by forty-six years of age, he had lived a full life.

My mom was twenty-one with two small boys at home when she took a waitressing job at the Village Green Inn. She was beautiful and intelligent, and she possessed a sharp tongue she was not afraid to use. It didn't take long for the two of them to zero in on each other. The failings of previous romantic relationships didn't dissuade her from looking for a partner who could check most of her boxes. My father, a pro-business conservative, was twenty-five years her senior. My liberal-minded, left-leaning mother came from an embattled family who strongly supported labour and the New Democratic Party. The attraction between them went beyond the physical, but there was no shared passion in the things that made them sing. Their differences were exacerbated by the complexities of a newly emerging world. My mother felt as if the world was pulling itself apart, and my father saw the operation of a mega-machine making progress, albeit clumsily at times.

The Cold War, and its two main political ideologies, capitalism and communism, was being waged throughout every region of the planet. A game of chess involving multiple players, impacting the lives of billions, and sandwiching people between opposing ideologies, horrifically at times, who wanted no part of this global domination game. All eyes had been on Castro and the Bay of Pigs, followed by Kennedy's assassination in 1963 and the US flooding into Vietnam. Throughout South America, the Middle East, and Africa, democratically elected politicians were being assassinated and replaced by puppet dictators who supported foreign business interests, in effect giving their countries' resources away for pennies on the dollar. Lumumba, Dag, JFK, Che, MLK, RFK, Malcolm, Hampton, and scores of others were eliminated for posing a threat to the now firmly entrenched establishment.

The months leading up to my birth were not short of big moments. NASA sent the *Mariner 9* to begin mapping Mars and sending out probes to look for oncoming traffic that could mean big-time disaster for planet Earth. In the first week of January 1972, the Irish Republican Army (IRA) exploded a bomb in Callender Street, Belfast, injuring over sixty people. The month ended with what became known as Bloody Sunday, with the British Army ultimately killing fourteen unarmed civilians.

On January 31st, there was a military coup in Ghana, which ousted the civilian government. On the same day, the US launched *HEOS A-2* for interplanetary observations, while John Lennon was getting under the skin of some high-ranking officials.

Richard Nixon became the first US president to visit China, opening the doors for American businesses to move in and utilize, some say exploit, cheap Chinese labour, advancing the age of corporatism and growing trans-corporate hegemony.

The United States continued nuclear testing at the Nevada National Security Site, a US Department of Energy reservation located about 100 kilometres northwest of Las Vegas. The residents of Las Vegas not only felt the seismic activity but also saw the mushroom clouds from the downtown hotels. St. George, Utah, received the brunt of the fallout, as the wind carried the radioactive material straight through southern Utah. A notable increase in cancer was reported from the mid-1950s through 1980, eventually leading to massive protests throughout the US.

On April 2nd, Israeli Prime Minister Menachem Begin visited Cairo, Egypt. Four days later, Egypt cut diplomatic relations with Jordan. One week later, the USSR and Iraq signed the Friendship Treaty.

On March, 21st Oberdan Sallustro was kidnapped in Buenos Aires and later executed by communist guerrillas.

On April 16th, *Apollo 16* was launched, resulting in the fifth crewed lunar landing. Five days later the *Copernicus*, the Orbiting Astronomical Observatory 3 (OAO-3), was launched.

On May 4th, The Don't Make a Wave Committee, a fledgling environmental organization founded in Canada the previous year, officially changed its name to Greenpeace Foundation.

John Lennon was back in the news after claiming on the *Dick Cavett Show* that the FBI was tapping his phone.

On May 22nd, President Nixon visited the Soviet leader Leonid Brezhnev in Moscow to sign the Strategic Arms Limitation Talks (SALT) Treaty. Six days later, after Nixon had lost favour with some of the brokers who helped put him in the White House, "plumbers" broke into the Democratic National Committee headquarters, triggering what became known as Watergate signalling an internal coup d'état.

On June 1st, Iraq nationalized the petroleum companies owned by British Petroleum (BP), Royal Dutch Shell, Compagnie Française des Pétroles, Mobil, and Standard Oil of New Jersey. A week later, in a show of support for Iraq, OPEC moved to prevent companies whose interests were nationalized in Iraq from increasing production elsewhere.

In July, the US government negotiated an arrangement that allowed the Soviets to buy up to $750 million of American grain on credit. The Egyptian president, Anwar Sadat, expelled twenty thousand Russian military aids; and top US health officials admitted African Americans had been used as unwitting guinea pigs in a forty-year syphilis experiment.

August 10th marked the day of The Great Daylight Fireball, an asteroid that passed within fifty-seven kilometres of Earth's surface, entering the atmosphere at fifteen kilometres per second over Utah before passing northwards and leaving the atmosphere over Alberta, Canada. Meanwhile, I was preparing to make my arrival.

On September 5th, Israeli Olympic athletes were taken hostage in Munich and later killed by the Palestinian Black September group.

Civil unrest in the Philippines prompted the US-backed President Ferdinand Marcos to declare martial law. His wife, Imelda, the world would later discover, owned three thousand pairs of shoes.

These events and countless more were energetically locked into every cell of my being before I took my first breath on September 25th, 1972. After cleaning me off and holding me in her arms, the head nurse, a petite Scots woman, peered into my squinting eyes. She whispered to my mother and Nana, "This little fellow is an old soul. He didn't have to come back. He came back because he wanted to."

Am I here because I want to be here? Did I exercise free will long before I was born into this world? Why would I want to come back? Perhaps our souls do have a twofold core directive: first, to awaken to who and what we are, and second, to align ourselves with our highest passion. We are all plugged into the world's energy vibrations well before our mothers give birth to us.

CHAPTER 5

DRIVING FORWARD

"Oh, what a tangled web we weave when first we practice to deceive."
— Sir Walter Scot

April 25ᵗʰ, 2010

I awoke to the sound of birds chirping outside. Their singing reminded me that life continues regardless of the actions I take. I am but one person among almost seven billion, with concerns and feelings that matter little in the bigger picture. *Stop with the self-pity! Get your ass out of bed and move!*

Candace came downstairs and joined me in the kitchen to help make breakfast. She knew I was leaving for a work-related trip, but I intentionally provided few details, knowing I was leaving her to quietly speculate. As I rushed around the kitchen, putting together my meals for the day and getting water and anything else I may need for the trip, she asked me when I planned to return.

"Not sure," I said. "I hope to be back Wednesday night at the latest, but if not, first thing Thursday morning." There were no ifs and buts about returning home later than Thursday morning, as we were scheduled to fly out of Victoria the same day for a trip to Las Vegas for our friend's fortieth birthday. Fucking hilarious! Going to yet another place I have no desire to go.

"Do you have to go this week?" she asked.

"I don't want to go." I put my hands to the side of my head and moaned. "God, I really don't want to go."

"Cork, what's going on?" she asked.

"You know what's going on. Our business is suffering, we're both burnt out, and we're trying to do it all. Vegas costs money, the kids' sports costs money, everything costs money, and that's what I'm trying to make." She stood there staring at me while I gathered up the last of my things. "I don't know what else to do. I'm tired, and I can't think straight."

She didn't have the answers, or even a response to the long shadow I had cast. I usually shared every thought, hope, and concern with her, but I did not want to burden her with the responsibility of allowing me to walk out the door, knowing she might be letting me go forever.

I called my boys into the room to let them know I was leaving and that I would probably not see them until the following week. As always, I told them how much I loved them, making sure to stress the importance of being on their best behaviour for Mom. They could sense an air of melancholy that had settled over their super-human dad and seem to feel the need to hug me a little longer and a little stronger than usual. I turned to my son Kahlil, kneeling to look him in his eyes, and telling him that he was the man of the house while I was away. "You need to help Mom out a little more than usual and make sure all the chores are getting done. No battles with Drédyn, ok? Develop your patience." I wanted to instill a sense of pride in him that he could fill my role, even if it was in a small way. I gave them all one last hug before walking heavily out the door and into my car to begin my trip into Mordor.

I shouldn't have left them. I shouldn't have left Candace with so much unsaid. We were more disconnected from one another than we probably had ever been. I was already missing them terribly. *Where did I go wrong?*

The two-hour ferry ride from my home on Vancouver Island to the terminal in West Vancouver gave me more time to consider what I was about to do. For the last sixteen days, I had had little else on my mind. Not trusting my judgment, I decided to confide in three of my closest friends. These were educated men, respected in their community, with families of their own. Was I looking for a group consensus? If they all said no, would that have kept me from going? Yes, I'm certain of it. But there was no consensus. One of the three showed concern, but essentially only offering an ear to listen without trying to dissuade me. The two others were keen to join me if I decided to do it a second time. So, why was I still so uncertain? My anxiety increased as the ferry moved around the peninsula, making its final approach to the mainland.

Its wide doors opened, and I could see berth number two awaiting us. A rush of sea air whipped in through my window, and I took another deep breath to calm myself. I had made this ferry trip countless times, but today's approach felt eerily different. Darkness had descended. I felt the ferry being pulled by an invisible force toward the docking berth. I recalled Sir Walter Scott's observation in *Marmion*, "Oh, what a tangled web we weave, when first we practise to deceive," picturing the fly moving toward the spider's web, entranced by a mysterious spell. *Who is the fly, who is the spider? Why do I feel I am being deceived?*

⌒◯

My arrival in Vancouver took me back to a not-so-distant past that looked to be someone else's life, though I knew it had been mine. Candace and I moved to Vancouver right after she graduated high school. She was pursuing her education while I chased my dream of becoming a professional bodybuilder. The city cultured me. I met people from all walks of life and was given opportunities to do things I probably never would have done if

I had remained in my rural hometown. I took on well-paying jobs outside of my regular duties working at Olympic Athletic Club; I modelled for an advertising company, appeared in a music video, and worked as a body-guard, more aptly described as a glorified babysitter, for TV personalities John Tesh and Connie Sellecca. That was the best paying job I've ever had. Not because it paid me the most, but because I had so much fun doing it. Vancouver also gave me a direct line to some of the best professional athletes, health experts, and coaches in the world. The city was beautiful, and at times epic, providing me with everything I believed I needed.

We left Vancouver and returned to our hometown once we decided to have kids. We believed that a rural environment, with the support of close family, would be beneficial to our children's upbringing. Moving was not an easy decision for us, as our work and many of our good friends were in Vancouver. It required a commute between Duncan and Vancouver for two years until we got a foothold on the Island. During the first year, Candace and I would take turns remaining on the Island with Mariah while the other worked in the city. We would often meet at the ferry terminal, one of us walking off while the other was walking on, allowing us about ten minutes to hug and kiss before passing our daughter from one to the other and separating again for the next three to five days. We were fortunate that we both had jobs where we could be flexible with our hours. Mine much more so than hers.

A lot of people thought we were crazy, but looking back, I fondly remember those years as being the best of both worlds: the slow-paced life of the valley, which allowed me to be much more present with my daughter, and the fast-paced life of the city, which meshed well with my work. I could quickly shift from first gear into sixth simply by taking the ferry from the Island to the mainland and from sixth to first on the return voyage. Now, ten years later, I was revving at an insanely high rpm, yet I was still sitting in neutral.

What had I been thinking? Oh yeah, where did I go wrong? So much had happened since the opening of my fitness facility, The Playground. It all seemed to be a blur, with conflicting events overlapping, making it difficult, almost impossible, to distinguish between the good, the bad, and the ugly. Of course, I reminded myself that there was a time in my not-so-distant past when I thought everything was good, that everything that happens was meant to be.

Do I still believe in this shit? It allows me to fully embrace the concept of living fully in the "Now" and being at peace with anything that happens, no matter the outcome. There was one year in my late twenties when I went about every single day, from waking in the morning to going to bed at night, with a genuine smile on my face. For one whole year I managed to see the world in all its beauty. The ugly spectacle that had previously displayed itself so readily vanished before my eyes, and taking its place were endless possibilities, possibilities I wanted to fill with love and service to others. I had studied and read all the books authored by the priests of the New Age religion. My good friend Dev was the first to call me a New Age Hippie, as I was the guy striving to merge spirituality and the disciplined reality of the twenty-first-century human experience.

Those days of being called a New Age Hippie and engaging strangers in philosophical dialogue ended years ago. No longer was I saying to my friends and clients, "It's all Good." However, I kept the faith, believing my vision would return. When we struggle, faith is quite often all we have. Even then, it can be a real bitch to muster enough of it up to go forward, but forward we must go.

The other vehicles and their occupants started to crawl off the ferry deck, so many different lives with so many different things to do. I reminded myself to accept every event as a unique experience grown out of millions of years of previous events. I am an infinite part of the universal legacy that binds us all together. Yet, I play the same questions, irritating me like a festering sliver, "Where did I go wrong? Where did the passion go?" I'm trapped in a giant maze that offers no clear direction back to happier days, left with only a flickering memory of the man I used to be. I desperately want it back.

I turned the key in the ignition slowly, my mind playing out a car bomb exploding. The voice inside my head whispered, "Don't turn the key! Don't do it!" But the engine turned over smoothly and joined in the communal hum of the other vehicles.

The grey sky began to break, allowing the sun to penetrate through parting clouds. The weather forecast for the next 24 hours showed a 20 percent chance of rain. Something was looking good. The sun always helps to lift my spirits. I can be having the most challenging day, working on just a few hours' sleep, but if I get some rays on my face, I'm happy. Maybe I have strong genetic memories linking to my ancestors who revered the sun for the bountiful crops it helped produce, or perhaps it's as simple as being low on vitamin D. Whatever the case, I'll take whatever I can get.

The signals that had been trying to steer me away from continuing were more like alarm bells; twisted testicle, high-strung hairdresser, and my drinking into oblivion. What other messages did the Universe need to send my way to wake me up and steer me back on course?

I arrived at Rick's apartment early, ahead of Chris, as I wanted to speak with him privately. I'd brought the hiking gear I thought I'd need for an overnight excursion: snowshoes, compass, multiple layers of clothing, headlamp, multi-use tool-knife, enough food for one person for twenty-four hours, first-aid kit. I didn't yet have our drop-off and pickup locations or the maps, items that Rick promised he would get me, things essential to my agreeing to go. I pushed the buzzer for Rick to let me into his apartment. I hear "two zero six" over the intercom. The six-floor building located in Yale Town looks to be fifty years old. It's in decent shape, but it's in a prime area for new development. I give it five more years before someone tears it down and builds another fancy tower.

The door was open a crack, and I knocked before walking in. The apartment was styled in an Asian-Buddhist Party theme. Like so many people I know, Rick's façade was supposed to evoke non-attachment. It fit well with the chic persona he portrayed: upscale, downtown hairdresser who mingled with some of Vancouver's social elite, clubbing at their private events and parties. As soon as he had made his way out of his bedroom, I reminded him I was still noncommittal. I told him I needed the maps, or I was walking. Rick went on the defensive, taking what I said as an attack.

"I don't know you," I said. "What I do know is from what I've heard and what I've so far seen. I don't mean to disrespect, but it's imperative you know how fucking serious I'm taking this. I have three kids and a wife at home."

"Yeah, yeah, I understand where you're coming from. I have a kid too, and a girlfriend," he said. "I'll find those maps."

He started rummaging around his apartment, looking for his two maps while having a one-way conversation with me. I took a seat on his couch, hoping to release some of the tension that was running throughout my body.

"If you're interested in doing it again after this run, we could probably line it up once every couple of weeks," he yelled from the other room.

"Sure," I said, more to appease him than anything else. "Did you find those maps yet?"

"Yeah, right here."

The two maps were insufficient and lacked detail, but they at least gave a north-south direction and some critical land bearings to help me get home if I got lost or, Heaven forbid, if hell broke loose. No sooner did I get the maps in my hand, then Rick got a text from Chris saying he was on his way. We went outside to meet him, timing it exactly right, as Chris pulled up on his motorbike, a new Buell Lightning, XB12Scg. That makes an excellent first impression! Rick made the introductions, allowing me to speak privately with Chris.

"How long have you been in Canada?" I asked.

"I've been here close to seven years now," he said, with a strong English accent.

He was cordial but not very talkative, so I pressed a little more. "Why are you doing the hike?"

"Don't know yet if I am. I came here to meet you and ask Rick a couple of questions."

"Sounds like we're in the same boat," I added.

"I'm not worried about getting stuck in a boat with you, mate. It's getting stuck with him," thumbing over his shoulder in Rick's direction.

"I was told by my friend that once he gets on the mountain, he's golden. The other guy, Sinisa, he'll have a difficult time, but Rick assured me he would help him if needed. My friend told me you climbed to Everest's base camp."

"Yeah, I did that last year with my girlfriend."

"Must have been amazing," I said, politely digging for some details.

"Great experience..."

Rick cuts him off, "Everybody ready to make some money?"

I looked at Chris and said, "I'm in if you're in."

"Why the fuck not?"

We arranged for a time and place to meet later that evening. Fredo picked me up and took me back to his place to rest before the big night. His nicely furnished sky-rise apartment was on Howe Street, close to the waterfront.

"Seen *Jackass*?" he asked as he started a video.

You've got to be fucking kidding me! Why am I surprised?

"Haven't had time to watch too many movies," I replied as I took a seat in the living room and began watching the crazy, weird stunts these people were pulling off. I've never found these types of movies funny. I find them depressing, as they remind me of how warped our culture has gotten, supporting acts that hurt and embarrass others. I can see the irony in it, as my own life was being mimicked on the television, with guys climbing into shopping carts, then allowing their friends to push them down steep hills. "That's me, isn't it, Fre?" I asked, pointing toward his giant flat-screen TV. "Are you the guy pushing me down the hill?"

"Piece of cake, buddy, as long you wear your helmet."

Did he catch my meaning? Probably not. Fredo was not responsible for me, and neither were Rick, Chris, or Sinisa. The painful truth slapped me again, reminding me of how alone I was. I positioned that shopping cart at the top of the hill and climbed into it all by myself. I had four hours to go before the packing team was to meet. I could feel the wheels on the cart begin to move. It was going to be a long night.

Rick had a safe house off Broadway and Main Street. We transferred 108 pounds of BC's grade A herb from three big duffle bags into our four backpacks. Trying to stuff that much marijuana into one backpack wasn't easy. The packages were vacuumed-sealed to compress them and eliminate the smell, but even so, twenty-seven pounds still took up a lot of space.

After getting our hiking gear on, we made our move to Rick's Nissan Pathfinder. The four of us moved as quietly as possible through the dark alleyway, trying to avoid any unwanted attention. I envisioned a SWAT team surrounding the entire city block, busting us before we made it to the vehicle. Rick opened the back hatch, and we threw our bags in as quickly and quietly as we could. Once the last pack was on board, I stepped back to survey the load.

"The latch isn't going to close," I whispered to Rick. He tried to push the rear door down, but it wouldn't fasten. I could see the bags would need rearranging if he was going to lock the latch. I told him my thoughts and suggested to the other guys that we all get into the vehicle while Rick rearranged the bags. It made no sense standing around, looking conspicuous. Was I being paranoid? If you had asked me then, I would have said, "Yes, a little." If you were to ask me now, years later, I would say, "No, absolutely not."

Five minutes later, we were on our way. Ten minutes after that, we stopped at a large, brightly lit service station so Rick could fill his empty gas tank. Wow! Let's scrunch five guys and four large backpacks of ganja in a Pathfinder running on empty and attempt to drive through the heart of one of Canada's largest cities.

If that wasn't bad enough, the argument that ensued immediately after between Rick and the driver, Carl, should have prompted me to open the door and jump. Rick hadn't coordinated ahead of time with Carl to pick us up on the US side of the border the following day — something he had confirmed was being looked after. Nothing was as it seemed. It was complete folly! The inner dialogue was at full volume. *Why am I not asking to be let out of the vehicle?* My inner voice sounded like a broken record, continuing to grind along, trying to build momentum, with a stoppage in play every couple of hours. *Just a little farther,* I assured myself. *See it through.*

CHAPTER 6

SUN RISES

"Our abode in this world is transitory, our life therein is but a loan, our breaths are numbered, and our indolence is manifest."

— *Abu Bakr*

April 26th, 2010 — 1:00 am

It's true what they say about aliens among us. We have one leading us. He has become every bit the cracker. For the first hour and a half, he led us in the wrong direction. When he finally realized he had made a wrong turn, he was everything but apologetic.

"We've got to push harder and make up for all this lost time," he orders.

The first three hours are straight up, and we are carrying close to forty pounds on our backs. Rick begins talking to himself, cursing, the words barely audible, as I'm at least twenty feet behind him. He walks at a fast pace, almost a slow jog, and Sinisa immediately starts to trail behind. I look over at Chris and ask him, "What do you think?"

"Fucking crazy, mate! Rick has gone bloody bonkers."

I holler up ahead to Rick to slow down. "Rick, we can't all keep this pace!" My headlamp can't find him through the narrow animal trail. We continue for ten minutes until Rick and Sinisa are out of sight, Rick in front and Sinisa behind. I hold up and stop on the trail, which brings Chris to an abrupt halt behind me.

"I think we should wait for Sinisa," I say. We pull out our water to take a swig. "This is a gong show! Is he using drugs?"

"No, I don't think so, but he was saying something about hitting his head last week and probably having a concussion," Chris says.

"That would explain it. The question is, what are we going to do?"

Sinisa approaches. "Hey, how are you making out?" I ask.

He offers an unconvincing "I'm all right," as he slowly sits down and lies against the trunk of a large tree.

I think we don't have time to spare for these micro rests, but he's not going to make it unless we make the time. On impulse, I ask them if they think we should continue or abort. There is no hesitation. "I'm finished," Sinisa says.

"Let's get clear of this place and head back the way we came," adds Chris.

"Ok, we're going to have to go and bury the packs and come back for them at a later date," I put in with total agreement.

We find a spot among the giant cedar trees, bury the packs, and start walking in the opposite direction of Rick. My compassionate, human conscience kicks in.

"Guys," I say. Chris and Sinisa stop and turn around to look at me. "We need to let him know we're going back. Why don't I run up ahead for no more than five minutes? If I don't see him, I'll come right back, and then we can get out of here."

Chris is as pissed at Rick as I am, maybe more so. "Fuck him!" he says.

I agree with Chris's sentiments, making it difficult for me to argue my point. "What if, as you said, he is suffering from a severe concussion?

We could be letting him go out on his own to die." I hate to see that as a possible reality, but I can't shake it. "I know we aren't responsible for him, but I would feel like shit if something bad happened because we weren't there."

Both Chris and Sinisa consider what I said. "Yeah, maybe you're right, mate," Chris acknowledges. Sinisa nods his head.

I immediately take off at a jog, feeling the spring in my feet without the green bud weighing me down. *What am I going to tell him if I find him?* The truth, of course. I looked at my watch before I left Chris and Sinisa on the trail. It was 12:03 am, and my watch now says 12:12 am. I come out of my fast jog and into a walk, yelling out Rick's name as I arrive at a shallow brook, no more than four feet across, and see that the trail picks up on the other side. "This is where I stop, Rick!" I yell out before I turn to head back to Chris and Sinisa. But I hear Rick coming down the trail on the other side of the briskly moving water. *What perfect timing.*

He stops at the edge of the water, facing me. "Where are Sinisa and Chris? What the fuck is taking you guys so long?" he snarls at me.

"We are heading back. We're not continuing," I say flatly.

"What do you mean? You guys can't quit this. We have a fucking commitment to uphold!"

"You can shove your commitment up your ass, you piece of shit!" I explode, barely managing to hold myself back from attacking him. "You managed to get us lost and add well over two hours to our time. Did you stop to consider for one second the strain you've put on your *team*?" I made sure to stress the word "team," as he had been using that word from the first day I met him, but he had no idea what it meant.

Somewhat to my surprise, Rick pulls a 180 right there on the spot. "I'm sorry, man. My head hasn't been working too well. I'm pretty sure I have a concussion."

"Yeah, Chris said as much. Another good reason for us to turn this thing around and go again another day." *A day that will never come.*

"But we can't turn around. There will be people waiting on the other side to get this. They'll be pissed if they come as far as they did for nothing."

"That's not my problem, Rick. Chris and Sinisa are done. I'm done."

"I'll make it up to you guys, I promise."

"Your promises don't count much with me, nor do they with the others."

"Please keep going, I'm begging you. I'll be in a heap of trouble if I don't get this job done."

Something sways me. Perhaps I am still holding onto getting my promised $10,000, or maybe my heart aches for what Rick is going through, like what Frodo felt for Gollum in *Lord of the Rings*. My affinity for Frodo and the burden he has to carry, the responsibility thrust onto him, is akin to the load I have been carrying for the last decade. Rick is my Gollum. Like Frodo, I wanted to rid myself of him, to beat him. But the things I saw in him were mirror reflections of what I see in myself. If I give up on Rick, I am giving up on myself.

"I'll go back to Chris and Sinisa, and we'll put this to a vote. I'll tell them that you are sorry and that you will make it up to us. How you plan on doing that beats me. And, Rick, if they do decide to jump back on board, you better apologize and kiss their ass."

"Yeah, yeah, for sure, man. It will be good from here on out." He continues talking, making excuses for himself, but I have already turned around to begin jogging back to Chris and Sinisa. By the time I reach them, Sinisa has recovered substantially from that first three-hour push.

Chris asks, "Did you find him?"

"Yes, I did. Right at the point, I was going to turn around. Funny, hey?"

Sinisa asks, "What did he say when you told him we were going back?"

"Well, he had a moment but regained his composure somewhat. He said he was sorry and that he would make it up to us if we pushed on. He said that he would smarten up and behave himself."

Sinisa, perhaps because his energy has returned, is thinking on it.

Chris is not impressed. "Screw him!"

"Sinisa, what do you want to do?" I ask.

He looks up at me from where he is sitting before pulling himself up onto his feet, a stretched-out six feet four. "I think we should continue. We've come this far."

I look back at Chris. There is no need for me to say anything as I know he knows what I'm thinking. Chris turns to look down the trail that would lead us back to our homes and away from Rick. He stands there for a few seconds, scratching his head as if it will help him think better.

"If you think we should continue, we'll continue."

We walk the trail for another two hours until the path is no longer clear. In front of us towers seventy degrees of gnarliness: a three hundred-metre slope that requires climbing on all fours, utilizing our hands as much as our feet to pull ourselves up. It is challenging to say the least, but on any other day — minus the weed we are carrying and one-third the company — this hike would supply me with everything I love about the outdoors. Once we crest the slope, we decide to take a ten-minute rest to hydrate and refuel, and that is when Sinisa alerts me he is out of water.

The snow is now deep enough to warrant strapping on our snowshoes for the five-hour push to the summit. Within an hour of strapping on the snowshoes, I begin experiencing pain on the inside of my right knee. With every minute that elapses, the pain worsens. I know what is happening. My right iliotibial, the IT band, which runs on the outside of the thigh, is becoming tight, putting severe tension on my medial ligament in my knee. It's like taking an elastic band and twisting it around two pencils. You keep turning the pencils around and around until the elastic is at the point of snapping. To relieve the tension in my IT band, I need to release the pressure. The only method of release at my disposal is stretching and massage. I tell Rick my knee is about to snap, and I have to try to work it out. He doesn't say a word; he just marches on. I find a safe spot where I can spread out to stretch. I dedicate ten minutes to stretching my right gluteus maximus before turning my attention to digging my knuckles into the side of my leg, where the IT band is located. I massage for a solid five minutes before getting back up onto my feet. The precious fifteen minutes spent on rehabilitation are worth it. The pain is still severe but manageable. Rick, Chris, and Sinisa are now long gone, but I don't care. I have their tracks to follow and the silence of the mountain all to myself.

Our path takes us past a ledge that overlooks the majestic scenery of the Cascade Mountains. I can see Chris just up ahead and know I could reach him within the next five minutes, but I decide to stop so I can appreciate what very few people ever witness. I sit and hang my feet by a ledge overhanging a sheer drop of what looks to be one thousand metres. The sun is just starting to rise in the East, and I can feel the warmth of the orange glow as it reaches out to touch me. I wish I had brought my camera to capture what God looks like in all her glory upon rising. Considering everything I have been through, I am surprised at being so overwhelmingly in awe of this moment and filled with gratitude for all I have.

CHAPTER 7

DUALISM

"You can't stop change any more than you can stop the suns from setting."

— *Shmi Skywalker*

1974 — 1979

My parents were together for four years before they separated in 1974. I was two years old. The circumstances behind why they ended their relationship depends on whose story you listen to, circumstantial evidence put forth only to gloss over their shared ineptitude to create a long-lasting, healthy partnership. They tried, but they couldn't emulate the idealized, cookie-cutter image of Ward and June Cleaver. My father wanted the bachelor's life, but a version that included a wife who would take care of the home and, when needed, double as a hot date. Having a child didn't keep Dad from living the life he had grown accustomed to.

My mother left my father for another man, finding a replacement she believed would check most of her boxes. My father never forgave her, though they were cordial with one another up until his passing. My father's replacement was a man named Frank Nichol. As a Scotsman, he was more likely to toe the Douglas line than my father, who respected but never saw eye to eye with my grandfather, the family's patriarch.

Within months of my father and mother separating, I was given the nickname Korky-Cat. Korky, a black-and-white cat, is a character from a UK comic strip who behaves like a human and is accepted in a world of humans as only a comic character can be. Supposedly my aunt gave me the nickname because of my copper-coloured, corkscrew hair, and high-energy personality, but I concluded years later the reason the name stuck was that some people in my family preferred not to call me by my father's name.

By the time I turned four, Korky-Cat was shortened to Corky, with a "C," and it has stuck with me to this very day.

I can vividly remember the first time I experienced myself as being separate from the Other. I was closing in on my fifth birthday, entering the initial stages of self-discovery, what Jean Piaget, the famous cognitive psychologist, classified as the stage of concrete operational thinking. I was beginning to use logically consistent mental structures to organize my view of the world. I was awaking to myself, noticing a difference between what I felt and what I perceived to be my rapidly growing Universe. Pleasure and pain morphed into joy and fear, which opened doors into new realms. This waking moment was the first of five significant massive mind expansions I would experience throughout my life.

My first five-year bubble consisted of daily events and occurrences that many in my generation grew up with. I was blessed to have siblings to play with and battle against, TV shows that worked to educate and condition, and a community that kept me from slipping through the cracks. I was immersed in politics and world events, as the Douglas Clan frequently discussed polarizing hot topics around my grandparents' dinner table.

Jack, my grandfather, spoke with passion whenever worldly matters were being discussed. You could hear his voice boom throughout their old Victorian home whenever a topic touched a nerve for him. There was never any concealing of the atrocities and hardships that people around the world had endured through the two world wars, Viet Nam, apartheid, and every place colonialism usurped and pillaged. These topics were all discussed with vigour, quite often becoming an oratory that would take on a life of its own.

I conjured pictures in my head of a bigger world that quite frankly scared the hell out of me. For all the knowledge that had been heaped onto me, there was no proper filtering, no proposed solution to address the suffering that was felt by countless others. I was comforted knowing I was safe within my bubble, that what took place out there couldn't get to me while I was under the protection of my family. But then something happened. Though I was physically safe, I had the stark realization there were children in the world who weren't. At five years of age, I felt those children had been betrayed by the adults entrusted to look after them.

One dark, rainy night, I awoke to the sound of thunder and my heart racing. The rest of my family had long gone to bed, and I was the only one awake, alone with my thoughts. For the first time in my short life, I saw myself objectively, with past experiences coming under the microscope as if I were looking at someone else. Then, my head began to ache badly. Never had I experienced concentrated pain such as that. It felt like my head was going to burst open. I didn't know what to do. Any time I was in distress I always went to my mother so she could soothe and alleviate my pain, but not this time. I knew what I felt could not be remedied by a mother's soft and loving touch. I was intrinsically aware that what I felt was due to the environment I was growing up in. For the first time in my life, I didn't trust the people who represented my pillars of strength and knowledge.

My head kept pounding, and tears began to stream down my face, but I refused to make a sound. I needed to escape the pain. I needed to run. My body moved automatically as if responding to someone else's command.

There was no thought to what I was doing, only that I wanted the pain to stop. Not just the pain in my head, but the pain other innocents were experiencing daily. I ran out of the house and into our large front yard, which sloped down to the main road. The rain was pouring down, soaking my pyjamas instantly. I crouched beside our three-foot-high rock wall and stared up toward my house and all the comforts it held.

Besides the unusualness of a five-year-old boy running out of his house on a dark, rainy night, I must add that whatever prompted me to go was much more potent than the fear I had of the witch whom my mother told me lived up on top of our roof. Up until this point, I thought nothing would ever have gotten me outside at night on my own. My mother used the witch story, a short-cut parenting method that had lasting effects, to keep me inside the house whenever I was frustrated with my family and threatening to run away. Sobbing, I hugged myself tightly and called out, "Please make this stop, please make the hurt go away. I don't know what to do. Make it go away."

Ask and you shall receive. The pain in my head immediately began to subside, followed seconds later by a man's voice that came from behind me.

"Corky," the voice said.

I was too nervous to look to see who was there. Geesh, I was only five. The voice spoke again, this time louder and with an authoritative tone that reminded me of the male role models in my life. But this voice lacked their edge, and instead exuded a confidence that helped to soothe my worries.

"Corky, do not be afraid. Everything you are, and everything that is, is meant to be."

"I want to make the hurting stop," I said, referring to the hurt of others as much as my own. The voice understood me.

"To make the pain go away, you will do what is necessary. In time you will make it stop. Do not be afraid."

And that was it; the voice was gone. Now, we can dissect and psycho-analyze the mind of my younger self so we can accurately label and cat-egorize what brought on that voice, but does it matter? Whether it was a construct of my mind or one of God's angels, I have since concluded:

we have the mental capacity to find the right tools to make sense of the world we live in when we need them most. The voice was firm but caring, and the words he spoke comforted me greatly that night, as I believed the simple truth: there was no reason to be afraid — even if my world conveyed the opposite.

This first significant moment in my life coincided with the release of *Star Wars*. Even though my mom kept covering my eyes, I discerned the essence of the film: altruism, spirituality, science, good vs. evil, all constructs my young mind tried to grasp. It helped galvanize my understanding of this chaotic and violent world I was living in, putting me on a path to train and become something like a Jedi.

Over the next few years, I had recurring headaches that matched the severity of the one I had on that eye-opening stormy night. The family doctor couldn't diagnose my condition, or perhaps they knew but thought it best not to discuss with me. What's not to know? I was a sensitive kid who felt the chaotic machinations of a barbarous world, compounded by the internal conflicts within our family and the continuous uprooting of our home to move somewhere new, on average, once every ten months. We moved fourteen times over a ten-year period, as Mom was regularly seeking a fresh start, gambling precious time and energy we used to create our last home and network of friends.

Moving into a new school halfway through the year posed many challenges, like trying to gel with kids who had already created their group dynamic months earlier. When you are uprooted as often as I was, you learn to be mindful and take more notice of the people around you. Our instincts drive us to try to fit in, or at the very least, to not stand out, yet there were a few factors beyond my control that always brought unwanted attention my way. For starters, I had copper-red, curly hair, my nickname was Corky, and my mother had married a man with the last name of Nichol. I would get called everything from Ronald McDonald, Corkscrew, and Porky Pickle. My new classmates were always amused, thinking the circus had left one of its talking monkeys behind. Fortunately, I also had a few talents. Having two older brothers and three uncles who constantly pushed me to keep up on their adventures helped make me a good athlete. I was fast and tenacious. This carried over on to the soccer field and placed me at the head of the pack in our school runs. My athleticism usually gave me instant credibility and won me favour with *most* of my peers and many of my teachers. However, this didn't deter the bullies from zeroing in on me, and perhaps even more so once I started garnering the attention they sought. Even if the name-calling never happened, my desire to fight injustice any way I could would, sooner or later, always lead me to square off with that one boy and his pack of followers who enjoyed making other kids' lives hell. I wasn't the biggest, but I was backed by the training from my eldest brother and my uncle Grant, two fighters who never shied away from fisticuffs. No matter their size or how many of them there were, I rarely backed down. Though my stomach would get twisted in knots, I understood from a young age that some fears had to be confronted face-on.

It wasn't all war and hostilities on the school playgrounds, though. Most of my time was spent playing with friends, who always made for a culturally diverse group. I never differentiated between my Asian, Indian, Indigenous, or Caucasian friends, though there was no shortage of back-minded, ignorant rednecks who espoused racism and bigotry toward minorities when I was growing up on Vancouver Island. Such attitudes were socially acceptable between the 1970s and 1990s, but ran counter to my family's values. My grandparents' large acreage was in the middle of one of the largest First Nation reserves in BC, and functioned as the Douglas family headquarters from 1963 up until the passing of Nana Gina at Christmas of 1985. I was fortunate to spend time with the Khowutzun people and learn from the elders about their heritage. The stark contrast between their traditional lives and the conditions in which many of them now lived grieved me. Garbage would often pile up outside dilapidated houses. There was a lot of domestic violence, usually attributable to alcohol, but the underlying cause was the expropriation of First Nations' land and the destruction of their traditional way of life, with many of their own people selling them out. The Douglas family embedded themselves in this community, finding they had more in common with their neighbours than with the other families who had long since settled the Cowichan Valley. The divisions so visible out in society were replicated in my grandparents' home.

Conversations that started out as healthy discussions would often heat up, with the tone escalating from one of disagreement to one of contempt and condescension, and — if we were lucky — ending with a bit of mockery. Most of us knew to keep clear and avoid the crossfire, leaving the hostilities to the adults who could quickly turn a matter of difference into an attack on character. Everyone talked as if they were an expert.

I was six years old the night my nana went at my mother. I don't know why they were arguing but assumed my nana must have thought my mother was being insolent and felt justified at clawing at her face. The high-pitched death screams frightened me more than the blood running down my mother's cheeks. My family, who once were warriors, preached a code of conduct that was not followed within the confines of their own home. No longer were they fighting the good fight, for we had turned to fighting each other. My headaches continued for another two years.

CHAPTER 8

INTERVENTION

"There was the old myth of divine intervention. You blasphemed, and a lightning bolt struck you. That was a little steep too. If punishment is at all proportionate to the offense, then power becomes watered. The only way you generate the proper attitude of awe and obedience is through immense and disproportionate power."

— Norman Mailer

April 26th, 2010 — 1:00 pm

"There's a vehicle coming. Jump in the bush," I yell at Chris as I scurry off the road.

"Do you think it's our ride?" Chris whispers as the truck comes to a stop on the road where the snow line begins, thirty to forty metres away from where we are lying tight against the bank.

Two weeks earlier, on April 12th, I was down on my knees praying for divine intervention, hoping for an end to my misery. Now, my knees are frozen in a bank of snow and I am uncomfortably conscious of my inability to steer my own ship. I hear two doors open and close, followed by the faint mumbling of voices. Will Rick call us over? Is it our ride? There's no way I'm going to pop my head up and look.

"Look there, tracks."

"It's the Border Patrol! We're fucked!" I whisper to Chris. The tracks left by Rick's snowshoes, the ones we followed, ended next to where the officers parked their truck. I didn't need to be a Level One tracker with Search and Rescue to know these guys are going to follow them back to where they meet up with ours. They will see where we went off the road. We're trapped.

I start pushing myself away from the bank and say to Chris, "We've got to go." But as I'm saying it, the two Border Patrol officers are already following Rick's trail back to us. Thirty metres, twenty metres, and my heart is racing in anticipation for the final moment, ten metres.

"Right there, look!" One officer says to the other. *Three, two, one.* "Freeze, mother fucker! Put your hands up, now!"

One guy focuses intently upon me with his 9 mm drawn point-blank at my chest. My hands start moving slowly up into the air, automatically obeying his order, but, as if they have a mind of their own, they stop at chest level, and I smile. The guy's voice notches down a decibel as he repeats his order.

"I'm not packing, and I'm no threat to you," I say.

The officer lowers his gun ever so slightly, and his look of malice changes to one of curiosity. "Why are you smiling?" he asks me.

I laugh to myself, thinking back to when I was down on my knees on my bedroom floor, praying and begging for it all to stop. I look up, slightly over his head, at the blanketed sky. *Universe, this wasn't what I had in mind.*

I drop my gaze to meet the officer's eyes. "It's a long story."

The load I had been carrying, in both the literal and metaphorical sense, had been cut away from me. I knew that the coming months, most likely years, were not going to be easy, but at least the train had come to a crashing stop.

Or had it?

CHAPTER 9

FINDING MY PLACE

"Perhaps it's impossible to wear an identity without becoming what you pretend to be."

— Orson Scott Card, Ender's Game

1980 — 1987

My desire to be a force for good made sticking up for those who could not stick up for themselves a natural thing to do. I would confront the kids who went out of their way to pick on others, though I confess my hypocrisy, for I recall a handful of occasions where I dished out what I was fighting against. Occasionally, the clashes got physical. By the time I turned eleven I had been in a lot of fights. Sometimes the altercations would end with a little bit of shoving; sometimes, there was a bloody lip and nose, rarely mine. More than once, I tried walking away, turning the other cheek as my mother had encouraged me to do, but that usually end in my either being spat on or hit from behind.

When I wasn't in school, I was playing games with friends, riding bikes, building forts, climbing trees, and jumping off towering cliffs that ran alongside the amazing Cowichan River. Things that so many kids these days don't get the chance to experience.

I was nine years old when I got my first job, delivering the *Victoria Times Colonist* newspaper. Earning my own money gave me immense satisfaction. After collecting the monthly fees from the nice people I delivered to, I would go to Bruce's Grocery and buy everyone in my family their favourite chocolate bar and soda-pop. I would sit outside the store's doors, drinking my pop and opening the door for the customers before returning home and sharing my wealth with my family. I learned many valuable lessons from that paper route. It required me to get up ninety minutes earlier than usual and miss my favourite cartoon, *Star Blazers*. Oh yeah, it took discipline, but it was worth it, as it proved to be invaluable to the development of my character.

What should have been one of my best childhood memories turned out to be one of my saddest. Someone stole my delivery money from underneath my mattress, adding weight to my belief that something was seriously wrong in the world. I was confused, angry, and much too young to adequately put my feelings into words and get the justice I felt was owed to me. I was mad as hell!

My childhood had its fair share of challenges, but there were also magical trips, adventures, and wise guides who dropped nuggets of truth, adding to an empty vault I wished to fill. One of many wonderful moments took place at school on a cold winter day when my grade five teacher, Mr. Patterson, shared an exciting piece of news that was regarded with little interest by most of my classmates, save for my three besties, Eden, Stefan, and Jinder. There was an article in the *New York Times* titled "Ideas and Trends; Clues get Warm in the Search for Planet X" that discussed the possibility that a giant planet, five times bigger than Earth, on the outskirts of our solar system was a brown dwarf star that was in an elliptical orbit around our sun:

Something out there beyond the farthest reaches of the known solar system seems to be tugging at Uranus and Neptune. Some gravitational force keeps perturbing the two giant planets, causing irregularities in their orbits. The force suggests a presence far away and unseen, a large object that may be the long-sought Planet X.

— JOHN NOBLE WILFORD January 30th, 1983

Hearing about such discoveries and reading about others in the magazines my mom and uncle John collected would send my imagination into hyper drive. I was never without a cache of interesting topics that stimulated my brain. *National Geographic, Omni, Scientific American*, and *Popular Science* provided me with information on what most intrigued me: astronomy and ancient history.

My confidence in myself and my place within my pack peaked as I came to the end of grade six. I was happier than I had been in a long time. For the second time in my short life, I had made it through one school for two consecutive years. That joy was short-lived, though, as my uncles persuaded me to join my cousin Bill and attend the school on the other side of town. They tried convincing me to get a jump on others by starting junior high one year early, as my current school was a K–7 elementary school. I wasn't sold, so they guilted me by saying Nana Gina, who worked at the school as the head secretary, would be disappointed if I didn't go.

I would have to make new friends all over again, but I was comforted knowing I had been down this road before and always came out of it all right. I never thought this time would be any different. I was wrong. My cousin, who has since grown into a fine man, was troubled in his youth. He grew up in the care of my grandparents, aunts, and uncles, as his mother's circumstances prevented her from caring for him properly. Other than when he was at school, he spent little time with kids his age. He had difficulty fitting in and would often resort to telling outlandish tales to impress others, stories his schoolmates would call him out on. I knew the underlying reason my uncles urged me to switch schools, and it bothered me they gave no thought as to how this change would impact me. Their soul focus seemed to be what I could do for Bill.

I thought my days of fighting battles at school were behind me, but as soon as I started grade seven, life got more complicated. Quamichan Junior High was a much larger school than I was used to. I was no longer hanging with kids; I was surrounded by young men and women who cared more about brand-name clothing, hairstyles, music, and who liked who. Materialism 101 was the new course being rammed down my throat as 1980s pop culture descended on us. Groups became more pronounced, and you were considered an outsider if you didn't find your place within one quickly.

My first day at school was hell. I was standing on the front lawn, minding my own business, when two boys approached me, their scowling faces tipping me off to stand on guard.

"Are you Corky?" one boy asked.

"Yes," I said, making sure to give nothing else away.

"What kind of a name is that?" the other boy said snidely.

"Ah, yeah, it's just a nickname my friends and family call me."

"Your cousin said you were going to kick our ass when you got here. Is that true? Are you going to kick our ass?"

I discovered Bill had alienated me well before I had even decided to change schools. Bill, the outcast, had been picked on, and he was never given the right tools to deal with it. My family tried teaching him how to defend himself but Bill wasn't a fighter. So, they looked to someone who could fight for him, pushing me to be the pugilist and make others pay for ostracizing him.

Those first few months were some of the most challenging days of my life. I tried keeping myself from getting involved in Bill's affairs, but it was to no avail. When my uncles found out I wasn't sticking up for him at school, they became angry with me.

"Turning your back on Bill is the same thing as turning your back on your entire family," said my uncle Grant.

For the first time in my life, I looked at death as a way to escape the pain I was experiencing. But I persevered and quickly learned the art of diplomacy, finding my way to make new friends, including those two boys who confronted me on the school lawn. I also helped Bill to get along better with others. The people I battled during those years weren't bad. They, like me, had not been given the proper tools to function effectively in society. It was apparent that we were collectively not on track to become fully functioning members of a larger community, and no one person was going to help us remedy this.

I was seeing the world play out at a microcosmic level, and aware of my hesitancy to being unceremoniously initiated into a system I resented. The chaos I saw across the planet was hitting closer to home than ever before. I was now fully immersed in a critical life-altering phase that I count as my second waking moment. The view I held of myself and my place in the world radically shifted. I broke from the Douglas Clan by taking back my father's name. I wanted to be free to make my way without being confined to any one group. Fontana was the name I was given at birth and the name I used until my parents separated. Honouring my father was the first step of many in claiming my life for myself.

I carried a sizable chunk of disappointment during my teens.

My uncle John, who was like a second father to me, left me hanging when I really needed him; reneging on his offer to let me live with him during my darkest days in Junior High. Shortly after my nineteenth birthday, he told me, "I thought you would be on your way to becoming a lawyer." His words were like a slap in the face, as we had never talked about my pursuit of higher education; in fact, he had shown no interest in my career path for the previous six years, though he had significantly influenced my life up until that point. I took note not to behave as condescendingly and as arrogant as he did.

I pawned my prized collection of *Star Wars* figures and vehicles to my uncle Grant, who never paid me the total amount promised. Not getting the last $100 I was owed was disappointing, but seeing my collection destroyed by his two young boys within months of getting them crushed me. Grant took offence to my complaint about his not paying me, and decided to teach me one of his lessons by choking me outside of the gym we both trained at, telling me in his *Dirty Harry* voice, "Get back inside the gym and train your legs, boy." With tears in my eyes, I went back into the gym and trained my legs harder than I had ever done before! Thanks, Uncle.

These same uncles used to hold me by my feet and hang me over the side of our second-storey deck. I would cry out for them to stop, as most young boys would do, until one day, when I was around six years old, I realized if I didn't react to their antics, they would no longer have the satisfaction of seeing me freak out. It worked, and I learned a valuable lesson.

My mom lived cheque to cheque. Food was always on the table, but it was sparse at times. On a few occasions throughout the winter months, we ran out of oil to heat the house and had no funds to top up the tank. Sleeping under multiple layers of blankets wasn't terrible, but it added to the distance I felt existed between those who have and those who don't.

When I asked my dad what he would have liked for me to be doing professionally, he said, "I hoped you would have played baseball."

What was disappointing was that he only watched me play a couple of games out of the three seasons I played. After he and my mom split, I only saw him once every four to six weeks. I don't have any memories of throwing a ball back and forth with him. My mom took me to a few of those games, but she would sit in her car and read her book, preferring not to denigrate herself by associating with *those* parents who were loud and raucous in the bleachers. I was a good ballplayer and would have done more with it if my parents had shown more support.

For all the disappointment, there were great times too. My dad shared his love for fishing. I spent thousands of hours catching thousands of pounds of salmon and cod with him. He taught me the art of patience as I learned to sit still on a boat for hours on end without saying a word.

The quiet days on the boat were balanced out with days and nights spent at the hotel he managed. The hotel staff were like a surrogate family who were extra nice to me. I got to order whatever I wanted from the hotel restaurant, swim for hours in the pool, and have the television all to myself.

The animosity I held toward my two uncles was not permanent. Along with my aunt Lisa and my other uncle, Rob, they gifted me with many memorable weekends camping, sailing, exploring, rebuilding cars, and learning about all things, big and small. Both of my parents had a plethora of friends from all walks of life, spanning multiple generations. I am blessed to have been afforded time spent with people from different cultures who ran the full spectrum of socio-political ideologies. I aspired to become like Master Yoda and fortunately acquired many tutors to teach me along the way. Mom had passed on her love of books and instilled in me the determination to question the dogma others accepted as fact. She epitomized the complexities of the human condition while remaining resolute in sharing the knowledge and magic that flowed through the Universe. But the day came when we needed to cut the umbilical cord. Shortly after starting grade ten, I decided it was best I move in with my eldest brother, Scott. It was time for me to take the next step.

CHAPTER 10

EYES ON ME

"If you're squeezed for information, that's when you've got to play it dumb: You just say you're out there waiting for the miracle to come."
— *Leonard Cohen*

April 26th, 2010 — 1:10 pm

The two US Border Patrol officers begin ordering us onto the road, directing us closer to their truck.

"What were you guys doing up here?"

I quickly respond ahead of Chris, "We were up here hiking and got lost overnight."

"I call bullshit! You guys are here to either pick something up or drop something off. Which is it?"

I look right in his eyes. "No, just out hiking and got lost. Where are we anyway?"

"You are in the Snoqualmie Park Reserve. Are you Canadian?"

"Originally from England, as you probably guessed, but now reside in Canada," says Chris.

"Canada, born and raised," I add.

The second officer glares at me. "You have crossed the border illegally, as I'm sure you're aware." Both he and the other officer are efficiently quick in their movements. I assume this is just one of many busts they've been involved with over the years. He calls over to the officer with his head poked into the cab of their truck, calling headquarters. "Hey, Shannon, better have them send two more vehicles."

Officer Shannon shouts back, "Already on it."

He orders us to place our hands behind our backs, securing our hands with zip ties. We sit on the icy ground about fifteen feet apart from one another and about twenty feet away from their truck. *Am I in shock?* I feel in control despite this out-of-control situation. *The shit just hit the fan! Yes, I know, and I received what I asked for.*

One of the officers cuts into my thoughts. "Is someone coming to get you?"

As the word "No" shoots out of my mouth, we hear a vehicle heading up the road. Any remaining credibility I had is shattered; I know it is Carl. I pray he has the smarts to turn around while there is still time.

"Who's coming in the fucking SUV?" the officer yells at us as he pulls his 9 mm back out of his hip holster and holds it in two hands, straight-armed, pointing down at the ground. Shannon moves to the back of the truck, sliding out a long drawer on rollers specially built for the truck's box. Reaching into the box, he pulls out an automatic assault rifle, spinning just in time to point directly at the windshield of Carl's silver Infinity SUV as it comes to a stop thirty feet away.

Both officers yell at the driver to get out while intermittingly yelling at us, "How many are there?"

"I don't know!" I say.

The SUV stops, and Carl slowly begins to exit his vehicle with his hands on his head, as directed by Officer Shannon pointing the assault rifle at him.

"Who are you? What are you doing here?" Shannon and his partner stand tensely, following the procedures of engagement. These guys are professional. I respect that. Shannon and his partner take little time getting Carl down to the ground and fastening his hands in front of him. Carl tells them, "I came to visit my grandma for a couple of days. Decided to get away from civilization and go for a drive into the mountains to do some writing."

"Do you know these two?" Officer Shannon asks.

"No," Carl says, shaking his head while checking us over.

"Well, if you've got nothing to hide, you don't mind if we check your vehicle out, do you?"

"No, go right ahead," says Carl, acting unfazed by what is happening.

While Officer Shannon searches Carl's rented SUV, his partner gets on the radio, checking back in with the command centre. He notifies command that they have apprehended three people — two packers, and one driver with a vehicle — and need some assistance. He gets off the radio and says to Shannon, "You got anything?"

Shannon pops his head out from the back seat. "Sure do! We've got enough Egg McMuffins and Quarter Pounders to feed an army."

"Gross! Who eats that shit? It's poison." I chime in.

If I wasn't certain forty-five minutes earlier, when Shannon had pointed his gun at my chest, I am sure now that I'm not going to walk away from this without serious repercussions. It's clear to the officers we'd been packing something from Canada into the US, as Carl's vehicle doesn't contain any contraband, just enough food to feed a platoon of hungry packers. Though we continue to deny the accusations levelled against us, I can't hide my true feelings from our captors. The second officer looks over in my direction, taking note of the amused look on my face. "I don't get it. Why are you smiling? Does this seem funny to you?"

I can't help but be condescending. "Funny? No, not funny at all. But amusing? Yes, absolutely-fucking amusing!"

"Why is it amusing? I don't think it's amusing," Shannon jumps in.

"Because my friend and I," as I nod in Chris's direction and ensure I don't say anything that will incriminate me, "are two of the unlikeliest candidates for backpacking contraband across the border that you two will ever encounter."

Snap! We hear a branch break farther up the road, close to the spot Chris and I had been hiding in a little over an hour ago. The second officer draws his gun and moves toward the noise as Sinisa pulls himself up and out of the tree line and onto the road. He's smart enough to have ditched his pack, but by this point it doesn't matter. They will comb every inch of this area and find all our packs. Sinisa would tell me later he was trying to get close without alerting us to determine if it was safe to come out. Stepping on that branch may have saved his life. Considering how exhausted he was, he may well have died on this mountain.

I can't help but reflect on the absurdity of my present situation, for how couldn't I have known what was going to happen? I have been spiralling out of control for months, if not years, acting no different than an addict who can't say no.

Once Sinisa is zip-tied and sitting on the ground, Shannon asks what we were packing. "Don't make us go looking for it. If you tell us now where to look, it will make us way happier and easier to deal with."

Again, we deny carrying anything other than what we have on us, which of course is highly unlikely, as neither Chris nor Sinisa had brought a secondary pack as I had done. The officers are angry, talking among themselves. Ten minutes after Sinisa is caught, two vehicles and three more Border Patrol officers arrive. Chris and Carl will be driven in one vehicle and Sinisa and I in the other, leaving the third officer to drive Carl's vehicle down the mountain, back to the command centre.

Sinisa and I are told to get in the back of the cab with our hands still strapped behind our backs. I ask the driver if he will make use of the seatbelts, but he ignores me. I'm not sure what is worse, the fully cranked hillbilly music, or driving at high speed, swerving back and forth on the road, whipping Sinisa and me hard between each other and the doors of the truck. I think they want to teach us a lesson.

"Would you care to slow down? This guy isn't doing too well." I ask nicely.

Sinisa has no strength to brace himself against the sudden jerking of the wheel from one side of the road to the other. Having his hands tied behind his back doesn't help. My feet are placed eighteen inches apart on the floor and my inner thighs are engaged so as to shorten the distance I slide from one side to the other. The driver ignores me and continues to speed down the mountain as if he were driving in the grand finale of the off-road rally championship series.

Five minutes down the mountain, as we emerge from the mountain track onto the open road, the driver eases off the gas and straightens out the steering wheel. I close my eyes and rest my head against the cold window. Beyond exhausted, I struggle to replay static-filled memory clips from the previous twenty-four hours, linking every step back to the side of the cliff, where I witnessed the majestic sunrise. Under other circumstances I would have been jubilant, reminded of how powerfully charged and connected to the Source we all are. The power of our intentions, even when directed by blind ignorance, will manifest if we focus hard enough. I've received what I have asked for, but I failed to dot the i's and cross my t's when sending my emotionally charged prayers out to the Universe. The idiom "The devil is in the details" is a truth I'm mindful of, yet it was lack of detail that placed me in this predicament. Setting a goal means nothing unless a well-thought-out plan is in place to support it. My inability to anticipate and react with prudence enabled the devil to run wild and leave a mess in my path.

My head raps against the window, pulling me from my thoughts. The driver pulls into the Border Patrol command centre. The vehicle that is transporting Chris and Carl pulls in behind us. I'm mindful that another day is ending; the darkness is consuming the daylight. The extreme exhaustion of not sleeping for thirty-six hours, accompanied by the beating I had put my body through, is finally catching up with me. There is no more adrenaline to assist in fighting or taking flight. The gravity of what just went down weighs heavy on me. My heart aches, as I know my actions will hurt the people I had sworn to look out for. *I want to go home.*

We are escorted into the command centre and separated into individual holding cells. We are kept apart so we can't coordinate our stories. Every one of us denies involvement in illegal activity, other than crossing the border without proper authorization, but I am under no illusion that will not change. There is a one-foot-square window in the door to my cell, which allows me to look out into the main room. It's brightly lit with fluorescent lighting, illuminating the white floor, walls, and ceiling with an intense sharpness.

At some point, the door to my cell opens, stirring me out of my half-sleep. An agent walks in with my paper bag dinner — processed cheese and ham sandwich on white bread and a small bottle of water. I'm famished, so I gladly accept. Before the agent leaves the room, I politely ask him if they would turn the air conditioning down, or if that isn't possible, maybe they could give me a blanket?

"I will see what I can do," he says as he walks out and closes the door behind him.

Ten minutes elapse, and the AC is still pumping cold air into my frozen box. *Is this another way to punish us?* At least I wasn't being water-boarded. I sit back down and devour the little sandwich, washing it down with the water. I rest my head against the concrete wall, and my eyelids slam shut. Once again, just as I start drifting into a deep sleep, my door opens, jolting me awake. A senior officer enters, carrying a pen and some lined paper.

"Here's your opportunity to come clean."

I tell the agent my Miranda rights had been read to me immediately following our discovery on the mountain. "I understand. I know what my rights are."

"If you cooperate fully, we will make sure to mention it when your file gets passed on to the judge. Be assured, if it's shown you didn't cooperate, it will play out in the amount of prison time you serve."

Ouch! The stark realization I will have to serve time in a US prison is setting in.

"I don't have much to add other than what I have already told you. We were out hiking and got lost. I have nothing more to add until I have my lawyer with me."

The agent frowns at me. "Your decision." He walks back out the door, taking the paper and pen with him.

Damn it! What if all three of those guys write a statement, and I'm sitting here like an even bigger fool than I already am? I need to think straight. I lie on the concrete bench and curl myself up as tightly as possible to maintain as much warmth as I can. The chill is deep in my bones. I have no energy left to shiver. My eyes close, and I fall asleep.

Something wakes me. A noise? I grapple with the possibilities as my eyes struggle to open. The light is so bright! I question where I am, my brain running a quick compute as to what has just gone down. *Was I dreaming?* The horror of waking at that moment makes my arrest that much more real. The twenty minutes of sleep is just enough time to give me a slight reboot to my operating system. I get up and look out the cell door window to see what made the noise. *Oh shit!*

I see Carl standing over a large desk. One agent is next to him, and another sits in a chair on the other side of the desk. The agent places a note on the top of the desk. Carl picks up a pen, leans over the paper, scribbling what I assume is his signature. They lead Carl back to his cell. Chris stands a couple of feet back, inside from the door to his cell, writing on a pad of paper, using the cell wall for support.

So, two out of the four mules are writing their statement, but I have no idea to what extent. I assume that Sinisa is also giving his account of what happened, which leaves me standing alone by the train wreckage while everybody else has moved on.

I need to find some clarity quickly. *Fat chance! Do you know where you are? Just breathe deep and slow everything down.* I sit back on the concrete bench, placing my feet flat on the floor directly under my knees. My hands are placed palms down on my thighs, and I'm sitting as erect as I possibly can, slowing my breath as I do. No answers come. There is only darkness and extreme disappointment. Images of my wife, children, friends, and clients pop in and out of my mind, adding to the mix of emotions churning inside me.

Our words are powerful, especially when packed with fervour.

Did I ask for this? Did I make it happen? We are all entwined, playing a role in each other's lives, but our ultimate destiny lies within each of us. I desire to be free, yet it's only humility and a dash of deliverance I can taste. Goethe springs to mind: "Destiny grants us our wishes, but in its own way, in order to give us something beyond our wishes." I try to console myself with the thought that some good will come out of this, but any genuine appreciation for it will be a long time coming. "As soon as you trust yourself, you will know how to live." Sadness, fear, anger, and disgust with myself sweep across me in waves. Each feeling intermittently grips me before washing away back into the dark, stormy sea of my mind.

A loud creak comes from the main room. I can hear the rumbling of a truck engine. Officer Shannon and his partner are back from the mountain, bringing with them our four backpacks. They proceed to empty the contents — 108 pounds of evidence — onto the floor. They now have what they need to convict us. *I wonder how long I will be going away for. Oh God, grant me some sleep and send some help.*

Asleep within seconds, I find myself back on the mountain, at the spot where I stopped to watch the rising of the sun. The view is majestic. When I look across the vast divide between the massive mountain tops, I feel myself getting lighter on my feet. The heavy pack that had been weighing me down is no longer strapped to my back. Shedding the physical burden came as a relief, but it is the symbolic unloading of the weight I had been carrying that makes me scream out across the valley at the top of my lungs, "I am not carrying this load for you any longer! Do you hear me? I am done!" Where the sun is beginning its ascent, atop the range of mountains directly to the east of me, two giant doors open. The sun sits directly behind those doors, illuminating them with a golden radiance that silently invites me to enter, to walk off the ledge I am standing on, trusting the air beneath my feet to support me.

I hesitate, not because of lack of faith, rather because of its presence. Another world is out there waiting for me. I can feel it. I yearn for it, but it must wait. A noise is behind me. I turn around to look back through the trees but see nothing. When I turn back, the doors begin to shut.

Do you hear that? I ask myself, hearing the same noise again. No sooner do I ask the question than the entire landscape begins to fade away, slowly bringing my attention back to a world that is more dream-like than the one I have just experienced. I order my body to stand so I can check the time on the big clock hanging on the wall by the officer's desk. My eyes focus straight ahead to where I see Rick standing. He is wearing a complete set of new clothes: jeans, skate shoes, and a blue windbreaker jacket. He glances in my direction and smiles at me awkwardly before they lead him to the officer's desk. It's 12:30 am, and the entire crew, including the marijuana we had been transporting, is under lock and key. Case closed!

I am filled with anger. I am attributing a good chunk of my pain, strain, and mental degradation to this schmuck, who led us to the point of no return before abandoning us in this waking nightmare. And yet, what right do I have to be angry with him? I knew the risks. I knew both instinctively and intellectually this was folly. The light bulb in my head turns on. Tell them the truth, ending it with Rick as the team leader.

I knock on my door window, and an agent in his late twenties comes to ask what I want. "I would like to write my statement now."

"Yeah, sure thing," he replies before closing the door. Fifteen minutes pass, and I have just started to fall asleep again when my door opens and in steps Agent Shannon.

He's holding a pad of paper and pen in his hand. "So, Mr. Fontana, you're going to share your account of what happened?"

"Well, it seems it would be the right thing to do."

"You would be doing yourself a favour."

Then why does it not feel right? Why do I feel like I'm trapped in a bad movie?

"Do you like your job, Agent Shannon? Do you feel any sense of reward from doing a good job?"

"You're a different cat. Anybody ever tell you that?"

"Yes, but not quite in those words," I say, visualizing the panther as it steps into a spring trap that snaps down on its paw.

"You're going to take some time to figure out, aren't you?"

"I'm still working on it," I say, half-heartedly.

He hands me the pen and paper and gives me some advice: "Take your time and try to recount as much as you can."

Before he exits, I stop him, "Shannon, do you know someone by the name of Graham Rowling?"

Shannon's eyes widen, and he moves his head back and to the side. "You know him?"

I don't know what I see in his face at that moment. Is he surprised? He looks it. Something tells me there is more going on than I know.

"I have been training him for the past couple of years."

"Graham is my counter on that side of the border. We have worked together a handful of times," he states.

"I would appreciate it if you called him for me. I would rather he hear of my arrest through you than other channels in his department."

"You are full of surprises, aren't you?" Shannon says, holding my gaze for a long moment, awaiting a response that doesn't come. He leaves the room, and I start working on my deliberated statement.

I was introduced to Rick on April 19th, 2010. He offered me $10,000 to pack twenty pounds of marijuana across the Canada/US border. Rick, as far as I know, was the primary facilitator in this job. He organized and led our group meetings, delivered the marijuana, and handled the transport logistics from Canada into the US. I sincerely apologize for breaking the law and deeply regret the pain I will undoubtedly have caused my family and friends back home.

Of course, there is much more to the story, but for all accounts and purpose, I am giving them what they want: a neatly wrapped, open-close case that will add another feather to Shannon's cap. As far as Chris and Sinisa are concerned, this is Rick's operation, so they're protected by their own ignorance. I know Rick will get pressed hard to give up names, but if he is smart, he will keep his mouth shut and take what they throw at him.

Around 2:00 am the following morning, we leave the Border Patrol command centre and are transported to Whatcom County Jail, thirty minutes away. Chris, Rick, Carl, and Sinisa are transported in one vehicle with Shannon's partner, while Agent Shannon transports me alone in his truck. Aware of the odd-numbered separation between the two groups, I wait for Shannon to open the dialogue to figure out his intentions.

"Fontana, I have to say, we don't come across guys like you every day. You don't quite fit the bill for a character who would be humping small amounts of bud for such a ridiculously low amount of money."

"Is that a compliment?"

"In all seriousness, why would you get involved with this guy, Rick?"

"I told you."

"Sure, you did, but there are parts missing to the story."

I look out the window before changing the subject. "You must be looking forward to dropping us off so you can get home and into bed." I long for the bed I share with my wife.

"No, I still have hours of reports to get done first. You will get sleep before I do." Shannon understands where my mind is. "The system isn't perfect, but it's the best one we've got."

"The parts that are missing to my story is what drives me to get up every morning and do the things I do." I want him to know there is more to me than what he sees at surface level. I discuss my children, The Playground, and the work, everything but the details of the past twenty-four hours. He seems to accept that, easing up on pressing me for additional information when it becomes clear none is coming.

We drive the last few minutes in silence. Shannon pulls into the jailhouse parking lot and turns the engine off. He leans his head back in his seat and stares straight ahead, his hands resting on his lap. Silent for what seems like an eternity, he turns to me. "How do you think we came across you guys?"

What is he insinuating?

"Well, I had thought that was obvious. The helicopter does a scheduled fly-by and discovers our tracks. The rest, you know."

He looks at me, "Hmmm," then turns and gets out the truck.

Something is awry. Only seven people on average are apprehended each year doing what we did. I've read that thousands of people make it safely across every year. Couple that with the fact this had been the first trip Chris, Sinisa, and I have done. Perhaps there were eyes on us from the get-go. *Eyes on us, or eyes on me?* His question, "How do you think we came across you guys?" is going to gnaw at me.

CHAPTER 11

PROCESSING

"My toughest opponent has always been me."

— *Muhammad Ali*

April 27th, 2010

I t's 3:30 am by the time they process us at the local jailhouse. I have
been up for forty-eight hours with only a nod of the head here and
there. I have only stayed up this length of time once before in my life,
back when I was fifteen years old. After finishing school on a Friday afternoon, I worked my shift at the gym before working that evening's graveyard
shift at one of the local gas stations. Saturday morning I went straight
from work to a friend's wedding then finished the night off with another
graveyard shift, not making it to bed until fifty hours later. I know what
exhaustion feels like, but this time is different. This time around, I have

none of the usual comforts that I can find in the sanctuary of my bedroom.

Whatcom County Jail offers no additional comforts over the place we have just left. Breakfast turns out to be a handful of plain Cheerios and some weird blue creation that looks like a mixture of spam and oatmeal, resembling a dead, blue SpongeBob. It tastes sweet, and the texture is unpalatable. The dry Cheerios are going to have to suffice.

The guards pair me with Chris in a cell for one hour before switching him out with Rick. Random occurrences like switching cells don't just happen in jail. I am weary of Rick, more now than I ever was. He walks in while I am sleeping. I wake up and roll on my hard bunk, acutely aware that there are no smells to pull from in this cold brick building. The food and the people who inhabit this place are devoid of life, soulless.

"Crazy, heh?" Rick says to me as he walks to the little window beside the metal bunk bed.

I say nothing, letting my silence inform him that I'm not in the mood for talking. Besides, someone may be listening — information inadmissible in court, but information that still holds value.

Rick doesn't get the hint. I cut him off as he starts talking again.

"Not interested in hearing what you have to say, Rick. I'm going to face the consequences and try to move on from this." I won't be able to fall back asleep with Rick in the room. Best to get myself up and look out into the hallway, which opens into a general corridor where we were processed hours earlier.

After ten minutes, Rick says, "Hey, man, listen. Just as long as everyone knows that we were all in this together. I was just another mule. Right?"

"Sure, Rick, whatever you say." His eyes flare with contempt; my response does not sit well with him.

Ten minutes pass before he motions me over to the bunk I was lying on earlier. He points to a swastika inscribed on the underside of the top bunk, a symbol I'm certain represents the nickname he has given Fredo. Rick looks at me and shakes his head back and forth while whispering, "No way." *Is he implying that we shouldn't say anything about this person?* I nod my head in acknowledgement, all the while holding myself back from hammering him in the face with my fist and saying, "Of course we don't say anything about him, you fucking idiot. Do you think you need to explain that to me?"

Later that morning, a police transport van picks the five of us up to transport us to the federal courthouse in Seattle, another two-hour ride. We speak little to each other, except for Rick, who gives a sermon about the team sticking together. We remain silent, openly wearing our indifference as he looks us over. His hands are clasped tight in front of him and he's breathing fast. I can feel his anxiety growing; it's only a matter of time before he pops.

The drive into Seattle whips me back two weeks to when we had come for the Black Eyed Peas concert. *How could I not see then what I see now?* My eyes are opening a little wider to a reality I had once known but lost sight of long ago, and the Black Eyed Peas play quietly in my head. "Where Is the Love?"

Underneath Seattle's William Kenzo Nakamura US Courthouse, a secured parkade is used to take prisoners in and out. The holding cells in that courthouse, like most modern courthouses, are in the basement of the building. We are held together in a large cell until taken individually to the lawyer assigned to our case. My lawyer, Darren, takes the work handed to him from the government, helping to keep the machine rolling. I know he isn't going to move mountains or get me out of doing time, but he doesn't pretend not to notice the system he helps to support is wrought with imperfections and a tremendous amount of injustice. I like Darren. A lawyer in his position is a paper pusher and little more. They are here to assist in the facilitation of documentation for the government. Unless I have the money to buy my way out of the trouble I'm in — which is essentially greasing the corporate wheels —the system will make use of me in some other way.

Darren and I discuss how to move ahead. My first suggestion is to have him phone Candace and explain the situation. My stomach rolls as I picture Candace's reaction on the other end of the line.

"Are you ok?" Darren asks, looking concerned.

"Yeah, I'll make it."

"I will ask her to get some character references together for you as those will be important."

My mind wanders to the faces of the people who will soon know of my whereabouts. "I want to plead guilty," I say.

"I recommend you don't. I need the time to research other cases like yours, reach out to the lawyers representing the others, and get those references from your wife."

After we've finished with the lawyers, we're transported to Federal Detention Center, SeaTac. FDC SeaTac is halfway between downtown Seattle and Tacoma. It's a high-security facility that looks like a ten-story apartment building on steroids, with a reinforced perimeter that makes getting in or out near impossible. I imagine this place is holding some interesting characters from all walks of life, and I'm getting the chance, whether I like it or not, to meet these undesirables.

When we arrive, they direct us into an empty holding cell to await processing. The room is long and narrow, and I can feel the chill coming off the concrete walls.

One of the guards orders me to face the wall and spread my feet wide on the floor and place my hands high up on the wall so he can remove my ankle and wrist shackles. He taps my left arm, where I have the names and symbols representing my two sons tattooed on the inside of my left forearm. "Let me see that tat," he says, pointing toward my tattoo of Master Yoda.

I turn my head and shoulder toward him. "Yoda wouldn't be happy with you at all," he snidely remarks.

"Are you sure about that? Have you ever, for one second, considered that the republic fell a long time ago and the master you serve is the empire?" I shoot back.

"What?!" He falters, struggling to find something smart to say back.

"You know there is truth in what I say."

We are issued our "standard bedroll" of bedding and towels. They measure me for size before handing out my prison clothes: a white cotton t-shirt, tan trousers, a matching tan shirt, two pair of underwear, two pair of socks, a pair of cheap boat shoes, and an identification card to be carried always, except to and from the showers. For the second time in twenty-four hours, I must strip off my clothes before bending over to spread my cheeks for the guards to determine whether I am concealing any weapons or contraband. The level of degradation and humiliation people experience daily is not lost on me. I understand the necessity, but it does little to alleviate my contempt for the empire.

They pair Sinisa and me together in a cell separate from Chris, Carl, and Rick. All eyes turn on us when we walk in the doors, and then the cheers and jeers start. Many of the guys look wildly menacing and combative, and I make sure to avoid direct eye contact with anyone as I scan my surroundings. I know there is a protocol to follow, but I won't find it in the handbook the prison gave me. I feel relieved when we get to our cell. It's about eight feet wide by twelve feet long, with two separate steel bunk beds, a sink, a toilet, and a one-foot by two-foot-wide window. *At least there's light.* And a new bunkmate.

"Hey, I'm Billy," says the mid-thirties white guy. "When you use the shitter, make sure to hang something on the door to notify your celly. Breakfast is at seven, lunch at twelve, and dinner at five. And be careful who you associate with. You don't want to get caught up with the wrong people."

"Thanks for the heads-up."

"No problem."

"What are you in for?" I ask.

"My girlfriend and I got hooked on Oxy and we couldn't kick it. It got bad enough where we started breaking into pharmacies." Another sad case.

"Sorry to hear that. It's an epidemic. People getting hooked on powerful narcotics being given out like candy by the US medical profession." I said, letting him know there was no judgment from me.

CHAPTER 12

FLASHBACK

"Our enemies are innovative and resourceful, and so are we. They never stop thinking about new ways to harm our country and our people, and neither do we."

— *George W. Bush*

April 28th, 2010

The doors to the cells automatically unlock at 05:30, waking me with a loud metal kerchunk. I've finally slept a solid six hours straight. I lie there on my back for the next ninety minutes, motionless, patiently awaiting the call to breakfast, working to unravel where I went wrong and wondering how to get back to my former self.

What else am I evading?

I quickly learn that specific tables in the cafeteria are spoken for, which I don't care about, as I'm not planning to stick around for too many days and have no desire to make friends.

At breakfast, Sinisa and I get a chance to discuss our court cases.

"Sinisa, there is a big difference in how the law relates to an individual or group who do nothing more than transport, as opposed to someone involved in the organization and distribution. The higher you go up the ladder, the more severe the punishment will likely be, but that too comes down to who you know and how much money you have," I say. "Emphasis is on who you know."

"I understand." He nods while swallowing a spoonful of tasteless slop.

Following breakfast, Sinisa decides to walk laps around the upper mezzanine. "I'll join you for a few laps, then go put my head down for a nap." The mezzanine is an eight-foot-wide walkway connecting forty cells on the second floor and overlooking the common area below, including the guard's booth, showers, and cafeteria. We observe what is happening from up here while we do our laps: one guy is getting tattooed, four others are gambling, playing cards, and a few guys are working out. As we walk, Sinisa tells me about living through the Bosnian war, the first period of mass genocide in Europe since World War II. Listening to someone who lived through that terror helps relieve me of some of the self-pity I am carrying. *What drove me to be reckless for so little gain?*

Back in my room, I roll onto my side to better see out the small window. It is a clear day, and I can see the southern base of Puget Sound. The water is no more than three kilometres away, and the loss of freedom I've taken for granted stabs me in the heart. My wife and children are about 250 klicks from where I lie, but they may as well be halfway across the world.

The disconnect between Candace and me has been growing these last three years. Our schedules are jam-packed, but we are always adding more to our plate and pushing ourselves hard to succeed in all areas, including volunteering for most of the well-known charitable foundations in our region. What I aspire to goes beyond building community. I want to dedicate my life to a progressive movement that enforces human rights for all people. Candace supports me in my desire to build bridges, but it isn't her passion. It's not that she isn't interested in socio-political issues; for her, it is about practicality. She spends her time on things she has immediate control over. *How is she going to cope with this?*

I always try to make the best of every situation, no matter how bad it may seem, but building upon this catastrophe will entail a lot of time and effort. *Take a deep breath, and you'll get through this. In... out... in... out.*

I close my eyes, and the darkness envelops me. I take another deep breath, and as I exhale, a bright light flashes in my mind, jolting every cell in my body to attention. My eyes open, and I spring up into a sitting position on my bed. *No fucking way,* shocked by a memory that has lain dormant for 2,772 days.

My cell acts as a time machine, teleporting me back seven and a half years to a warm autumn day, my thirtieth birthday, when I was pondering the same thoughts as the ones coalescing in my mind now. This is when I started to veer off course. World events had been agitating me more than I cared to admit. Concerns and conflicts, which I had no immediate control over, had been brewing. I had been sucked into consuming the news for months, spending hours upon hours every day immersed in it, prior to the 2000 US presidential election. I had concluded that our governing social-political system was beyond corrupt, that a person's vote didn't count, and that we were living in a fascist authoritarian state dictated by the corporate oligarchy. The president of the United States is generally described as the most powerful elected official in the world, but I saw this position as being held by mid-level businessmen, top level administrators at best, who read their scripted lines and posed for cameras. I was obsessed with knowing who pulled their strings and to what end, driving me to delve deeper into my study of the shadowy world of politics, which proved to be as much a blessing as it was a curse.

My research on Al Gore and George W. Bush didn't produce anything that seemed shockingly unusual or unexpected. But I was able to find snippets of information that gave me solid background about them, information I believed painted an accurate picture of their lives. Not surprisingly, both candidates came from influential political families. However, the Gores' legacy didn't stretch back as far as the Bushes'. Gore was raised in a liberal, progressive family and gained popularity for championing the environment and the internet. My research into Bush led me down a rabbit hole. I read what I could find on the Net and make good use of our public library. Once again, just as I had done in my late teens and early twenties, I became an information addict, looking to connect the links in a very long chain. Rather than focusing on philosophy and theology, I focused entirely on geopolitics and the leading influencers behind the most prominent movements that shape the world as it is today.

President G.W. Bush wasn't the sharpest tool in the shed. He lacked polish, but he was personable. He was dressed up and promoted as the guy you would want to invite to a ball game. Hell, he owned the Texas Rangers! Could he have had this level of success without the help of his father and his prime influencer, his mother? I don't believe so. How much control did his family wield in shaping his destiny, and for what purpose? My research pointed to the Bush family connecting to a long-standing and influential network that sat high on the ladder. I came to believe they may have been sitting on the top rung with select company.

By the time the 2000 presidential US election rolled around, I felt I had a good read on what was going on in the world. I didn't trust Al Gore, but he came across as the guy who had to roll up his sleeves and work a little harder to get to where he was. Sure, he had his own family connections to the political elite, but his inheritance within the establishment wasn't as blatant as Dubyah's was. I felt jaded that our system is heavily influenced by people who are accepted into the club based solely on who they know rather than merit. I understand how the pyramid system operates, and by no means was I in direct opposition to it, but the thought of a smug guy like Bush and an arrogant guy like Cheney, the CEO of Halliburton, winning the presidency made me want to vomit.

The election was stolen from Gore, and he barely protested, eventually selling out and supporting the team's narrative. What choice did he have? My stomach was tied in knots over how easily democracy could be subverted, and I was sure there were millions of others who felt the same way I did. After the election, I vowed to do everything within my power to change the system that rules us. The mission for grassroots change had always been at the forefront of my thoughts, but I wasn't doing nearly enough to quantify it as a serious contribution. We needed a revolution, but not one mired in blood and loss of life. We needed to stop the blatant corruption taking place at all levels of government and business around the world. *How am I supposed to help make that happen?*

Less than a year later, on September 11th, the lives of millions were radicalized. This calm, cool cat was now simmering on the inside. I wanted to hammer the fuckers who justified killing innocent people, chalking it up to necessary collateral damage, so they could continue with the execution of plans that had been years in the making. The poison and treachery that seeped in through the cracks of every empire throughout history came to mind. Where was the honour, the justice, *the love*? And what had I done with my time since Bush won the election? No imminent revolution was at hand, but there was a sparking of one, coinciding with the conception and birthing of our second child. Kahlil was conceived days after Bush stole the election and born three weeks before 9/11.

Realistically, how was I supposed to make any real difference? I was a good trainer, a good father, and, I believed, a good husband. I had also learned to grow and take to market small amounts of quality herb. For all accounts and purpose, I had a great life, but it was beginning to lose its lustre, as I was not contributing to my community in a substantial way. I wanted nothing more than to sit in the same room as guys like Bush, Cheyney, Powell, and Rumsfeld. I wanted to speak with Kissinger, Putin, Gates, Annan, and Vieira de Mello, but I knew I would be out of my league. Most of these people would chew me up and spit me out without any effort. I needed to learn so much more.

CHAPTER 13

FOUNDATION BUILDING

"Each workout is like a brick in a building, and every time you go in there and do a half-ass workout, you're not laying a brick down."
— *Dorian Yates*

1988

My sophomore year at Cowichan Senior Secondary School brought me more freedom, and with it… more responsibility. I worked a part-time job so I could pay for the extras, but the thing I really needed — structure to help guide me onto the right path — was sorely lacking. I harboured resentment against a world authority I didn't understand and pushed back against those who had been entrusted with protecting me. I was breaking away from the key influencers who were instrumental in my upbringing. I wasn't abandoning all that I'd been taught but I was consciously questioning my place in the world, understanding there was an established process to follow, critical to unlocking the doors that lay ahead of me. My body was morphing, and the testosterone surging through my veins was compounded by the weight training I did every day. The frustrated angst that had been bubbling to the surface the last few years, a common occurrence for adolescent boys, was tempered by my time spent training in the gym.

Fortress of Fitness Gym was my saving grace, my second home. It gave me an outlet to vent the pent-up anger I was carrying. I funnelled my frustrated energy into a source of strength. Weight training was a discipline I could easily measure. Every pound gained, every extra repetition, and every weight I added to a lift showed me the value of what working hard, in all areas, could do for me. I was fortunate to train with some of the most intense athletes my province was producing at that time. The owner, Kim, and some other freakishly big guys took me under their wing and pushed me to excel. Kim gave me the opportunity to better myself, including entrusting me to train his newer clients when I was just seventeen years old.

I missed more classes than I should have during my senior years at high school, but I still received decent enough grades to attend college. My friends found it amusing when I would have to bring a letter to my teacher, explaining my absence from class, as I wrote and signed these notes rather than having a guardian sign for me — and didn't try to hide the deception as so many other students did.

Please excuse my absence from class yesterday morning as I had a conflicting engagement that kept me from attending. ~ Daryl Fontana

I often played poker with my brother and his friends on a Tuesday night. Staying up until 2:00 am was worth it, as I won nearly every time we played. Walking away with an extra $50 in my pocket when money was scarce was well worth missing the occasional morning class. Outside of school, work, and working out, my time was spent playing sports, reading, hanging with friends, and cruising into neighbouring cities, looking for adventure and excitement.

Once a month we would gather outside of the town boundaries to rip wild through the night with outdoor pit parties. They would start with the keeners showing up early to get the fire going. Most people would wait for night to fall before descending in droves, half-liquored, looking for a good time. My angst and teenage emotions were not mine to own alone at those parties. After a couple of hours of drinking, the first fight would break out, a couple would break up, and two people would hook up for the first time — all acceptable behaviours to those coming of age.

I experienced my first love before starting grade twelve. Sarah Staschuk set a new standard for the Wow-O-Meter! She possessed many of the qualities as my previous crushes, only now they were in a woman's body. Sarah was mature, bright, witty, beautiful, sexy, athletic, and daring, and she shared my curiosity for the world. We met in the summer of 1989 at the King Coho resort while I was visiting my dad. I had been fishing out of this popular destination spot for the past seven years, and never had I seen someone as beautiful as her.

Dad and I came in from being out on the water all day. We did well, catching our limit, a mix of coho and spring salmon. Once I had cleaned the fish and helped store the boat, it was time to sit back and relax. At sixteen, for the first time since elementary school, I felt I had a solid handle on my life. The sound of the waves rolling in and softly crashing upon the beach enhanced the warmth of the early evening sun that was pleasantly shining down upon my face. My eyes closed as I took in a deep breath of sea air, and when they opened, two beautiful young women sprang up from behind the log that was twenty feet in front of me. I assume they had been sunbathing, as both were wearing bikinis that left little to the imagination. Though I remained calm and collected, I was no longer relaxed, for these lovely creatures had shaken up every hormone inside me. One of the girls was my dad's friend's grand-daughter, Marnie. The other, I would soon discover, was Sarah. Sarah and Marnie were best friends, two mainland city girls vacationing their summer away on Vancouver Island. I was attracted to Marnie, but Sarah captivated me. I was happily being thrust into a new phase of developmental growth.

For the remainder of that summer, I seized upon every opportunity to make the two-hour drive north so I could spend time with them. Though our time together was short, we fell for one another. We may well have stayed together longer if it hadn't been for the distance between us and the pressure I placed on her to visit me. She was entering grade eleven. Convincing her mom and dad to allow her to travel by ferry to see me wasn't going to fly, but I was annoyed she didn't make more of an effort and presented her with an ultimatum. I still carry feelings for Sarah to this day, as I will never forget the light she emanated and the magical kisses she gave me.

Like most everything else, things that seem to go the wrong way wind up going the right way. Eight months later, I met my future wife.

I was introduced to Candace through a good friend, and we started dating a few weeks later. In the beginning, I was less interested in her than she was in me. She was only fifteen years old to my seventeen, an age difference that bothered me, but more than that... I still had feelings for Sarah.

Though we were both young, she was as much a mother to me as I was a father to her. She loved me unconditionally. I pushed her to excel, going as far as threatening to break up with her if she didn't put more effort into her studies. Our future was wide open.

CHAPTER 14

HARDENING

"If you're gonna be stupid you gotta be tough."
— *John Grisham, The Testament*

April 28ᵗʰ, 2010

I snap out of my memory travel, back to the reality of lying on my prison bunk, with the prayer I said on my 30th birthday looping through my mind:

Universe, hear me now. Today is my birthday, and I am asking you to grant me this wish. I want to succeed in accomplishing the goals I have set forth. I want you to work through me without me having to plan every detail and action. Turn off the switch that allows me to see what you see. I wish to enjoy a simple life with my family. Wake me up when my children are a little older and a whole lot stronger, at which point we will usher in the worldwide revolution.

Why would I ever wish to put myself to sleep? The truth is, we can't do what we came here to do if we keep reminding ourselves that we created every moment of it. I wanted to ground myself, but getting dropped in a US federal prison is not what I had in mind. And here I am, awake again.

I finish my lunch and make my way over to the main door, where I wait for a guard to escort me to my meeting with my lawyer. There is no visitation on Tuesdays, Wednesdays, or Thursdays other than client-attorney meetings and, since it is a Wednesday, the visiting room is relatively quiet when I walk in. The guard prompts me to take a seat by the far wall and await the arrival of my lawyer, Darren. I notice someone else sitting there. I don't recognize him until I'm nearly over to his seat. It's Carl, and he's now wearing glasses.

"How are you making out?" I ask him as I sit to his left.

"I'm doing all right. You?"

"I'm keeping my shit together, but I will admit it's been a pretty rough ride."

"Yeah, it has," he agrees. His eyes are sunken and he looks exhausted but still, to his credit, he seems relatively calm and collected.

I waste little time, knowing we will be separated soon and might never have a chance again to confer about what went down.

"The lawyer they sent me is an idiot. He has no clue as to what he's doing."

"That bad?" I ask.

"He just sees an arrest he needs to process."

I can't help but laugh. "I know what you mean. Even though Darren, my lawyer, genuinely wants to help, he's been trained to push paper. It doesn't matter, as I'm not going to fight it. I'm going to hope for the best and prepare for the worst."

Carl looks at me intently. "What do you think that would be?"

"Darren says somewhere between six months to a year is most likely. It depends on the judge."

"Well, I don't know what direction I will be going in," says Carl, "but I'm not taking it in the ass for Rick, that's for sure."

The guard calls Carl's name, and he goes to meet his lawyer in an adjacent room, leaving me alone momentarily to question the timing of our chance meeting. Within seconds of Carl's departure, Darren walks into the room. He motions me to one of the tables, and I walk over, taking a seat across from him.

"How're you doing, Daryl?" he asks.

"I'm ok, thanks," I'm in no mood for small talk. I just want to know how my wife and kids are doing. "Did you reach Candace?"

"Yes, I did."

"How is she?" I ask, dreading the answer.

"She was understandably upset, but she kept herself together. She asked if you were ok, and I assured her you were."

"Thank you."

"I talked with her about getting those character references, and she is working on that today. She will hopefully have them for me tonight. I have been able to put some money onto your phone account here so that you can call her later."

"Thanks so much, Darren. I appreciate you doing that for me," I say.

"I've put in the paperwork to change your plea to guilty. You'll be arraigned tomorrow back at the federal courthouse. Candace will be making the trip to be there."

I go back to my unit and immediately try calling Candace, but I don't have authorization to call her number. It must not be approved.

"Try after dinner, man," says a man next to me. "If your lawyer just submitted the phone number this afternoon, it's probably not in the system yet. It might take six to eight hours to get verified."

I want to smash the phone onto the keypad but get a grip on my rage. My separation from Candace is killing me. I want to tell her I am ok, that everything will be ok. But I can't. It would be a lie.

I decide to do a workout, hoping it will burn away the feeling of help-lessness that has descended upon me. I just completed a gruelling fif-teen-hour hike and then got bounced around from jail to courthouse to federal prison with very little sleep. I've barely eaten, and when I did, it was the furthest thing from what I consider to be food. Rest is surely what the doctor would order, but I am setting the prescription aside, knowing this workout will serve a second purpose.

No matter how much a person tries to remain unnoticed, they will eventu-ally be called out and inspected by the inmates who hold sway within the tight quarters of any "correctional" institution. Why wait for them to come to me? The level of intensity I put out will make my presence known very quickly.

There is no gym, just a 1,600-square-foot courtyard with what looks to be four twenty-foot-high concrete walls. There is one basketball net and that's it. I need more. Two separate groups are training on the lower level underneath the opposing set of stairs that give access to the second floor. The step risers from the stairs are used for doing chin-ups, and the handrails are used for training shoulders and triceps. I walk to the south set of stairs first to find the neo-Nazis training. The vibe I'm getting from these white boys is not conducive to moving me in the right direction. I casually make eye contact, seeing nothing but hatred in their eyes. They look at me like a pack of feral dogs about to pounce. *Can people like this be reformed? Can they heal?*

No way in hell am I going to allow myself to be discarded along with these lost souls.

My next move is important, because if I forgo training with these guys and train under the northern stairs with the group that comprises the Hispanics and Blacks, I will be conveying a message that I am looking for inclusion elsewhere. It will be the same as flipping them the bird.

As I approach the other side of the room, I quickly scan the group of five hanging out under the northern stairwell. One of the five is training, and the others are kicking back in conversation. I stop walking when I'm six feet from the guy nearest me and wait for my presence to be acknowl-edged. All eyes stare at me coldly.

"Do you mind if I jump in?" I respectfully ask the guy who is training.

He gives me a quick, disgruntled nod. "Let's see what you've got, white boy."

Forty minutes later I am standing motionless in a pool of my sweat. I'm working to slow my breath and bring myself back to the reality I had momentarily escaped from while completing one of the most intense workouts I have ever done in under an hour.

As I turn to grab my shirt from the railing, I look up to see all five guys looking at me. No words are spoken, but they acknowledge my demonstration of warriorship by saluting me with a nod of their heads and a pump of their fists.

After my shower, I meditate on my bunk.

How many years has it been since I meditated with consistency? Why did I stop doing something that served me so well?

An hour later, I make my way down to the seating area, where I wait for dinner. I'm famished, but dinner is still half an hour away, so I continue to read the John Grisham novel I picked up that morning.

"Can I sit here?" I look up to see a Caucasian man, near my age, gesturing at my table.

"Of course," I say, placing my book on the table. "I'm Daryl."

"Matt," he says.

We briefly make small talk until the details of his case start to emerge.

"I'm also from BC," he tells me. "Extradited five weeks ago on charges of conspiring to export three thousand pounds of weed. I've been fighting this extradition for years."

I consider the possibility this guy has been planted by my captors to lift information from me. The possibility seems likely. I think carefully before saying anything.

"How are you making out?" I ask him.

"They put me in solitary when I first got in here, still shaking that off."

Prison is already changing me. No longer am I an open book; naively trusting others is a thing of the past.

I get through to Candace after dinner. She says she is doing ok, but her voice indicates otherwise. She has character references from three of our good friends, each of whom is held in high esteem within our community. She doesn't want to tell the kids what has happened until we figure out what lies ahead. Her sister Tawnya will make the trip with her the following morning so that they can be there for my arraignment. I have no words for her other than, "I am so sorry." She's unreceptive to my apology and offers no words of support, just silence.

I return to my grey and lifeless cell so I can be alone. I lie on my bunk and roll through the twenty years we have been together. Special moments — from our first kiss to the conceiving and delivery of our children — flash into my mind. Sleep eventually saves me from misery.

CHAPTER 15

BAIL HEARING

"If anyone comes to you and does not bring this teaching, do not take them into your house or welcome them."

— *2 John 1:10*

April 29ᵗʰ, 2010

Sinisa and I have to be at the main entrance of our unit by 7:00 am. We get rounded up with inmates from other units who are also having their day in court. While we wait, we take the opportunity to talk privately. Sinisa tells me he has been receiving candy bars from the guy who has a cell three down from ours. *This guy, who supposedly likes blowing up buildings, is trying a wee bit too hard to become his buddy.*

"You shouldn't take anything from anyone around here, unless you can pay for it. I don't want to see you forced into returning any favours," I say.

It takes thirty minutes to get through all the security checks and elevators. When we get to the final holding cell deep within the basement, Rick and Chris are already there along with six other guys. Carl is missing. I assume he's fired his lawyer. The guards cuff us at the ankles and wrists, then shackle us together like a train of ten cars with me as the caboose. We shuffle onto the big blue prison bus. I recall driving past a similar prison bus years before, wondering about the different characters who were on it. What was their story? How did they wind up on that bus? The only story I wonder about now is my own.

As soon as we take our seats, Rick turns his attention to Sinisa and me, his eyes wide and bloodshot, "Remember, I'm just another mule. This isn't my show."

"I know, Rick. You're just like us," Sinisa says.

I know Sinisa is lying. "Rick, I'm only going to say this once. You continue to focus on looking after yourself; it's obvious how well it works for you," I say. His eyes flare with resentment, then he turns his back to me and quietly faces the front of the bus.

We arrive at the courthouse and unload into our holding cells, the hours creeping by ever so slowly. It is torture sitting with Rick. I empathize with what he is going through, but he didn't care how we felt and never apologized for how he treated us. No one speaks to him despite his attempts to be friendly.

Rick, to my surprise, is called to go first and alone. An hour later it is my turn and Chris's turn to enter the courtroom. I manage a meek smile for Candace and Tawnya, who are sitting on the benches directly behind the area designated for the defence team, represented today by Darren. My heart pounds. I ache to take her in my arms. I want nothing more than to snap my fingers and make the last couple of years go away so that we can start fresh.

Judge Tsuchida appears deeply moved while discussing our case. Chris and I are respected members in our community, unlikely candidates to be involved in a story normally designated for the back page of the newspaper. "I wish you gentlemen the best possible outcome in what I can only say is a most unfortunate case. I sincerely hope you and your families can weather this storm and get your life back on track. God speed."

Judge Tsuchida grants us both bail. We can return home and get our affairs in order before returning to the US for sentencing. Unfortunately for Sinisa, his refugee status makes him a flight risk, as he has few ties to anyone or anything in Canada. He has to remain in custody until sentencing.

Back in the holding cell, Rick is lying on a bench in the fetal position, staring at the wall opposite him. As soon as our cell door closes behind us, Rick sits up and launches into one of his tirades.

"Fucking awesome! Thanks, guys! Throw me under the fucking bus!"

Where does a guy go after becoming unhinged? In Rick's case, he goes mad. The veins in his neck bulge as the blood begins flowing heavily back into his pale white face.

"I was just another packer! This isn't my shit! You guys didn't back me at all!" he screams.

"We got some snitches over there? Someone's going to get gutted tonight," says a menacing voice from the cell next to us.

Chris attempts to calm Rick down, whispering so the others can't hear, "C'mon, Rick, watch what you say. Nobody wants to die in here."

Rick jumps from the bench and begins pacing back and forth along the entire twelve feet of the room, opening and closing his fists. Seething with anger, he continues, "Well, maybe you guys should have thought about that before you fucking hung me out to dry."

"That cage isn't going to protect you forever, rat!" The gangbangers next to us start laughing and adding more threats.

I feel like the Hulk is trying to wrest control from Bruce Banner. The camera in the corner of the room constantly watching us is the only thing that keeps me from slamming Rick's mouth shut. I direct all my rage into staring into Rick's eyes. "Shut the fuck up, Rick, you whiny little man! Take some responsibility for what got us here."

His fists and jaw are clenched. No doubt he disagrees with me, but at least he shuts up and gives me a minute to think about the guys in the next cell. We will be coming face to face shortly and will be transported back to the prison on the same bus. A guard speaks over the intercom, instructing us to exit into the small corridor and file into a single line. As we begin filing into our line, I look directly at the guys who had issued the threats. Five badass dudes stand before me, one of whom is cut from a different cloth altogether. I suspect he is the guy who made the initial threat against us. I conjure the look of death and stare hard. They all turn from my gaze except for the leader, who stares straight back until the guard forces him to turn away to assume his position in the train chain. The power behind our eyes can often communicate more effectively than words.

We return to SeaTac just as the sun is setting. Darren said earlier that day that Chris and I would be moved to an immigration centre within the next few days, and would be held there until our paperwork was processed. Now it was just a matter of waiting.

After dinner, I decide to ask one of the guards for a racquet ball to teach myself to play handball, a popular game played in most American prisons. The rules are simple enough: think tennis with the wall acting as the return net.

I play on my own for well over an hour, working hard to get my hand cupped just right so as to have better control when hitting the ball. By the time I finish playing, my right hand is raw from the repeated smacking. It was worth it, because I had given my mind a break from the constant shifting of raw emotions that were still swirling inside me.

The next morning, following breakfast, I decide to walk laps around the mezzanine. Sinisa joins me somewhere around lap fifteen. We walk the next five or six laps without speaking a word, silently sharing the uncanny experience of living out what we have only ever watched in the movies. By the time we approach the fortieth lap, our pace has slowed considerably, as our heads are down and we are perusing our court documents. We are deep in discussion, unaware of the man who is approaching us head on. I fail to see him until he is no more than five feet in front of us, stopping to my right, inside the walkway, obstructing my way.

He looks to be in his mid-thirties, and he's solidly built, five feet eleven inches tall, weighing a lean 175 pounds. He was bigger than the average Hispanic I had seen in SeaTac, or for that matter, anywhere else. His dark brown hair was neatly combed back and the fact that he has buttoned his standard issued collared shirt right to the top tells me he takes care of his appearance. He carried himself with a quiet confidence that instantly throws me into fight-flight mode, although I tried not to show it. We stopped in front of him, puzzled as to what he wanted. I nod my head slightly forward with a look that expressed my acknowledgement of him and a willingness to hear what he has to say.

I assumed his attempt at a half smile was to disarm me and ease my concern. "My friend wants to know if you would join him on the court," he says coolly.

I looked at him inquisitively, recognizing him to be one of a handful of guys I saw earlier in the week playing handball. I made no attempt to hide my suspicious reluctance.

"He wants to have a game of handball with me?"

"Yeah."

I don't trust anyone in here. I didn't trust myself to say or do the right thing unless given a considerable amount of time to think it through. Who could blame me? I was on heightened alert, aware of my surroundings, knowing full well, regardless of the outside factors that influenced me, that I was the one responsible for where I was. The last thing I needed was more trouble. I worked to quell the apprehension that rose inside me, making myself look as calm as this messenger does.

"Well, I'm not that good, as I just started playing yesterday, but why not? I will be there in five minutes."

"Good," he replies with approval and then walks away.

I returned to my cell to drop off the documents I had been looking at with Sinisa and put on my standard issue plain white t-shirt.

Just as I was about to step out of my cell to make my way to the court, my cellmate, Billy, stops me, "What was that all about?" He looks concerned, a little jittery, possibly high from the drugs he would sometimes take during the day.

Yes, there are drugs in prisons; the contraband brought in by family and friends during visitation and the drugs prescribed by facility doctors. My cellmate and countless others are given pills for everything from pain management to depression. Many of the guys, including my celly, would crush the medication into a fine powder and snort it for a fast and heavy hit.

"What was what all about?" I asked him, not certain as to what he meant.

"Rico came and spoke with you on the walkway," he says, pointing to where I had been standing a few minutes prior. "What about?"

How do people pick up on things so fast in here, and why does he care so much?

"His friend wants a game of handball. I said I would play. Is everything cool?" I asked.

His hesitation to answer adds to my discomfort. "Yeah... you're good. I'm sure it's legit."

"You don't seem so sure."

"Well, Rico's friend would be his boss, and he doesn't make a habit of inviting just anybody to come join him."

"I'm intrigued. Who am I playing handball with?"

"He's the highest ranking member of La Familia in SeaTac."

"And...?" I asked, pressing him for something more before I make my leave.

"He's as big as they get on the inside. It's his business to know everyone else's business. He probably just wants to see where you fit in."

"I guess I have nothing to worry about, as I'm not planning on fitting in here at all. I will be gone, hopefully, by Monday." I turn and walk away, aware I am leaving my protected space, hoping that only good will come from this meeting.

When I walked into the large concrete room, I saw my opponent warming up on the court, smacking the ball effortlessly against the north-facing wall. Rico stood beside the lone door to the room with his back to the wall. I stopped a few feet in front of him, waiting for his direction. Rico nods in the Boss's direction, signalling for me to walk out onto the court. The Boss didn't say a word, simply held out his hand for me to take the ball from him. I guessed him to be in his early to mid-fifties, near my height, heavier set, with a slight rounding of his belly. His Mexican decent was not as prominent as Rico's: both his skin and hair are lighter in colour.

For the next hour he schooled me in handball. He had me running from side to side, easily placing every shot with amazing precision on any one spot on the court. There was little dialogue between us, and what was said had only to do with teaching me how to play. His messenger, Rico, never moved from the door, watching us quietly for the session. As the minutes ticked by, I relaxed, and felt a little more at ease.

I don't know how long we would have spent there if a guard had not come to the door, calling me. "Fontana! Go pack your stuff. You're being transferred."

I turned to my playing partner, "Well I wasn't expecting to have been leaving so quickly but I'm not going to complain." I extend my hand to thank him for the lesson.

He took my hand in a firm grip and his eyes lasered in on mine. "Keep your eyes open and don't trust anyone."

CHAPTER 16

MICHEL

"I believe that imagination is stronger than knowledge. That myth is more potent than history. That dreams are more powerful than facts."
— *Michelangelo*

April 30th, 2010

Chris and I are transported on Friday afternoon from SeaTac to the Northwest Detention Center in Tacoma, Washington, a notorious immigration centre that holds non-US citizens facing deportation. We are told we will be penned up for a month, even though our paperwork processing takes no more than a few days. Everybody wants to get their cut, including Geo Corp, the private company that lobbies the government for longer sentences. The prison system needs an overhaul; it's inefficient, outdated, and unjust.

The Northwest Detention Center (NWDC) doesn't lack any of the shortcomings I had heard about. It's actually much worse than I'm expecting. The entire air ventilation system at the NWDC is interconnected. The air that blows into the cells connects to ventilation pipes for the showers. Whatever goes through those water pipes vents off through the air pipes. Chris and I smell shit coming through the wall vent in the cell we share. At first, I think there is a farm in the vicinity spraying manure on their fields. I make a complaint to the guards but never get a response. On day four, we get sent to the doctor, as we have developed strep throat. No one told the new detainees from Somalia that it isn't acceptable to defecate in the showers. I can't fault the Somalians because they are accustomed to standing in latrines. Over a few days, feces built up in the pipes, and we breathed in ripe human excrement for three long days. The doctor gives us each a heavy dose of antibiotics to combat our streptoccus infection..

A few days later I am scheduled for what is supposed to be a routine medical exam. *Why didn't they do the exam when I was here the other day?* I am escorted to a holding cell full of other foreigners, most of whom are waiting to see their lawyer. As I step in, a man sitting on the bench next to the wall on the left side of the room gets up and walks toward the door. I move to his left as he passes and walk the five paces to the spot he just vacated. I take a seat and immediately start focusing on my breath — *in... out... in... out...* trying to tune out the chatter and encourage a stream of consciousness to flow through me. *Where did I go wrong?* Every major event and every person of significance in my life from the last ten years fires from my memory: The decision to leave Vancouver, our home, for seven years. Opening a health and fitness centre, The Playground, with the intent to use it as a vehicle to connect with and inspire others. My network of friends and business associates; my extended family, the ones I adore and love, and the ones I love but could do without.

The cell door opens again, and I'm doing my best to tune out the voices and shuffling of feet as one person leaves and another comes in. My eyes remain closed, and I'm aware that the last person to enter has made his way to where I'm sitting. He stands close to my right. I open my eyes and recognize the slender man who was previously sitting where I sit now.

"May I sit beside you?" he asks, with a noticeable French accent. I slide over so he can wedge himself in between another guy and me. "I see you were meditating."

My head nods in acknowledgement but in no way invites conversation. I close my eyes and resume focusing on my breath. He, however, continues to converse.

"You used to meditate all the time, then you stopped."

Does he know me?

"Yes. I used to meditate regularly," I say while giving him a look that says, "Who are you?"

"There is nothing more to do," he says. "Everything you need starts from here."

"How did you end up here?" I ask.

"I was pulled over for having a tail light out. I didn't realize my visa had expired the week before. Now I am waiting to fly back to France." he says with indifference.

"Sorry to hear that," I say.

"It is a small inconvenience. I will fly back and get my paperwork in order, then return."

"You don't hold any resentment for the time lost in here?" I ask, surprised to find someone else who likely makes the best out of every situation he finds himself in.

"No time has been lost for either of us. If we hadn't made our way in here, then we would not have met." His energy, the frequency in which he vibrates, feels perfectly tuned to me.

My first tattoo, the Yin-Yang surrounded by fire, comes to mind. This peculiar fellow points toward the tattoos on the inside of both my wrists and forearms. "Do you mind?" he asks, as he leans in slightly, admiring the names of my three children inked in old English font. I turn my arms over so that my palms face upwards.

"Those are the names of my kids, their birthdates, and the symbols that represent them."

He smiles. "I dabble in numerology. Do you mind if I take a closer look at the birthdates?"

"Uh, yeah, ok," I say, with little interest. He takes a hold of my right wrist, turning it gently to get a better read of my daughter's name and birthdate. He looks up at me with an elated smile.

"Oh, wow! When she walks into a room, she lights it up. She's plugged in socially. A leader."

My hard edges melt away. I'm smiling now. "That symbol means 'light.' When she was born, I found my truth, I saw the light. The best way I can explain it, I was born again," I say.

He nods with appreciation, before turning his attention to my middle child's name. "Kah-lill?" he says, making sure to confirm the pronunciation before calculating my son's birth number. He places his right hand over his heart, patting it softly, as he breathes in deeply and releases a long sigh, "This one... much love and compassion for others."

My mouth drops open, and I sit there in disbelief while he struggles to find the right words in English to describe what he knows in French.

"He is going to be a guide. He will be a... great leader."

I'm not sure he is getting his words right. "What do you mean, guide? Leader of what?"

He cocks his head, thinking. "He will help others on their journey."

"The symbol above his name is Mandarin; it translates to 'love.' When he was born, I was preaching the power of love, hoping to make the world a better place." I talk about myself as though I'm talking about someone I used to know. Someone whose passion was lost, along with his voice. The six-foot rule I once used to engage others was abandoned long ago. Everyone had once been on my world-changing radar. I'd engage strangers in conversations about philosophy, political affairs, and other topics that, in essence, affected them whether they had ever given much credence to them or not. It had been paramount to my existence. And yet, here I sit, feeling like a fraud.

The immigrants who are cramped in this cold room with me slowly begin to fade from my senses. I am no longer picking up their chatter; all movement outside the immediate space surrounding me and this curious fellow diminishes into a silent, grey blur. There is a heaviness to the air that slows all movement and inhibits my thoughts. What will he say about my youngest child's name and the tattooed symbol above it, a portrait of Master Yoda?

George Lucas's *Star Wars* saga affected me profoundly, as it did so many others of my generation. Using the image of Yoda to represent wisdom not only paid tribute to Lucas but also personified the energy surrounding the identification of Drédyn's spirit. When Candace showed me the positive pregnancy test, I felt a presence and someone yelling in the background, "Hey! Wait for me!" A third child was not in our plans, but Drédyn was saying, "Damn, with your plans, this must happen!"

My strange new friend looks up at me and laughs, popping the dream bubble I am floating in. "This one…" he says, still laughing, "with this one, there is only one chief in the room. And, he's the chief."

My dam of blocked emotions that has been keeping me from fully engaging broke in that moment, and I join him in filling the small room with our laughter. This man, this stranger, has helped me zero in on what is most important in the universe.

"Do you mind if I have your birthdate?"

"No, go right ahead," I say, telling him my birthdate, eager to hear him convert numbers into meaning.

A look of affectionate concern passes over his face. "You're a healer, Daryl." He breaks our eye contact. "But you're not able to heal anyone until you first heal yourself."

Stomach punch! I recognize the truth of what he says, but hearing it shakes the pillars of my already crumbling foundation.

The door opens and my name is called to see the doctor. I don't want to leave, but I stand up.

"Daryl, remember. There is only one thing you need to do."

I wait on his words of wisdom for what seems an eternity.

"Meditate."

"I didn't catch your name," I say, knowing the guard is not going to wait patiently much longer.

He extends his hand, and once I take it, he says, "Michel."

I cock my head and grin, not missing the irony that Michael is the healing archangel, the protector and leader of God's Army.

Thirty minutes later, I'm back in my cell. I can no longer contain the raw emotion washing over me, and the tears flow. I cry for my children, my wife, and all the disappointment arising from my failure to stay true to what mattered most to me. I cry myself clean.

CHAPTER 17

THE DREAM

"The place where you made your stand never mattered. Only that you were there...and still on your feet."

— *Stephen King, The Stand*

1990

The summer of 1990 was sweeter than other summers, as it followed my recent graduation from high school. I did enjoy certain aspects of my school years, and there are a few teachers to whom I owe a gratitude of debt. They were patient, encouraging, challenging, and understanding, embodying the cliché "It takes a village to raise a child."

Finishing high school presented me with more freedom, but what to do and where to go, I did not know. I was seventeen years old, in the thralls of summer heat romance, a full two months going steady with Candace.

I wasn't thinking too far ahead. I didn't feel any urgency about anything I was doing until I had my third life-altering moment.

A group of my friends and I decided to spend the day at one of our favourite swimming holes, the Forestry Pools, with plans to play capture the flag. We split into two groups of four and took off in different directions. Our mission was to get to the opposing team's side of the river and steal their flag, in our case, the brightest coloured shirt from each group. The river was neutral territory, and if you were tagged on the opposing team's side, you were taken as a prisoner. I was hiding behind a cluster of bushes, five metres up the cliff, on my team's side of the river, spying on my buddy Ken, who I thought was guarding his team's flag. I watched him walk downriver about twenty metres and take a quick look around before diving into the water. I made my move, quickly stepping out from behind my hiding spot and diving into the deep dark pool before he could resurface. I was going to swim the twenty metres, stealth-like, and one metre below the surface to avoid detection.

Once fully immersed in the water, I opened my eyes, anticipating the blurred vision but not the surreal sensations that came with it. The cool, clear water was now warm and exaggeratedly fuzzy, heavier, thicker, making me feel like I was moving in slow motion. I could see Ken swimming toward me three feet under the water's surface. His entire body looked to be inside a thin silvery membrane. I continued swimming toward the other side, extending my arms forward and back while kicking my legs hard. My lungs were feeling the ache from the lack of oxygen. I needed to make it to the other side before he got to me. When I was ten feet from shore, I stood up and took a deep breath, as much from a need for the precious oxygen that would feed my burning muscles as from my total disbelief that I was standing in a setting that no longer appeared real.

In less than sixty seconds, the sky had changed from clear and sunny to overcast and dark. I looked to my right to find Ken, but he was nowhere to be seen. There was no one around, the silence reinforcing my realization I was all alone. The wind stirred, and instantly goosebumps covered my wet, dripping body. Knee-deep in the water, I looked directly in front of where I was standing, up to the horizon, and felt an impending, dark force slowly coming my way. There was nothing to see, only a gut feeling telling me there was a force, massive in size and dark in nature. The fear of the unknown suddenly gripped me tight, just as it did when I was a five-year-old boy on that dark rainy night.

My conscious mind came to attention, realizing I must be dreaming and could wake myself up if I wanted to. Immediately, acting on command, my eyes opened. I was lying in my bed. I moved to sit up, raising my head no more than a few inches off my pillow, then my eyes closed, and I was standing back in the place I had just been, knee-high in water, only this time the dark presence had moved considerably closer to where I was. Initially I felt this presence coming from the other side of the planet. Now, it *felt* to be somewhere on the North American continent. My fear intensified, panic set in. *Corky, wake up!* Again, my eyes opened, and I was back in my bed. This time I was able to lift my head a few inches further before my power was cut once again, my head dropping back onto my pillow, returning me to the river. *What is happening to me?* The looming presence continued to advance, gripping me so tightly I was finding it difficult to breathe. *Corky, wake up!* Back in bed, I desperately tried to rise, nearly making it the entire way up before my eyes closed, and I fell back one last time. My eyes sprang open, and I was aghast to find myself standing back in the river. By this point the presence had halved the distance between us.

"Wake up! Wake up! Wake up!" I screamed out loud, pushing myself up in bed, breathing so hard and fast I was nearly hyperventilating. I sat there for a minute, slowing my breath, making every effort not to move a muscle, nervous that I was going to return to the riverbank and come face to face with whatever it was that seemed so intent on finding me. After convincing myself I had finally woken from a horrible nightmare, I worked up the nerve to reach over and turn my bedside lamp on, illuminating my room and driving the darkness back into the corners. My cat was lying at my feet, undisturbed by the commotion that had rocked me awake. I glanced up at the clock hanging on the wall and saw that it was 1:18 am. I decided to get up and use the bathroom, hoping to wash away the cloud that had descended upon me. I walked to my bedroom door, reaching out to grab the handle. As soon as I touched it, I immediately snapped back to the river, standing knee-high in the water again. My heart stuck in my throat, and 1 froze in position, no longer able to scream at myself to wake up. The dark looming presence enveloped me. This was my day of reckoning.

Before losing myself forever to this foreboding presence, I snapped from standing in the river to hovering five feet above my sleeping body. I was now staring down at myself, lying motionless in my bed. I had never experienced so many varying degrees of fear. I wanted inside my body more than I had ever wanted anything in my life. My will to live fuelled the fire that lit every cell inside my body. My mind fired like a bolt of lightning into my sleeping body, and I instantly shot straight up into the seated position I had been in only moments before. I sat motionless for a minute before reaching over to turn on my lamp. I looked down at my feet to see my cat sleeping undisturbed, then turned my attention to the clock on the wall: 1:18 am. I decided against going to the bathroom, preferring to sit and process what had transpired while waiting for the sun to rise.

The need to rationalize and neatly box up that lucid dream was important to me, otherwise I was sure to flounder like a fish out of water. I felt like I had been abruptly punted from the small fishbowl I was finally comfortable in to a much bigger tank that was going to require additional learning and the application of new skills. That waking dream came on the heels of reading a slew of mind-bending books: Stephen King's *The Stand*, Frank Herbert's *Dune*, Doris Lessing's *Canopus in Argos* series, and Isaac Asimov's *Foundation Trilogy*. My mind was rapidly tapping into a network of Imagineers who collectively pushed me to explore new possibilities.

There were few people I could turn to for help in trying to decipher what this strange waking dream meant. Fortunately, one of those people was my mother. Paula was fondly called the Oracle by a few of her friends. She had read Freud, Jung's dissertations on dreams, and countless other books on psychology. Even though the emotional closeness of our relationship sometimes skewed her analysis of the facts presented to her, she was still able to paint a clear picture that helped make sense out of what I experienced.

My world was expanding. My days of hiding and playing small were over. A powerful force had awakened in me.

CHAPTER 18

HIGHER EDUCATION

"In that nanosecond of enlightenment, I knew that the human spirit survives the death of the physical body and I understood that my wandering soul needed to get back into its earthly habitat."

— *Janet Bettag*

1991 — 1993

My lucid dream acted as a jump-start for my radical ideas. Step one was higher education. I had missed the deadline to enrol in the fall program but was able to get into Malaspina College (now Vancouver Island University) in the spring of 1991. I juggled school with three different jobs. I worked the desk at the Fortress, selling memberships, training new members, making protein shakes, and keeping the gym neat and orderly. I worked evenings as a doorman, providing courtesy and security, for two local bars, which always seemed to attract the nonsensical, confused, and dysfunctional. Being my mother's son, I naturally played the counsellor more times than I can count, occasionally resorting to physical dominance by removing those who needed counselling the most. I also worked in construction, digging trenches, pounding nails, and roofing. During the long days of summer, working under the hot blazing sun, I felt like I was in the French Foreign Legion. I would go home to eat, then hit the gym for ninety minutes, spending my last reserves of energy.

The courses I took at college helped to broaden my knowledge. Growing up I had developed a crude but honest interpretation of how our social system was managed. The college classroom provided me with an opportunity to explore some of my firmly held convictions. I now had an arena where I could sort out and express my geopolitical views. I took aim at the Persian Gulf War and the newly created North American Free Trade Agreement, NAFTA. I was comfortable discussing world events and social issues with my classmates, but I was not satisfied with my level of education.

The desire to learn was akin to feeding a constant hunger, and college helped narrow my focus onto what I was most passionate about. However, my drive to excel rooted itself in the physical form via bodybuilding, becoming my primary teacher for the next five years. Initially, I had started weight training so I could be a stronger, more versatile skateboarder. I rode my board a lot back then, skating with my good friends Gord and Stefan, using it as my number one means of transportation. Within six months of joining the Fortress of Fitness Gym, I had gained ten pounds of muscle and doubled my strength in lifts. The skating got kicked to the side, and sadly, so did Gord.

The natural progression to lift heavier weights was addictive. I started as a 135-pound fifteen-year-old who, although relatively fit, lacked strength, size, and power. My brothers, many of their closest friends, and the owner of the gym, Kim, guided me in this new arena. By the time I entered my senior year of high school, I had established myself as a regular fixture at the gym and was included in the workouts with the serious lifters. Our hometown was known for producing good athletes and fearless fighters who utilized weights to strengthen their game. Their intensity rubbed off on me.

Every second Saturday, we would get together for a monster leg-training day. Five to eight guys would set up around the squat rack, and we would take turns at the bar for the next three to four hours, increasing the weight as we progressed through each round. Many of those sessions would make me hurl my breakfast as we pushed our bodies and tested our mental capacity to the max. For me and a few others, the obsession that had us thirsting for the euphoric high that followed the pain would always saddle up alongside my fear of the next workout. Every workout I did was built around twenty-four hours of preparation, visualization, and final execution. By the time I left for the gym, I was both excited and freaked out because I knew what it would entail. I wanted to see how far I could push beyond my previous best, and there was nothing but myself to hold me back.

Looking back, I can see living a life raised in an invisible cage, but it was one that narrowed my focus and gave me the rudimentary structure I needed to help master my body. I recall a scene in Oliver Stone's *Conan the Barbarian* featuring a young boy chained to a large water wheel, which he had to push, around and around, all day long, for years on end. I had enough sense to know my future depended on putting in the time and pushing that wheel until I was strong enough to break away and claim my freedom. I spent years developing a higher standard for myself, breaking through new barriers on a physical level, but more importantly, dislodging the childhood chains that had kept me trapped in a small man's world. I was redefining my world through discipline and hard work, attempting to lay the foundation for a future in which anything was possible.

By the time 1992 was winding to a close, I was feeling good about myself. Candace and I had been together for two and a half years; I was attending college, was working steadily, and had signed up to compete in my first bodybuilding competition. In April of 1993, two months before Candace graduated high school, I entered the Gold's Classic competition. I was a nineteen-year-old junior competing in the men's division. This contest had always attracted a lot of competitors, with the light heavyweight class numbering ten participants, all of whom were in great shape. I came fourth. Some people were upset with the judge's decision, believing my size should have easily given me third. But I was happy to have overcome my fear of standing on a stage in front of hundreds of people while wearing posing trunks that looked like Speedo swim shorts.

The head judge saw me in the parkade after the end of the evening show and said, "Corky, you were awfully close in points to the second and third place guys. Are you going to enter the Provincial Championships next month?"

"I have no interest in getting back on stage so soon."

"But why not?" he asked me puzzled. "You would certainly win the Junior class."

I was given an opportunity to add to my resume, and I blew it off, believing I didn't need recognition from others. It wasn't about winning trophies or getting first place; it was about taking something as far as possible and being the best I could be at it — *my* best.

Coming out of that first contest lit another fire under my ass. I read everything I could get my hands on about human performance, fitness training, and diet. My thirst to be my best led me to read the biographies of champions from other disciplines: Muhammad Ali, Arnold Schwarzenegger, and Bruce Lee. Just as impactful, maybe more so, were biographies of Nelson Mandela, Mahatma Gandhi, and Martin Luther King Jr. These people, and many more like them, refused to be bound by limits that others had set. Their attention to detail in all areas, coupled with their unconquerable ability to focus and persevere is the stuff heroes are made of. I was feeling the best I ever had.

My feelings of joy didn't last. Two weeks after my contest, I was injured in a near-fatal worksite accident while working for a guy I knew from the gym. He and his partner were building three-storey condo units. It was a Friday afternoon, and my mind was on getting to the gym so I could work the 5:00 – 9:00 pm shift. I loved working at the gym on Friday nights. I would get to the gym and eat my dinner while talking to the regulars as they came and went. From 7:00 pm on, I would do my workout, clean up, then wait for my friends to visit me before they went out for the night.

Shortly after 3:00 pm, the general contractor came to me with an assignment, "Tomorrow there will be contractors coming in and out of the building, and I don't want them tearing up the new vinyl we laid down on the patio decks. I need you to grab 4 × 8 sheets of plywood and lay them down on every deck."

I knew getting the task finished in time to make it home and to the gym for 5:00 pm would be tight. I devised a game plan, carrying the boards to the third floor first and finishing with the ground level. I moved quickly, approaching the job the way I would a race. I knew I needed to move fast but I needed to pace myself as well. I had laid three sheets and entered the next unit in preparation to lay the fourth. As I walked into the unfinished unit, I noticed another contractor was standing outside on the deck. I waited for him to walk through the sliding glass door, moving to my right to give him space to move past me. I stepped onto the deck, holding the sheet between myself and the building, with my back facing the edge of the deck. There were three things I had going against me:

1. There was no railing.
2. I was rushing the job.
3. I had gained twenty-five pounds over the last two weeks, making me awkwardly out of step in my body.

As I attempted to lay the sheet on the deck, I inched my feet back toward the ledge, thinking there was enough room for me to drop it and step over. My foot went one inch too far, and I found myself frozen in a moment of absolute shock. That frozen moment was extraordinary. If you have a basic understanding of Einstein's theory of relativity, you may appreciate what I experienced next. My friend Lance was working below me and looked up moments before I made that painful mistake. He said he experienced time slowing down, whereas I stepped into a time portal. A few seconds before this life-changing misstep, I was moving quickly. With a flick of the switch, my movements seemed to slow. I was pouring over the side of the deck like thick syrup, and I knew full well there were no pancakes below to soften my fall.

I cursed myself for being such an idiot, all the while reflecting upon key moments in my life, many of which were memories I had buried away and long forgotten about. The thought of dying rushed through me, charging every cell in my body, but there was no fear, only regret. There was disappointment in the thought that my death would bring suffering to those I loved. I had racing thoughts of my children who had not yet been born. I could taste flavours somehow connected to future experiences that may never come. The syrup sped up the closer I came to impact. My mind whirled as my body twisted in the air, causing me to fall headfirst. Every thought instantly vanished from my mind except for one: impact.

This is it, dumbass, you're either going to be dead or in a lot of pain.

Fortunately, I twisted enough that my right hip smoked the edge of the second deck, spinning me around so I wound up facing the opposite direction and landing away from the building in an upright position. Impact! I landed with most of my weight over my left foot. My foot sank into the ground at least five inches, and I fell back onto my ass. I knew I had survived because the pain that rushed through me could only have meant I was still alive.

Lance rushed over in a panic. I heard over and over, "Are you ok?" I pointed to my left foot and grunted, fighting to hold myself back from screaming, "My foot, my foot!" He looked down and tried to pull off my work boot, forgetting to untie the laces. I yelled at him, "The laces!" As soon as he got the boot off, my toes twisted out to the side. Lance looked like he was going to be sick, and I began cursing as I realized training at the gym would be put on hold for a while. I was devastated.

The doctor told me I had dislocated every metatarsal in that foot, but the swelling was so bad they would have to wait a week before they could operate. Oh boy! Getting me into my apartment was difficult enough but trying to do anything else was near impossible. Whenever my foot dropped below my heart I instantly broke into a sweat, and the foot would pound as if someone was taking a sledgehammer to it. I felt like a key player in Stephen King's *Misery*. I underwent reconstructive surgery and spent the next ten weeks in a cast. Candace was a trooper during this time. She was in grade twelve, president of the grad committee, working twenty hours a week, playing soccer, and coming to my place every spare minute she had to help me out.

Moving was out of the question, so I had been relying on using a four-litre water jug to urinate in, but by the fourth day, I could no longer hold off moving my bowels. I devised a plan and waited patiently for Candace to arrive after school to help me execute it.

"Ok, I have an idea!" I said excitedly.

"What's your idea?" she said, her curiosity showing on her face. I asked her to get some newspaper from the table and lay it out on the floor beside my bed. I barely got the words out before she threw her arms up in the air. "No way, no way! This is where I draw the line."

I was puzzled for a second, then started laughing so hard that my foot began throbbing again. I fought to control my laughter as the tears ran down my cheeks, as much from the pain in my foot as from the image that had popped into my mind. "No, no, no! You don't understand," I said.

I explained the plan was to ease out of the bed while keeping my foot high in the air and sitting on the newspaper, using it to slide on toward the bathroom. I don't know who was more appalled.

The surgeon said I wouldn't be able to do the same physical activities I had been accustomed to doing in the past; sports that involved running and lifting heavy should be eliminated. I refused to believe this prognosis and moved ahead, planning my return to competition and turning to visualization to help me advance my healing.

Those summer months I spent recovering provided a lot of time to read. I added to my stack of books texts on metaphysics, near-death experiences, psychology, and the world's most prominent religions, hoping to gain insight into a world I knew little about.

CHAPTER 19

STAND TRUE

"There is no better teacher than adversity. Every defeat, every heart-break, every loss, contains its own seed, its own lesson on how to improve your performance the next time."

— *Malcolm X*

May 2010

While biding my time, waiting to be released from the Northwest Detention Center, I'm inspired to write a letter to my family, friends, and clients:

"I feel I owe it to the community that helped raise me to come forward and be truthful, to offer some insight into what led me down, or should I say up such a treacherous path.

The people born into my generation saw the end of the Cold War only to be replaced by the War on Terror and the continuing saga of "us against them." The exponential growth of technology and the speed at which information is shared has created an almost unbelievable worldly existence. Many were quick to capitalize while most watched idly, living relatively unscathed in the Shire, as trillions of dollars were being sucked from the apathetic.

What does this have to do with my arrest and the circumstances surrounding it? Everything! It wasn't the money that drove me to do what I did; it was my frustration at the world I was living in. Many people do little to affect the direction of their lives, while a minority have a firm grip on the wheel which steers us to a pre-determined destination. This world is one we all help to create, whether we push the big blocks or sit passively and play with the little blocks.

I dedicated myself to pushing, challenging, and lifting others by any means I had at my disposal. And though I succeeded in many areas of my life, I still managed to fail at what I held to be most important. I became blinded to the belief that what I did was for the betterment of all, and if by chance you were to experience some pain and discomfort that accompanied your growth, so be it, tough Love!

However, in my relentless desire to push ahead, I failed to recognize the chaos I created. For that, I sincerely apologize."

Candace is apprehensive when I ask her to film me reading it for a blog post. "Cork, I'm not sure we should air this."

But I want to fix the situation. "I think people want to know I'm ok. That we're ok."

My sincere attempt to show people I am still the uplifting and inspiring guy backfires. Some people feel I should keep my head low and show more humility. I can feel the wedge between Candace and me pushing us farther apart.

CHAPTER 20

BIRTHDAY DECLARATION

"The only limit to your impact is your imagination and commitment."
— *Anthony Robbins*

September 21st, 2002

Four days before my thirtieth birthday, my wife and I hosted a BBQ for good friends and family. September had been warm, and the final day of summer did not disappoint. It had been two years since we made the move from the big city of Vancouver back to Duncan. The days of commuting on the ferry for work were coming to an end. Mariah was now five, Kahlil had just turned one, and Drédyn was three months away from coming into the world. We had decided to start channelling our energy into our community, driven by a desire to connect with others and build a life that would bring us a tremendous amount of joy. A big gathering was the perfect way to celebrate new beginnings with our friends and family. It would also give me an ideal opportunity to speak openly with all who were attending, the people I cared for most, about the things I had only ever dared talk about in private.

Once the twenty different salads, roasted pig, baked salmon, crab, freshly baked bread, and countless appetizers were laid out, I climbed to the top of my children's play fort and called for everyone's attention.

"Hello, everybody! Thank you so much for joining us on this wonderful September day. Candace and I have been wanting to get everyone together for quite some time, and now that we have you here together," I took the time to look into the faces of all the people who formed my family, wishing to channel my thoughts and emotions clearly, "I couldn't be happier." There was no hesitation; my opening words were robust and carried well. But once I started speaking about my life's calling, my emotions began rising to the surface, like the first whispers of the wind brushing lightly against the sail. "I feel the anguish and torment that millions of children across this planet feel every day. Some will argue that things are working out just fine, that nature is taking its natural course, and that the growing pains we endure accompany progressive evolution. I agree with that sentiment, but this does not mean we are restricted from co-creating alongside evolution. I know I can do more to affect the quality of people's lives simply by bringing awareness to them."

My words echoed through my mind, critiquing the message I wanted to impart. Was I coming across as arrogant, claiming that I knew something others did not, that my path was more virtuous and noble than theirs? The questioning of my intentions continued to rush forth, as my desire to respect other people's views created doubt within myself.

"I don't have a set plan about how I'm going to affect the type of change I wish to see in this world, but I promise, I will dedicate my life to doing everything I can to make the biggest contribution in the lives of others, especially the lives of our children. It will likely mean I'll have to put my nose down and work harder than ever before, and I'm ok with that. If for whatever reason we don't see each other for long periods, I want you to know that you are always in my thoughts, and I love you very much." At the end of that unscripted speech, someone in the crowd started to sing, "For He's a Jolly Good Fellow." To my discomfort, everybody joined in.

Two things were made glaringly apparent at that moment: the first was just how much I disliked being in the spotlight, and the second was seeing how important it was to put myself out there if I wanted to advance the revolution.

CHAPTER 21

FACEOFF

"Don't roll the dice if you can't pay the price."

— *Ziad K. Abdelnour*

July 8th, 2010

It's been two months since I was released on bail, and I've been instructed to meet with Officer Shannon at the federal courthouse in Seattle. Shannon has some follow-up questions for me that need to be asked with my lawyer present. I replay in my head the phone conversation I had with Darren the night before.

"Darren!" I said, "I've told you repeatedly, I'm not giving my friend's name. Stop asking. Whose side are you on?"

"Sorry, Daryl, I just want to make sure you know they might hold this against you."

"I do understand, and better than you think I do."

~⚬

There was no respite for my exhausted mind. So much to consider and so much to do. Shannon had bombarded me with questions, but one in particular is eating at me: How do you think you got caught? That question had dug in to me deep, scattering pieces of broken memories that overlap to paint a distorted picture. My gut tells me our arrest had everything to do with me.

I meet privately with Darren for a few minutes before we sit down with Shannon. Darren instructs me to be forthcoming. *Is it in his best interest to do so, or mine?* Darren is a good guy, but he is just a low-level cog representing another low-level cog. We move to the fifth floor, where the offices of the District Attorney and its staff are located. Shannon is waiting for us with another, younger agent I have never met before. We exchange pleasantries and make our way into a private office.

"You're going to be 100 percent honest and put everything out on the table, right?" says Officer Shannon.

"Of course," I say casually.

We sit down at a small table. Darren is to my right, Shannon sits directly across from me, and the other agent is to his left. The younger agent leans back in his chair with a notepad and pen in his hand, watching me intently. Shannon leans forward in his chair and launches into a barrage of questions. The first handful of questions are ones he already has answers to, so I assume he is getting warmed up. The new agent gauges my response to every question, watching every movement in my face and body. This guy is the lie detector, and it is his job to make a note of everything he sees. I'm feeling at ease — until Shannon leans in to get closer to me.

"Bafaro is pointing the finger at you, saying this is your gig. And for us, that makes sense. There's no way you're just a mule."

I push my chair back and stand up. "This is bullshit, and you know it!" Pointing my finger at the floor and raising my voice, I say, "You know Rick is going to say whatever he can to save himself. You asked me before we started if I would be upfront and forthcoming with you. Well, I expect you to do the same with me. Let's stop playing games and get on with asking honest questions." Shannon's face softens to a smile, and I move to take my seat. "Shannon, why don't you ask your partner if I'm telling the truth? That's what he's here for, is he not?" The two agents look at one another.

"Who is this friend of yours that introduced you to Bafaro?" Shannon asks.

I laugh, clearly seeing how ironic my outburst was. "Well, you've got me there. That's the only question I won't answer."

Shannon leans forward again in his chair, hands clasped together in front of him on the table that separates us. "So much for being honest and forthcoming. Why are you protecting this friend? What has he got to hide?"

"Look, like I told Darren, my friend simply made the introduction. He thought he was helping me out."

"Well, it's no big deal then if you give us his name. If he has nothing to hide, you shouldn't worry about it."

"Really?" I say. "Is that what you think? Everybody has skeletons in their closet, including you, Shannon." The other agent chuckles under his breath. "Why would I turn the eyes of the authorities onto my friend who has done nothing? I am a grown man who made a stupid decision. I should be the one to pay for my mistake, nobody else." I'm certain he will keep pressing, but he ends the questioning right then and there.

"Thanks for your time, Fontana."

As if I have a choice in the matter.

After the agents have gathered up their paperwork and left, Darren says to me, "Holy shit! My heart jumped into my throat when you stood up and barked at him. I can't believe you did that. It was awesome!"

I say nothing as he presses the button in the elevator to take us down to the main floor. "That went well, don't you think?" he says.

"Geesh, Darren, yeah, I guess so." We both know Agent Shannon could relay to the assistant District Attorney — a DA with a reputation for being ice cold and ruthlessly tough on her opponents — that I hadn't cooperated. And that information could eventually make its way to the judge in charge of my sentencing. The judge has the power to give or take away, giving me anywhere from the minimum to the maximum sentence. I don't share Darren's enthusiasm. I feel like I've just fought another battle in the ring, coming out of it a little less unscathed than I could have. It would be months, maybe years before I ever feel any sort of excitement again. "I rolled the dice, and now we wait to see what fate awaits me."

CHAPTER 22

CONFESSIONS

"It takes two to tango; one dictates the steps and the other executes them effectively. That is how a great show is made."

— *Olaotan Fawehinmi*

Summer, 2010

Finding a buyer for The Playground while negotiating an exit out of our lease was painstakingly difficult. Looking after the business, dealing with my parole officer, and working with my lawyer consumed my time when finding an experienced family counsellor should have been my number one priority. The fallout from my arrest significantly hurt the business. We lost about 15 percent of our revenue. One of our most vocal detractors was the gym princess, who told anyone who would listen that The Playground was going to be hit by a drive-by shooter. People like that were the least of my worries. They annoy me but are seriously small-scale irritants compared to my real problems. Everything is relative, right? The layers of the fabric belonging to my being continued to fray. I realized I had been naïve, failing to interpret people's body language and words that hint at unspoken thoughts. My whole life, I've been taking most of what people say literally, my naivety obscuring a person's intent, taking their mild flirtations as appropriate communication. Easy to explain, as my modus operandi was exchanging energy with people in a mutually beneficial way. Projecting loving energy toward others is one of the healthiest forms of communication we have.

Yet, I wasn't prepared when people I considered good friends shared their true feelings with me. The news of my arrest seemed to affect various members of my circle differently. Most of my male friends and associates were puzzled but easily grasped the reasoning behind my actions. My three friends I had confided in prior to going felt awful for me — and relieved that they had been able to avoid direct involvement. The kids and young adults I train have never stopped supporting me, though they were shocked when they heard the news, forced to see one of their role models in a new light and to question societal norms they had previously never given much thought to.

The women seemed to express varying degrees of disappointment. Some were angry, some sad, and two women felt all the emotions — some more unexpected than others. Within weeks of my returning home, they confessed their love for me.

These confessions added extra weight to the doubt I already carried. *Was it infatuation? Did I lead them on?* They tried to absolve me of any wrongdoing, saying I had nothing to feel guilty about, but that didn't diminish my anguish. It takes two to tango, and I had been dancing carefree for years. I've had few role models who exemplified the spirit of Man I wanted to personify, but since dropping to one knee in the summer of 2000, I had eyes for no one other than my wife. I tell Candace about these confessions, and she doesn't flinch. Does she believe I'm fully committed, or is she just beyond the point of being able to make sense of it all? *Maybe she no longer cares.* I promise to pay more attention to the signals I'm sending out to others.

CHAPTER 23

FIRST OFFENCE

"The true measure of the justice of a system is the amount of protection it guarantees to the weakest."

— Aung San Suu Kyi

1993 — 1996

The summer of 1993 was life-changing for me: I nearly died, my uncle introduced me to my first indoor marijuana garden, and I met a traveller who would prove to have a significant impact on my life. It had been twelve weeks since my surgery and I was still on crutches when Candace and I left Duncan the end of August to move to Vancouver. I looked around for the gyms with the best trainers and top athletes in the Greater Vancouver area. My trusted sources told me if I was serious about advancing my bodybuilding career, Olympic Athletic Club was the place to train. Olympic used to be located on Arbutus and 12th Street, in the Kitsilano-Kerrisdale area, a forty-minute drive from where Candace and I were renting in East Van. Olympic was my home for the next three years. I met people from all walks of life there: the city's top professional athletes, internationally renowned trainers, therapists, health gurus, movie celebrities, and business tycoons, many of whom are still close friends today.

These wonderful people bestowed a wealth of knowledge onto a fledgling athlete and fitness trainer. Their collective advice, much of which I am sure to have missed, gave me many of the tools that helped me start my career.

We lived a quiet life. Candace was a full-time student with a heavy course load, and I was dedicated to winning my pro card. We were both driven to succeed, so going out and living it up, as most of our young friends were doing, wasn't really our thing. In fact, while we lived in the city, many of our friends we spent time with were much older than us. They had lived their party years, now preferring sushi and a movie to drinks and late nights. That worked well for us.

During those first two years in the city, I morphed my body from big to freakish. In seven years, from the first day I walked into the gym as a 135-pound fifteen-year-old, I nearly doubled my body mass on my five-foot-ten frame. I won the British Columbia Body Building Championship in 1995 as a heavyweight, weighing in on stage at 222 pounds. Even though I placed first, I was dejected by the way I looked, as my body could not produce a pre-stage pump, which is necessary to make your muscles appear fuller. I was flat, which I initially blamed on a mistake I made during my carb depletion and reload phase the week before the show. But now, looking back, I am sure my failure to get a pump had more to do with my being arrested by the RCMP one month earlier. Stress significantly alters the chemistry in a person's body, and mine was on cortisol overload.

The Crown Prosecution charged me with "importation of a controlled substance (steroids) with the intent to distribute." Someone had informed the police I was receiving parcels from overseas. I have always maintained that the use of most drugs should be the sovereign right of every person of legal age. You may object to that, and I am not here to convince you otherwise. However, I will state that I fully believe the resources we spend on battling illegal drug use, specifically the incarcerating of people who use, would be better spent on health and education and on creating programs that help elevate, not incarcerate. The hypocrisy that society perpetuates through the government support of alcohol and the over-prescribing of barbiturates, anti-depressants, and opioids has always been a bone of contention with me and was perhaps one of the reasons I never tried hard to conceal what I was doing. My decision to use steroids — gear, as we used to call it — was not one I made lightly. Even though many of my peers in the gym had been using them, I was cautious, understanding that taking any drug had the potential to wreak havoc with my body's natural chemistry.

I was also aware of how the public viewed users. It was ok to use just as long you never got caught. People like Sylvester Stallone, Arnold Schwarzenegger, and many of the world's top athletes depended on these substances to advance their careers, but they were forced to keep their use a secret due to the stigma. Guys like Ben Johnson — the famous, and then disgraced, Canadian sprinter who ran a world record-breaking 9.79 seconds, 100-metre sprint in Seoul in 1988 — had their careers destroyed. I wanted to be a bodybuilding champion, and the reality was, if I wanted to do that, I needed to do what the other guys were doing. After researching everything I could on the subject, I consulted with my doctor. He didn't condone it, but he did agree to work with me, keeping a close eye on my body chemistry by doing monthly blood tests. Until this time, I had been a casual weekend drinker, but once I committed to using anabolic steroids, I cut back substantially, allowing myself to drink only once or twice per year. Honestly, I was more concerned about protein overload than steroids, knowing my daily consumption of five hundred plus grams of protein derived from fish, eggs, chicken, and beef could make my liver quiver.

Following my win at the regional championships, I turned my attention to beating the charge laid against me. Fortunately, one of the owners of

Olympic, a man named Ralph, connected me with one of the many hired guns who worked for him. Ralph was a character, loud and flamboyant, who carried a lot of influence. He had his detractors, but he was always good to me, though he tested my gullibility meter every chance he got. He warned me about associating with certain "players" and advised me in no uncertain terms to stay clear of any illegal racket, believing my disposition was not suited for it. The lawyer Ralph put me in touch with was impressive, one of Vancouver's best: Larry Myers, an astute businessman who clearly understood what drove the machine.

Winning my case was dependent upon who I knew and how much I could pay. For all intents and purposes, I got off with "a slap on the hand." Was I happy to get nothing more punitive than fifty hours of community service and a two-year conditional sentence? Absolutely! But the slap on the hand felt more like a slap in the face because I was reminded of the gross inequality that exists within a rigged system. A person's decency takes fourth place, coming in behind money, influence, and status.

As with every other significant moment in my life, that arrest fell like one key domino, tipping other dominoes down the line that I may otherwise never have paid attention to. I spent my fifty hours of community service at Vancouver's Gathering Place Community Centre, assisting a whole range of people, including people on low incomes, people with disabilities, seniors, people from diverse ethnic backgrounds, youth, and homeless people. The Gathering Place provided engaging programs focusing on food and nutrition, health education, recreation, arts and culture, and community development. After talking with a middle-aged man in the laundry room one day, and hearing about his adventures, the dreams of his youth, and the unfortunate happenings that pushed him off his path, I felt the divide inside me widen.

CHAPTER 24

BIRTHDAY SENTENCE

September 25th, 2010

The days leading up to my sentencing are dedicated to as much time spent with my family, trying to give them the best version of myself, but the stress often gets to me. There are days I feel I am losing my mind. I have nothing to grab hold of to keep me from drowning in my misery. The emotional distance between Candace and me is widening. Her father is not pleased about my video blog confession. I continue pouring my finite resources into the sinking ship we call The Playground, and I've sold our next-door rental property.

My sentencing is scheduled for my thirty-eighth birthday. Candace and my dad accompany me to Seattle and sit while the judge reads out the charges against me. I'm asked if I have anything to say before she issues the sentence. I thought I'd be able to cope with standing before the court, but right now I feel like the five-year-old version of myself, kneeling alone outside in the rain. "I am sorry for bringing so much pain and anguish to my family. I am so sorry," I say. Unlike Judge Tsuchida, who had set my bail, this judge shows no compassion.

"You are not, in any way, representative of a good, upstanding American father. None of whom would smoke marijuana." I wasn't expecting those words to come out of her mouth, but she reminded me just how far to the right many people still are.

She gives me an eight-month sentence, to be served somewhere in the United States, starting in six to eight weeks.

CHAPTER 25

GOODBYE

"It is all exactly as it should be, when the robin sings on a glorious morning, and raindrops beat on the temple roof."
— *Ken Wilber,* The Atman Project

October — November, 2010

A week after my sentencing, my friends and family come together to help dismantle The Playground. The strain of the physical work pales in comparison to what I am feeling. Some of the equipment and office furniture is sold, and the rest we put in storage. I get the call to report back to the States after the gym is closed. I'm sentenced to spend my incarceration in Pennsylvania at Moshannon Valley Correctional Center, the MVCC, a medium-security immigration prison that holds up to fourteen hundred non-US detainees. It's a three-hour drive north-east of Pittsburgh in a small town called Philipsburg. They were sending me far enough away that visiting would be difficult for friends and family. Perhaps that is part of my punishment; total isolation from my loved ones.

I'm supposed to turn myself in to the US authorities no later than 3:00 pm on November 15th, at which point the US government will transport me to Pennsylvania. But I'm deterred by the thought of flying Con-Air, which could result in me flying from one facility to another for weeks on end. I've been preparing to enter prison on my own two feet, wilfully submitting and entering as a free man. This was a rite of passage I needed to make on my own terms.

November 13th, 2010

It's 4:00 am, and I've barely slept for thinking about my imminent departure from my family. I pull myself out of bed, make coffee, and sit down at the computer. Today's news highlights the tenth anniversary of the conclusion to the Florida vote count. Lawyers for George W. Bush fail to win a court order barring a manual recount of ballots, but Florida's Secretary of State intervenes, ending the recounting. This is a dark day for me, adding fuel to a bitterness I had buried deep inside me.

Out of the corner of my eye, I see Ken Wilber's book *The Atman Project* sitting underneath some papers on my desk and feel compelled to pick it up. I open it to where I had left a folded piece of paper inside, months prior. Having no recollection of what the paper is, I unfold it and discover it's a Christmas letter I had sent to my clients and friends eleven months earlier, five months before I was arrested:

Dear friends,

I am contemplating my next move in this magical universe of games, discovery, adventure, and finality.

Often, I wonder; what makes the world turn, my relationship to it, and how to best work with the machine that runs it? This abstract world is rarely simplistic, often confusing, and always challenging. Many people perceive a world with tight guidelines, rules, and regulations, and although they can learn to work with it, never can they fathom ever changing it.

Most people have been conditioned to see the need for order, and any opposition to it is usually met with stern reprimands, downgrading, or possibly termination. Let's face it, any time someone or some group stands up and asks for more, they are frowned upon and scolded harshly.

Please don't misinterpret what I am trying to say. I have great friends, a beautiful family, and I live in a place that many call Paradise. But I want more.

I refer to better education, better health care, less corruption, no fear, self-sustainability, more patience, determination, more desire, and more passion. To have anything of quality, one must be willing to step up, be a leader and create the "more" that they want.

Look around yourself today. Feel the magic, live it, breathe it. We are blessed more than we know, having the power and the ability to make this day and everyone after it a beautiful one.

You are all Angels, and I thank every one of you for helping to guide me through this incredible journey we call life.

— Merry Christmas, Corky

Wow! After so many years of remaining quiet, fearing I would be taken down, I had finally unabashedly spoken from my heart.

Mariah and Kahlil both have games today. We decide to keep everything status quo and have them play even though I am scheduled to fly out that afternoon. I drop Mariah off with her soccer coach early that morning, allowing me to have some alone time with her. She assures me she is fine, but I am worried her brave face is a mask meant to protect me as much as it is her. I long to jump back ten years, when it was just Mariah and me going on one of our many adventures together. What would life have been like had I not walked from growing weed to opening The Playground? Would things have been different? Would I have had more time with my daughter these last five years? *Universe, if in all your wisdom you deem it necessary I receive these hard lessons, so be it.*

Kahlil has had time to prepare for this day and holds himself together well. We say our goodbyes before I take him to his hockey game. I leave halfway through the second period to catch my flight, happy to have left him on the ice playing the game he loves the most. Candace and Drédyn walk me into the airport, staying with me until I have to walk through security. I give Dré a big hug. "Don't worry about me, ok? I am going to miss you terribly." To a seven-year-old, eight months is an eternity, but he stands tall, wearing the same brave face Mariah and Kahlil had donned earlier. When I stand up to say goodbye to Candace, all I can see is a wall. She is stone cold, showing no emotion, and I don't know how to break through to her. I could see at that moment that I had got so caught up in *my* mission, giving 100 percent of my energy to it, that I had neglected to save any for my cornerstone. There is no hug between us, no kiss goodbye.

Once I'm in my seat on the plane, I pull out the Christmas letter and read it again and again.

CHAPTER 26

CHAMPION REBORN

"There are only two ways to live your life. One is as though nothing is a miracle. The other is as though everything is a miracle."
— *Albert Einstein*

August 3rd, 1996

Weeks after winning the BC championship in June 1995, I decided to enter the 1996 Canadian Body Building Championships. I was now under the guidance of an expert trainer who was working out of Montreal, Quebec. I scheduled a flight for August 16, 1996, to meet Jean, my new trainer. He was openly excited about my arrival. He had arranged for my visit to coincide with the arrival of his other top prospect, an amateur heavyweight from the US, who was getting ready for the American championships, called the NPC National Championships.

Jean's excitement was short-lived, as I decided to drop out of the competition and most likely leave the sport for good. He was dumbfounded.

How could I explain to him something I couldn't quite make sense out of myself? I had awoken early that morning, August 3rd, and had taken three steps from my bed, making my way to the bedroom door. Nothing was out of the ordinary. My focus was on my morning meal prep and the day ahead of me. In the time it took me to make my third stride across the bedroom floor, I was jolted awake with my fourth epiphany. In a span of nanoseconds, my mind flashed years into the future. I saw myself standing on stage crowned a world champion. The image I held seemed so utterly real; I believed it had already happened. I knew it was still 1996, and the path to that vision, undeniably within my reach, required a sacrifice to my health and to something else I couldn't put my finger on. Until that moment, I had been 100 percent committed to becoming a champion in my sport. I never doubted my chances, believing with all my heart I was going to make it. And then, in a flash, it was over.

How could I go from 100 percent all-in to 100 percent all-out in the time it took to complete a single stride? Something told me I had learned everything I needed to learn from this foray into the physical. I had become a master in that arena, so continuing for the mere sake of winning trophies, making money, and gaining prestige no longer felt like it was serving my best interests. It didn't take long for the rumours to start flying. Some people speculated I had problems with my heart, while others thought I had some other illness. It's funny how people so often make things up when the reality they are subjected to doesn't make sense to them. Even the people I was closest to couldn't fathom why I had quit. There was more to life than spending most of my energy building bigger muscles. I had the respect of my peers, but I didn't want to be respected solely for what I could accomplish inside of a gym or on the stage. There was something of great importance buried inside of me, and I was determined to dig it up — even though I had no clue what I'd do with it once I found it.

The days immediately following this massive shift in perception came with news of life in unexpected places. On August 6th, NASA announced to the world that there may once have been life on Mars. Two days later, Candace surprised me with news she was pregnant. I had just gotten into my car with my friend, Stefan, when my phone rang.

"Are you sitting down?" Candace asked.

"Wow!" was the first word that came out of my mouth when she finished speaking.

I had closed a big door in my life to make room for something much bigger, much more important. As soon as I ended my call with her, I looked in the rear-view mirror and discovered my first white hair sticking out the top of my head. "Holy shit!" I said laughing, pointing the hair out to Stefan. "So it begins."

Over the next six months, we both continued to work, I continued to work out, albeit with a little less intensity, and we read the current literature for newly expecting parents. I spent a lot of time lying on the couch and staring at the ceiling, reflecting on how I had gotten to where I was. I would lie there for hours on end, the wheels in my head turning ever so slowly, my mind working to connect all the scattered pieces of a massive jigsaw puzzle. Numb, with little to no emotion, neither sad nor happy. I felt empty. I wanted answers, but I was skeptical of getting them from any outside source. The world in which I lived had been tainted long ago, full of individuals and organizations who were trying to sell others on their bastardized version of the truth.

I considered myself a seeker of truth, a spiritual man who adhered to fundamental principles taught by Buddha and Confucius, but who based his application of thought more on science than on religious dogma. Despite that, I was having a hard time ignoring the shared faith of billions of people who idealized-rationalized a monotheistic god, whether they followed the teachings of Jesus, Muhammad, Bahá'u'lláh, or any other prophet-type figure. I had friends who had sought deliverance from the worldly bonds that kept them prisoner by asking the Lord Jesus Christ to come in and free them. Those who were genuine in their desire to see anew spoke of seeing the world as it is for the first time. To be born again by the Spirit of God, you are given a new nature that longs for the right things of conscience.

After seeing its positive effects on others, I thought it arrogant not to consider the validity of this rite of passage. However, I wasn't willing to wager my salvation on any one cult figure. Instead, I decided to pray to the combined perceived reality of every living soul on planet Earth, with a liberated willingness to tune myself into the Universe, pledging my life to serve in any way the Universe deemed necessary. I wanted to realize Truth in its purest form, which can be neither manipulated nor controlled. I offered my last breath and life as payment for the Truth to be revealed. I didn't want to die, but my need for clarity trumped any fear of death. I had no choice but to surrender, trusting in the divine wisdom of the Universe.

Until this point in my life, I had been completely at the disposal of my environment, a machine that operates within certain parameters. My days became blurred, each one running into the next, presenting me with a mountain of things to do. I had no context. There wasn't a raising of the dead moment. There was no screaming "Hallelujah" from the top of my lungs, but as the days rolled on, I progressed, making headway toward bringing forward long-forgotten memories that were now in full technicolour and surround sound stereo. Memories I could now taste and smell. My mind went into overdrive, sorting every file, memory, learned habit, and belief. It was mind-blowing, the delight I had in being able to connect the dots between things that had happened when I was a kid, the emotional connections I had to them, and how those experiences and feelings helped shape me into the man I had become. Information poured out of the darkness the same way a waterfall pours from one cascade to another before making its way back to the source: Dark Water Fountain. The pieces fit neatly together. I could see all that came before me and much of what lay ahead, the good, the bad, and the ugly, embracing every single moment with full acceptance and gratitude. The energy force that had once scared me, the energy I had seen as existing outside of me, reintegrated, bringing with it the most powerful feeling of unconditional love for all. This revelation, which occurred shortly before the birth of my daughter, was the most impactful thunderbolt moment of my life. I was reborn.

When I decided to walk from my sport, I also decided to stick with the training. It wasn't until five years later, when I walked into a BC Ferries gift shop and picked up a bodybuilding magazine, that I saw the life I could have lived if I hadn't broken from my sport. One of the top body-builders in the world, Jay Cutler, was on the front cover of *Flex* magazine. I stood there smiling to myself, basking in serendipity. Supposedly, Jay was the guy who Jean, my trainer, was helping to get ready for the NPC Championships while he was getting me ready for the Canadian Nationals. Jay and I were of the same weight, height, and age. He became one of the greatest champions the sport has ever produced. How could I not smile? The morning I had taken those first few steps out of bed, I remembered flashing ahead ten years to a moment where I would be standing on stage competing next to him.

CHAPTER 27

WORLD REPUBLIC

"If a man will begin with certainties, he shall end in doubts; but if he will be content to begin with doubts, he shall end in certainties."

— Francis Bacon

September 25th, 1997

Quitting competitive bodybuilding allowed for new activities. My body trimmed down quickly from a powerful but slow 265 pounds to a much faster and leaner 200 pounds. I began rock climbing and snowshoeing, relishing the opportunity to get out into the outdoors every chance I could get. I took to practising yoga, as much to bring balance to my physical self as to respond to my need to incorporate the power of breath in my life, consciously holding my connection to the Source.

Mariah's birth helped ground me, highlighting the most important things in life, but at the same time my world was rapidly expanding, introducing me to new places, people from all walks of life — and the BC marijuana market. I took to being a parent with a tremendous amount of enthusiasm. Mariah was the most beautiful thing I had ever seen, another soul who returned more out of want than out of need. She was the jewel of everybody's eye, as we were the first of our friends in Vancouver to have a baby. She went everywhere with me. The women who ran the day-care at Olympic gym were always delighted when I dropped her off with them. I began packing her up Grouse Mountain when she was a couple of months old. She would sleep peacefully, snuggled into my chest, while I encouraged new clients to push hard for the top. In no way did she cramp our lifestyle; she only enhanced it.

Those were some of the best days of my life, most of them being spent with my wife and my daughter. My transformation — physically, emotion-ally, and mentally — was noticeable to everyone who knew me, and when I finally peaked, I dropped to one knee and spoke new vows to Candace, unrehearsed and from the heart. At that time, I was more confident of my place in the world than I had ever been. Nothing mattered more to me than Candace, Mariah, and the mission I was now on. And what about that mission? My self-created program's main function is to awaken those who are asleep and help support others who are doing good things for their community. After awakening to my truth and realizing what I was here to do, I went on study overdrive again. I would often reread the books that fired every cell in my body, marvelling at the new places to which they took me. Sun Tzu's *Art of War*, Miyamoto's *Five Rings*, Gibran's *The Prophet*, Napoleon Hill's *Think and Grow Rich* are a handful of those gems.

I returned to college full-time, hoping to replicate my experience the first time around and making sure to enrol in John Dixon's philosophy class. John was a distinguished professor and the acting president of the BC Civil Liberties Union. He was a real cool cat. The major term paper he assigned to our class was based on being given a baby girl to raise from infancy until she turned twenty-five years old. Upon that girl's twenty-fifth birthday, the key to power, the key that would give her sole ruling authority over planet Earth, would be bestowed on her by an alien race that has been keeping their eye on us for millennia. If we failed to provide her with the right education, training her to become a great leader, they would obliterate the world. The students' task was to decide how best to raise the child, and, in the end, John decided our fate. I didn't miss the reason John had chosen this topic. He knew how much I wanted to positively contribute to society. Knowing I had a young daughter, as I had taken Mariah to the occasional class, he saw and seized upon the opportunity to help make sure I galvanized my focus onto her. I received an A on that paper.

During the previous twelve months, I had taken a keen interest in hiking and snowshoeing the North Shore Mountains, a small sub-range of the Pacific Ranges, the southernmost grouping of the vast Coast Mountains that wrap themselves around northern Vancouver. Trading my long hours spent inside the confines of the gym for the spectacular scenery that was in my city's backyard helped to ground me. Anyone who spends a considerable amount of time alone in nature knows how the great outdoors can help shed the illusion that the material world, Maya, wraps us in. The view from the top of my world gave me the ability to hear from God in a way I had never experienced before. During one of my long treks into the mountains, I meditated on a quote I recently had printed on one side of my new business cards:

"A human being is a part of the whole called by us universe, a part limited in time and space. He experiences himself, his thoughts and feeling as something separated from the rest, a kind of optical delusion of his consciousness. This delusion is a kind of prison, restricting us to our personal desires and to affection for a few persons nearest to us. Our task must be to free ourselves from this prison by widening our circle of compassion to embrace all living creatures and the whole of nature in its beauty."

— Albert Einstein

155

That was when I first felt the call to go to Scotland, and once that call started, it would not cease. I boarded a plane and flew to Manchester, England, then rented a car and headed north to Edinburgh. My two days stay in Scotland's capital city coincided with the world-famous Fringe Festival, which saw the city streets jammed with performers and tourists from all over the world. It was quite a welcome. Edinburgh is rich in history, and I felt a strong connection to my family's heritage, yet instinctively, I knew my purpose for making this journey would make itself known elsewhere.

Circumnavigating the whole of Scotland would make for a great trip, I thought. Go west to Stirling, then north-west to Inverness, across to Aberdeen, and then south to Perth, watching for signs left by the Universe and allowing spontaneity to guide me. The scenic countryside was filled with never-ending farms where sheep roamed and horses grazed. Old castles could be seen in the distance, taking me back to another time in history, with scenes from the movie *Highlander* playing out in my head. *"There can be only one."* I had no desire to stop other than for a quick bite to eat or fuel my rental car.

In Fort William, the second-largest settlement in the Highlands, next to Inverness, I decided to look for a place to sleep for the night. I pulled into a gas station to fill up and ask the store attendant about bed & breakfasts in the area.

"Go stay at the Achintee Farmhouse," the man in line behind me advised. "Good people who run it, and a great view of the mountain. It's splendid."

"The mountain! Can you hike this mountain?"

Sounding somewhat surprised, the man said, "Of course you can hike the mountain. That's why the tourists come here. The tallest mountain in all the British Isles, Ben Nevis is. It's an ancient volcano with a hundred-year-old observatory sitting atop of it.

Goosebumps appeared on my right arm. "This sounds like the place I was looking for. Would you please point me in the right direction?"

"Yes, of course. It's a mile down the road, on the right. You can't miss the sign. It's at the base of ol' Beinn, right where the trail begins."

I thanked the man and then headed out the door. I had thought of calling the B&B first but decided to wing it. The man was right; it was easy to find, as there were a couple of good signs pointing me in the right direction. I slowly drove up the dirt driveway, a long gradual climb, hemmed in with the native pinewood trees. As I pulled into the open, the large farmhouse and another smaller residence came into full view. Five or six vehicles were in the parking area, leaving me to think there might not be any rooms available. Once I parked the car, I walked over to where I saw a middle-aged woman sweeping the stairs.

"Good day," I said.

She smiled warmly back, "Hi, a lovely day it is."

"I am hoping there may be a room available for a night or two."

"You are in luck. Someone cancelled this morning. It has the best view of Beinn. My name is Helen, what's yours?"

"Daryl." I began to share my reasons for being there as she walked me through the front door and into her spacious three-storey home.

"My husband and I have enjoyed meeting people from every corner of the world. Many who come here feel the calling like you did. They feel the land pulse through their veins," she said.

I followed her up the stairs to the top floor of the house, breathing in the scent of my new surroundings while paying attention to her running through the list of house items I should know about, notably the times for dinner and breakfast. My room was small but cozy. I walked straight to the big window that faced Ben Nevis, dropping my bags on the floor beside the bed.

"Thank you. Your home is what I was looking for. I think I'll take a nap before dinner."

"Yes. Relax, take your time, and enjoy. If you miss dinner, I'll leave a plate for you in the kitchen."

I thanked her again as she walked out of the bedroom, closing the door behind her. I lay down on the bed, which ran close alongside the large window that looked out at the mountain towering overhead. My body didn't move, other than the rising and falling of my chest as my lungs worked effortlessly to take in the salty, rich air. The yearning to silence the call I had heard a month earlier was no longer there. I was where I needed to be. I eventually dozed off, waking about an hour later to the sound of a door in the outside hall closing. Realizing it was time for dinner, I decided to get up and make my way downstairs. Splashing cold water onto my face helped wash away the last of the sleepiness that was still clinging to me. I felt refreshed.

Even if I hadn't been shown the layout of the house, my nose would have easily found the dining area as the smell emanating throughout was rich with what I soon learned was a mix of basil, mint, garlic, chives, coriander, and fennel. The dining room was spacious, decorated with a rustic décor of the type you might expect to find in this part of Scotland. The tables, cabinets, and side tables were all made of solid oak, and each table was covered with a patterned white tablecloth. The dining room could seat up to eighteen people at a time. There were three smaller tables, and one large table spread out through the room. Every seat was set with a placemat, drinking glass, and artfully arranged silverware. Two of the smaller tables were occupied, one by a couple who looked to be in their late thirties and the other by a couple who must have been in their mid-fifties. I felt a pang of regret about not having Candace with me. I considered taking the last of the small tables but decided against it, opting for one of the nine available seats at the large table in the centre of the room, the tenth being occupied by a man whom I presumed to be the man of the house.

"Good evening, sir," I said as I pulled my chair out. The man looked up from the newspaper he was reading and returned the greeting. I took my seat just as Helen entered with her hands full of steaming food and a small pitcher of milk.

"Your plate is hot," she warned, placing a delectable-looking shepherd's pie down in front of me. "Would you like a glass of milk with your dinner?"

"Yes, please." I was in Heaven. This place was rhythmically tuning every cell in my body; I felt centred, connected to an ethos that transcends time. Helen walked back into the kitchen, leaving me to satiate my hunger. The first bite of the pie didn't disappoint. "So good," I said out loud, more to myself than to anyone else. The man looked up at me and smiled, acknowledging my obvious satisfaction.

"The lady of the house never disappoints. I have made my stay here a handful of times, never once regretting I did."

His accent was nowhere near as strong as the other locals' but it was still perceptible. He was distinguished; the word "gentleman" aptly described his persona. He sported a full, neatly trimmed beard, most of which was gray, which suited his thick, wavy, salt and pepper hair. I'm not usually one to pay attention to the dress attire of an individual unless it is unique or over-the-top flashy, or the individual possesses a strong presence. His tweed jacket with leather elbow patches went well with his light brown casual slacks and his brown, three-quarter-top leather boots, one of which was crossed over the opposite knee, helping to support his newspaper. His reading glasses helped tie his entire outfit together, leaving me with the impression he was a teacher at one of the local schools.

"Do you live in these parts?" I asked.

"No, but I do consider it home and try to come at least once a year. My home and family are in London. I mostly work from there."

Oxford and Cambridge flashed in my mind, both of which I knew were an hour's drive outside of central London.

"And how about you, what brings you to the heart of the Highlands?" he said.

I grinned, feeling slightly foolish, knowing I was going to tell him the truth, "I know this may sound strange, but I didn't have any reason to come, just felt the place had been calling me." If he was surprised by my response, he didn't show it.

"How charming, and a wee bit adventurous?"

"Yes, definitely," I said, returning the smile.

"Has the call been answered?"

"From the time I arrived here, I felt like I was home."

"Yes, this land connects with one's soul."

I thought about what he said. I was connecting to something, but getting my mind to adequately translate my feelings into words was not easy. "Do you ever have moments in your life when everything you have been doing seems to lead exactly to where you needed to be? Not because you had planned it…" I paused, searching for the right words. "But rather you had been part of the plan?"

"Yes, assuredly so. I have spent many hours contemplating what is hidden in nature's eternal consciousness and marvelling at her beauty. Here's a question to ponder," he said. "Do you perceive being here, sitting at this table, one of chance, or one of intelligent design?"

"That's a difficult question to answer. Maybe a loaded question as well?" I said, amused with myself, knowing full well that what I said had the potential to take me down countless paths. "I have thought on this for a long time without ever being able to define my feelings about it."

"Sometimes, closing your eyes helps," he said encouragingly, while looking amused.

"Sure, I'll give it a try." I closed my eyes, thinking about the last three years and how they had led up to this day. I took in a deep breath, which helped the spinning wheels in my mind to slow. A picture flashed in my mind no more than ten seconds later. I opened my eyes and laughed. "I see myself standing at the helm of an eighteenth-century sailing ship. It's massive in size, outfitted with at least ten individual sails. Standing at the bow of the ship, looking out past the crew, I can see the open sea."

"What is going through the mind of the man standing attention on deck?"

"I am the master of my fate. The choices I make are mine to own, and yet intuitively, I feel something is guiding me, connected to something that continuously nudges me forward."

"The wide-open sea mirrors the sky above. You can use Heaven's celestial beings to navigate your chartered direction."

"And if you don't have a chartered course and don't know how to follow the stars?"

"Then do just as you did."

"Which was…?"

"You followed your heart."

"I've always believed I was meant to do something important, to contribute in a meaningful way to the global community. Yet, as I get older, that vision looks more like a fantasy of a young boy who is afraid to let go."

"Why the self-doubt?"

"I'm not sure, but I know I was guided here to be sitting with you now, and it would never have happened if I didn't make the conscious decision to act upon the feelings that had been churning inside of me. There is an internal relationship to 'I' and an external relationship to 'other,' yet I feel they are one and the same."

"Often, when we enter obscure realms of thought, common sense is an unreliable guide."

Just then, Helen stepped out from the kitchen to take the man's plate. "Adriel, I can take that for you."

He looked up at her with a smile. "Always a delight, Helen."

"Yes, dinner is delicious," I added. She thanked us both for the praise and offered tea. We both accepted, thanking her as she left the room.

Adriel turned and asked me, "How long do you plan on staying?"

"I think two nights. I'm going to run the mountain tomorrow morning and then spend the rest of my time writing in my journal."

"You are going to 'run' the Ben?" he asked, looking surprised.

"Yes, I feel the most alive after pushing hard to summit a peak. I think I'm addicted to the endorphin rush," I laughed.

"There are far worse things to be addicted to," he offered. "May I ask what you do for a living?"

"I'm an athletic trainer," I said, refraining from blurting out I had recently been introduced to growing marijuana and that it comprised half my workday.

"That seems fitting."

"I enjoy training people. Helping others is rewarding."

"I can see that in you," Adriel said.

"How so?" I asked.

He smiled, his warm brown eyes searching my face. "It's the way in which you carry yourself, the way you address a stranger, your interest to start a conversation. You are genuinely interested in others, for their own sake, not necessarily for your own."

This guy was so fucking cool. Talking with him affirmed what I held to be true, that there were great conversations to be had with people from all over. We moved into the living room, taking a seat next to the fireplace, where logs were already burning hot and bright. I felt spoiled, assuming firewood would have been a scarce commodity in these parts.

"I've been told, not sure if it's true, I'm a descendant of Sir James 'The Good' Douglas," I told him.

"The Good Douglas, or if you were fighting for the English, The Black Douglas. Great strategist, a master of guerilla warfare, taking victory when victory seemed impossibly out of reach. A prominent figure in his day." Adriel talked of James Douglas as if he had known him, firming up my earlier impression of him being a professor at some prestigious college. "The Douglas family is connected to the House of Moray and, before that, Freskin. They first appeared on record in the twelfth century, but you come from old stock that goes farther back than that."

"How far back do they go?"

"At least to the eighth century. The tale goes something like this: A battle took place in 767 between Solvathius, the rightful king of Scotland, and a pretender named Donald Bane. Bane was a hair's width away from victory when a nobleman charged forward, turning the battle in the king's favour. In the aftermath, the king sought out this gallant knight to whom he owed a debt of gratitude. When he asked who it was, somebody yelled, 'Sholto du glasse!' or 'Behold the black-grey man!' Sholto was the legendary ancestor to Clan Douglas, a powerful and warlike family who continued to rise in prominence over the centuries. His son William Douglas was the commander of the forces sent by King Achaius to the court of Charlemagne to aid him in his wars against Desiderius, King of the Lombards. It is believed William Douglas settled in Northern Italy, where his descendants became powerful lords under the name Scotti."

Adriel paused, aware I needed a moment to process the information I was downloading. My father's family, the Fontanas, had come from Northern Italy, making me wonder how many times our family lines crisscrossed throughout the ages.

"A century later," he continued, "Sir William the Hardy joined William Wallace's uprising against English rule in Scotland. He was captured and died a prisoner in the Tower of London. His estates were forfeited to the English crown. His son, Sir James Douglas, swore allegiance to Robert the Bruce and shared in his victories leading up to Bannockburn, earning his appointment as Warden of the Western March."

"When you said I came from old stock you weren't joking. However, I'm not convinced there is any relation. I was told by a relative who could have been pulling my leg. I've never taken the time to dig into it," I said.

"Ah, verifying our sources is due diligence used wisely. But if I were a betting man, I would wager Sholto is running strong through your veins."

I reflected on what he said. "I appreciate the compliment, but I think the fighting spirit that runs through mine and my family's blood has at times created more hardship than good." I expected Adriel to respond to what I'd just said, and wanting to steer clear of personal family dynamics, I shifted our conversation further back in history. "I would love to know how far back we all go together."

"Do you mean, how far we, as in *Homo sapiens*, go back?"

"Yes. I'd love to have the map of the world when Adam and Eve began their clan," I said.

"Are you a man of the Book?" he asked.

I chuckled. "No, not really, though I have read the Bible. My reference to Adam and Eve is made with the hope every person living on this planet can be traced back to the same lineage. Showing the world, with irrefutable evidence to back it, we are all brothers and sisters."

"I think we may be close to revealing this truth."

"How so?"

Adriel lifted his left hand in front of himself, and I noticed the plain silver band on his ring finger. He spaced his thumb and index finger two inches apart. "We are this close to sequencing the human genome. With this advancement in science, many great things will occur; tracing your ancestry back to the beginning of time will be one of them."

"That's cool. What else do you think we'll be able to do?"

"We will have the ability to cure disease and live much longer."

"Breaking down our DNA will allow for that?"

"It's a culmination of breakthroughs in all areas, including nano-technology, which will aid in the evolutionary advancement of our species."

"We want to be like the gods of the past. Don't you think this is dangerous territory?"

Adriel gave me a long look before responding, "Life is inherently dangerous, whether we live passively, always in search of meaning, or actively engaged, exploring our divine nature, co-creating, together."

"So much power in the hands of a few makes me worry the human race will become totally subjugated."

"Ah, to be ruled by the Titans. It would be naïve to think history won't repeat itself. For every action, there is a reaction. For every person or group working toward the betterment of humanity, others work to undermine it for their own nefarious goals. You are right to be cautious and to question people's motives."

"How am I supposed to make my way around in life if I can't trust anybody?"

He leaned forward to grab the poker for the fire, jabbing the biggest of the three pieces of wood. The flames crackled, and a handful of sparks shot up the chimney. "Trust, at its core, requires we attach a level of expectation to our relationships. Sometimes we are let down, and that is the way of it."

"Well, that's no fun," I said, only half-joking.

"Surrender yourself to truth, and you will no longer be blinded by the dogma and falsities owing to others."

The skin on my arms and up my neck was suddenly covered in goosebumps. "I surrendered last year. I prayed to the universe to reveal the truth, offering my life as payment, if needed."

Adriel looked surprised. "Is that so? And who guided you through this process?"

"Nobody."

"Hmm… I'm intrigued," he said, possibly questioning the validity of my answer. Our casual, friendly conversation amped up with a little more intensity. He removed his glasses. His eyes looked piercingly into mine as he waited on my answer.

"I just… decided to shut myself down, for a long stretch of time, many months. I needed time to process what I saw."

"What were you shown?"

I closed my eyes, making sure to take in a deep breath. "My mind entered into and became one with pure light. No physical body, no shadows, or objects were present. Nothing except for my mind and the light. I had always thought myself an atheist, but I suppose you could say I was born again."

"You found God?" Adriel sounded unconvinced.

"I don't know how else to describe it."

"Those who know God, those who have actualized themselves by self-attainment of realization, first had to take a leap of faith, letting go of their fear of death. Only those who are willing to surrender completely can experience the true nature of God."

I was amazed at how easily he put into words what I had been wrestling with for the past year. "I don't know why this isn't taught in school. I don't think this is common knowledge."

"There is a vested interest in keeping the masses ignorant of the power they possess."

And there it was. His statement made me sit a little taller. The goosebumps returned. He was expressing a truth I knew from everything I had learned but had never been able to definitively prove: most of us were owned, or at the very least, manipulated to behave the way others want us to behave.

"Sitting here with you right now feels a little surreal. It's as if I have been on this ride since the beginning of time, and all of those years led me to you right now."

"Perhaps this is providence?"

"Yeah, maybe. I suppose so."

"Being on the ride since the beginning of time is a long time. You must be tired," he said, laughing.

I laughed too. "Yeah, seeing through the lens of the conscious universe over hundreds of millions of years is both liberating and frustrating. I mean, I have great admiration and love for all that is but in a very simplistic, human way of thinking, I find myself disappointed with the collective's short-sightedness, with their 'What can we get out of this right now?' way of thinking."

"How do you plan to resolve your feelings of frustration?"

His questions were direct and straight to the point, requiring extra focus to stay with him.

"Maybe I need to reach out and connect with people who want to affect the same positive change in the world as I do. People need to wake up and realize more is going on around them. They can contribute a lot of good rather than add to the mounting problems we face together globally. If I can contribute and connect with others, then I'm confident the frustration I carry today would leave me."

"You sound sure of what you want."

"I think so, but I'm not certain about how to advance."

"Are you passionate about the work you do?"

"You mean my work as a fitness trainer?"

"Yes."

"I enjoy it, but I don't see how it can affect the change I want to take place in the world. Like Gandhi said, 'Be the change you wish to see.' I get it. Well, at least I think I do."

"We all have our paths to take, but when and where we can, we must try to do what we love while making sure we don't allow the outcome of our goals to imprison us."

I thought of the tattoo I had recently gotten on my left shoulder: a Yin-Yang inside of the sun. Striving to maintain balance was key to my success. The sun represented life, the passion that fuelled me, but if I was not careful and allowed myself to be driven by ego, the sun could burn me and those I love. So much to consider, so much to learn. Why did I refuse to choose simplicity? "Maybe it's best if I try turning off the part of my brain that seeks to overcomplicate. If I'm to be completely forthcoming...."

"Please do!" he said fondly.

"I said what I did because sometimes... everything... feels a little overwhelming."

"Wanting to do good for others is commendable. The world needs more people who wish to contribute, but I caution, don't get trapped into thinking that you must carry the load all by yourself. You are not alone with these thoughts."

We sat quietly for a moment as I pondered his words.

"I often wonder if there are people in positions of extraordinary power that help to carry most of the load. I envision seeing them sitting in front of a large control panel, flicking switches and pushing buttons that affect every aspect of our daily lives, from the minor details to the major worldly decisions."

"I think you may have watched *The Wizard of Oz* one too many times. Why take an interest in the people behind the curtain? To use a computer, do you have to know how to write code or build processors?" His voice deepened, perhaps in an attempt to mimic the voice of the wizard bellowing from behind the curtain. "Does living a life with purpose require knowing every detail of the inner workings of the machine?"

"For me, it's a resounding, yes." For the first time that night I could see Adriel doing some inner reflecting of his own. When I realized he wasn't going to add anything further, I continued, "If there are people, or an organization invisibly pulling all our strings, and these people think of nothing but furthering their self-serving agenda, then something needs to change."

"Or, do the people who operate the controls act from a purely benevolent level of service to others? Perhaps they look at the world the way you do."

"Perhaps there are two opposing forces, like the Empire versus the Rebel Alliance."

"Yes, some people would agree with that analogy. Every machine has a control panel, but there is not just one person behind it full-time. Yet, some commit their entire lives to sitting in front of those controls. The self-determined continuance to forge ahead, whether for altruistic reasons or purely greedy ones, has been running through the hearts and minds of men for millennia."

"I keep thinking about the Yin-Yang symbol. I don't wish to see the world balanced by 50 percent greedy people and the other half who work in service to others."

"The Yin-Yang expresses an infinite number of differing contrasts in life. There is the purest of white, the light, and the purest of black, the dark. There is only one Mother Mary, one Adolf Hitler, and billions of other unique souls we share Earth with."

I moved off my chair and knelt on the floor so I could reach a piece of wood to place on the fire. As I sat back into my chair, Adriel continued, "There is an opposing ideology very much like the comparison you used, the Rebel Alliance against the Empire, but it is not entirely black and white. One side isn't inherently bad and the other good, as they are both fighting for the same end goal."

"What would that be? World domination?"

"World order sounds more appealing. But in truth, our evolution has been inextricably linked to war, and wars will continue to wage until there is only one organization that sits at the head of it all."

"I'm not so sure I like the sound of that. Gives a lot of power to a small percentage of the populace."

"Or, a lot of power to the people."

"How do you give the power to the people?

"Hmmm... a near-insurmountable task. People have willingly surrendered their autonomy to a system that can be coldly efficient. Getting them to take responsibility would not be easy."

"It would take a revolution!"

"Perhaps," Adriel said.

"If enough people rose in unison, world leaders would have to listen."

"When people rise up, it equates to people not going to work, which disrupts people who are trying to work. I assure you, the people sitting at the control panel are aware of how volatile the system is, like a runaway freight train that requires more and more track to be laid; otherwise, the global economy will come to a crashing halt. There is not one main engineer, not one main conductor, just a bunch of passengers who are along for the ride. Some people keep to themselves, relatively quiet, allowing whatever course of action to be rolled out for them. Some are panicking; they do nothing other than increase the level of fear felt by others, making it difficult for those who are tasked with finding a humane solution to our problems to be able to act upon it. And of course, there are those sitting in the area reserved for first class. Many of them fail to see a problem at all. They think increasing the train's speed is a good thing as it will get them to where we have to go that much quicker."

"And where are we charging ahead so fast to, leaving behind the richness and beauty of a world that we may never get a chance to see again?"

"Good question. Where are we going?"

I watched him as he looked into the fire, his eyes reflecting back the flickering of the flames. He was in deep thought, making it a good time to excuse myself to use the washroom.

I looked out the window as I relieved myself of the milk and tea, amused it was still light out, despite the time of night. If I were back home, closer to the 49th parallel, I would see stars. While washing my hands, my mind flashed back once again, this time to the Cretaceous–Paleogene extinction event, which took place sixty-six million years ago. I have an overwhelming sense that we are trying to outrun something. Is it possible we are heading for another major world cataclysm? We have been struck in the past by enormous asteroids, and it's only a matter of time before we are hit again. Is global warming everything scientists are warning us about?

When I returned to the den, Adriel was gone. I wondered briefly if he had retired to bed for the night but assumed not. As I sat back down in my chair, he returned, carrying two short glasses and a dark glass bottle.

"I trust a man of high fitness standards would appreciate a dram of Scotland's finest."

"I strive for balance, Adriel. I would love a shot, thank you. Besides, today is my twenty-fifth birthday, so I think it's rather appropriate."

"Is it?" he sounded surprised. "Well then, I better fill our glasses to the top as today is your golden birthday."

"I am glad you returned. I thought maybe I was asking you too many questions, and you had escaped to your room."

We laughed.

"Emerson said, 'The glory of friendship is not the outstretched hand, nor the kindly smile, nor the joy of companionship; it is the spiritual inspiration that comes to one when you discover that someone else believes in you and is willing to trust you with a friendship.' Happy birthday, Daryl."

"Thank you," I said, feeling somewhat in awe of the man I was with. I shared what I had been thinking while in the washroom. "Do you think if the engineer and conductor knew an impending major cataclysmic event was on the horizon, they would share it openly with the public?"

"That depends entirely upon the time frame. Is it global warming we're talking about, or some other event?"

"What if it was an asteroid, one that would hit Earth in two to three years?" I asked.

"If people were to be informed of an impending Doomsday, we would have millions of crazed frightened people running around creating mayhem, and any chance of facilitating a plan would be compromised by people's self-serving needs of themselves and those closest to them. So, in this case, there would not be sharing of details with the public."

"I agree, people's instinctual drive is to fight and survive at all costs, even if it is at the expense of the whole group. No different than when a drowning person fights their rescuer."

"We come back to the need to trust. Specifically, do we trust in the ability of others to do the right thing for the greater good?"

"It would be a lot easier to follow in good faith if there was a system in place that held people accountable when they break our trust."

"I wholeheartedly agree. Egregious wrongdoing while working for the people, abusing one's position of authority should come with serious consequences."

"Perhaps," I hesitated before completing my sentence. "Perhaps there really ought to be a revolution."

"Not if it means the revolution causes more harm than good."

"The French and American revolutions looked to have been a step in the right direction."

Adriel gave me a questioningly look. "Yes, magnificently orchestrated and played out. It was one great revolution."

"One great revolution, not two?" I asked. "I thought both these revolutions were started at the grassroots. Wasn't it guys like Voltaire and Rousseau who created the fervour among the peasantry in France?"

"They had a part to play."

"It sounds like some decent people were trying to change the world."

"Many of whom who were discarded once they served their purpose," Adriel said.

"Discarded by whom?"

"The principles written in the American and French constitutions highlighted the mindset of a group of extraordinary gentlemen. Men who were devoted to a cause to bring light to man. They were dogged in their approach, with an immeasurable amount of patience, waiting for the day when they could break the chains. But history has shown repeatedly when one chain is broken, another one is made to take its place. More than two hundred years have passed, and with it, a return to the gluttony and waste we bear witness to, for the regents have returned and have claimed a strong footing next to that control panel you like to refer to."

I took a sip of my Scotch. "You have a good understanding of how the world operates. Are you in support of the current global operating system, or do you think it needs to be overhauled?"

"Both. The structure in place serves us well, but without question, it is not perfect. For mankind to have climbed out of the dark abyss, they needed to be strong; they had to do what was necessary to survive.

The blood spilled by Alexander and Khan forged empires, bringing people, places, and ideas together, spreading knowledge that helped us map our place in the world. But the ways of old no longer serve us. We have reached a tipping point where the energy and resources poured into conventional war are detrimental to the advancement of the human species. Our resources need to be diverted elsewhere. The daily waste of human energy is utterly gross and unconscionable."

"I believe most people want change, but they can't expect it to happen without any effort put forward."

"And what do you recommend people do?"

Adriel patiently waited for me to answer.

"I'm not sure. Maybe there is something people can get started on doing today. Whatever that first thing might be; getting exercise, eating better, reading, gardening, taking a class, volunteering. Keep looking for something new to challenge yourself, something new to learn. Join organizations that support your community. One thing will build on top of the other, and then soon we will be connecting to more and more people who are all aspiring to achieve that one higher ideal." Adriel nodded his head as I continued, "We need to make this world a better place! But everywhere I look, I see people who have this incessant need to tear others down."

"Yes, there exists a propaganda machine at work, so masterful, the operators make what they do look like the highest art form."

"How do you combat that?"

"More humour. After all, there's so much to laugh at in the world."

And what's there to laugh at?"

"How about George Jr. becoming the next US president?"

"Who's George Jr.?"

"Texas governor, son of the former president, George H.W. Bush."

"Oh, if I'm not mistaken, he's still serving his first term. I think Gore will make a run and get it. He's hugely into the environment, and it seems like more and more people are waking up to the need to change how we do things. I'm hoping this is the moment in history the good guys begin to pull away."

There was a weary look on his face. "The decision has already been made."

"How can you be sure?" I asked skeptically.

"A course of action is being followed that will take another thirty years to complete. Another Bush will be in the White House very soon, mark my words."

"Are you telling me that the US elections are pre-orchestrated before people know who they are even going to vote for?"

"Yes, sometimes."

"So, the people who are placed in power are just window dressing?

"Yes and no. There's still a modicum of responsibility, but the position has evolved over time to give people the veiled appearance they have a voice, that their vote counts."

"And yet it does not really give them a voice!"

"Yes, and obviously no. I say 'yes' because at the end of the day, and as you said, the public must take responsibility for where they find themselves standing. The direction we walk has much more to do with the personal desires of each individual."

"Do you believe there is hope for humankind?"

"Yes, of course I do, but because we have built this reality by means of force, treachery, and deceit, it makes it difficult for us to trust one another. Who can be trusted, who can be counted on? For thousands of years, we have waged war. Something that will continue so long as the public listens unquestioningly to those who are considered authorities, not realizing they are as programmed, mechanical, and predictable as everyone else. People would be horrified if they knew the true extent of their mental conditioning."

He was so matter of fact when he said this that a chill ran straight up my back. "You speak what I think, but it is an ugly thought to dwell on for very long." I said. His glass was near empty, and his tone of voice was infused with a little more heat.

"How did you come to know so much?" I asked, hoping to get some background information on this man.

"I read a lot," he chuckled. "The breaking down and analyzing of the human condition and how it operates under differing circumstances has been documented and studied for thousands of years. The material is there for everybody to read, but few have the means to access it. I am grateful to have been born to wonderful parents who continued on with a long tradition educating their children."

"Quite the family lineage you must have?"

"We both come from a wonderful lineage," he said as he gave me a gentle poke in the ribs with his finger. "Half a glass?" he asked, motioning toward the bottle.

"Yes, please." I was already feeling the first four ounces he had poured me. "I admit I am not well versed in the understandings of a good Scotch, but I am certain this is the best I have ever had. The writing on the bottle, is that Latin?"

"Yes, it is. This batch came from my family's private reserve." Adriel turned the bottle in his hand to read something on the label. "This bottle is from the year..." He stopped in mid-sentence, and I could see his mind working. "It was 1972, the year in which you were born, lad! Would you fancy that? A good omen I would say."

"An omen or another coincidence," I add.

"No, not a coincidence. Do not discount the magic that exists all around you. It's the magic that makes life worth living."

"Sounds like something my mother would say to me."

"She sounds like a wise woman. Daryl, our world reflects our own beliefs and convictions. You do realize you have the power to shape the world around you, don't you?"

"I do, with all of my heart, I do. But sometimes I feel I am helpless to contribute to a system that seems beyond repair."

"It better be repairable because it's the only system we have. Daryl..."

"Yes?"

"You may be my harbinger."

"Your harbinger?" I repeated, unsure as to what he meant.

"Yes, an omen, perhaps. I have been grappling with some issues at work. Much of what we have discussed tonight has helped me to see these problems a little more clearly. What if a worldwide, cultural-spiritual revolution was encouraged to spread?"

"I thought you said that could be dangerous." I could almost hear his mind working while he talked, and I was certain there was much more to what he was thinking than what he was saying.

"We cannot afford to play the game of chance. A carefully laid out plan would have to be set. The transference of power would be slow and drawn out."

"Are you planning something?"

He laughed. "Feeding the mind, lad, just feeding the mind."

We sat there quietly for a while, both of us staring into the fire, enjoying the silence.

"This planet has progressed, regressed, advanced, flooded, frozen, and been lit on fire many times over again. And yet, here we are still pushing as hard as ever to make sure that we continue with our existence. We are survivors, fighting with a never-ending desire to perpetuate our species," Adriel said, looking toward the fire.

"Sometimes it seems God wants to stop us from getting too far ahead of ourselves."

"God?! You and I, and every other creature awake to nature, is God. Your personal wants and desires are reflected in the collective consciousness of us all. Those who focus on purpose with intent will manifest the world in which the rest of us will see."

"What is it you see?"

"Assuming we make it through this next century, avoiding another Dark Age, how sweet would it be to survive as a world republic?" His last few words trailed off. Before I could respond, Adriel stood up and stretched his arms, bringing an abrupt end to our long conversation. "I must say I pulled an extra couple of hours and a couple of extra drops from the bottle tonight."

I stood up. "I suppose I should be getting some sleep too, as I want to hit Beinn early."

"You are in for a treat. I hope the morning weather permits a clear view. It has been a pleasure, Daryl." As he spoke, he extended his hand to shake mine. "Perhaps we will cross paths again."

"I would like that and thank you for the great history lesson and the delicious Scotch. It has been one of the best birthdays I've ever had." As I made my way to the stairs, I turned and asked, "Adriel?"

"Aye?"

"What does the Latin on the bottle translate to?"

"From one, learn to know all." He smiled once more before walking off to his room.

CHAPTER 28

CANNABIS

"The illegality of cannabis is outrageous, an impediment to full utilization of a drug which helps produce the serenity and insight, sensitivity and fellowship so desperately needed in this increasingly mad and dangerous world."

— *Carl Sagan*

October 1997

The return flight to Canada seemed to take half the time the outward flight did. Perhaps it was because my actions were aligning with my sense of purpose, like a radio tuning into a pitch-perfect clear broadcast, playing rhythmic beats that energized my body and cleared my mind. I landed in Vancouver fully committed to a mission of supreme importance, set on making changes that came to feel like the shedding of my skin. One of my first steps was to dissolve my business relationship with Kip, the guy who started me in the marijuana industry.

The late 1990s and early 2000s brought many influential figures into my life. I spoke earlier of John Dixon, who had spent his younger years studying at Berkeley and hanging with influential icons of that era like Janis Joplin and Joseph Tussman. I met Deepak Chopra, a man who spoke my language. His books helped me better articulate to others my spiritual awakening and aptly put into words what it is to know God. I incorporated Tony Robbins courses into my studies, which helped me strategize and better develop my master plan. I searched out and studied people I considered masters in their field, hoping to gain greater insight and wisdom so that I could, in turn, apply what I had learned to help educate others.

I have drawn as well as been pulled in by a variety of personalities, but at any one time in my life there has always been — and continues to be — at least one character who appeared to have embraced the darker side of the Force. These people are larger-than-life characters who desire to build their empire. I had grown up surrounded by intense, fierce warriors, many of whom were misguided, and most of whom, I believe, just wanted to be accepted. Kip was one of these warriors.

I first met Kip at Olympic gym the year before Mariah was born, shortly before I had decided to quit the sport. He was easy to spot, as he was one of only a half dozen guys who could lift as heavy as I did. I was at my biggest then. He equalled my strength for most lifts and bettered me in a couple of others. What set Kip apart from the other beasts was the way he moved. He was a big man, no doubt about it, but he didn't move like a builder; he moved like an agile linebacker. It came as no surprise when he later told me that was the position he played in college, a period of his life when he hid from the Canadian authorities by playing ball at a Northern Cali college.

Kip had a reputation as an enforcer and was known throughout the region. At six feet four and weighing a lean and muscular 250 pounds, he resembled Dwayne "The Rock" Johnson, though his attitude was more in line with that of Hugh Jackman's Wolverine character. His network of friends and associates spanned the continent; some were ex-military, others were the top MMA fighters of the day. He was a good-looking man, charismatic and confident. His intensity matched mine, making teaming up with him to work out a natural thing to do. Training together graduated to spending time outside the gym, which eventually led to him showing me one of his houses where he had an indoor cannabis garden.

Many cottage growers established businesses or used an existing business as a cover so they could tend to the maintenance and general operations of their gardens unnoticed. This is what Kip did.

I had been warned to stay clear of him.

"He's bad news, Corky. It's best to keep away from that guy," warned Ralph, the owner of Olympic. At the time, I was unaware of Kip's other business dealings or whom he associated with, so I ignored the warnings and learned more about an industry I fully supported on moral grounds. As the months passed, our friendship grew stronger.

I never bought into the cannabis fear-mongering that had been rammed down our throats by the so-called experts. Most people I knew back then were ignorant of the medicinal benefits marijuana provided. Few probably cared, but they did enjoy the temporary mind-bending effects minus the hangover left by alcohol. I had puffed recreationally with my friends but decided it wasn't something that gelled with my daily routine during my competitive training years.

Marijuana had been grown and used before the 1960s, but it wasn't until the decade of love and anti-war protests that BC underwent the birth of the marijuana-cottage movement. This movement took root in places like the Gulf Islands and the Kootenays, as they provided the ideal climate in which to grow and the ideal place in which to hide. People who wished to live closer to nature and stay sheltered from the encroaching world at large were attracted to these sanctuaries, as were the young, free-thinking souls who were dodging the Vietnam draft. The 1970s saw a substantial increase in the money and power being brought to the table. People who owned or had solid connections to companies that exported products to the US and Mexico started to hide the quality BC bud among their shipments. It wasn't a one-way street; cocaine and other illicit products were already making their way into Canada, which is why many marijuana exporters turned to importing cocaine, as the one could be traded for the other.

A combination of factors led to the sudden boost in production among American and Canadian growers in the homegrown marijuana industry, including Operation Intercept, President Nixon's 1969 initiative to tighten the Mexican border. Shutting off the weed supply from Mexico made many people look to Canada for their bud. The introduction of reasonably priced indoor gardening equipment made hydroponic marijuana intriguing and lucratively attractive. It didn't take long for new companies to open their doors to service the needs of people who were now growing with more complicated hydro systems. Everything a grower might need — specialized liquid food, lights, fans, growing mediums, sensors, and CO_2 equipment — was brought onto the market, with new and improved versions and equipment appearing from one year to the next. By the time the 1980s rolled in, there were new ways of doing things, including the aero-hydroponic method. The future of hydroponic gardens had arrived, and more people were getting involved.

It was an unprecedented underground movement that brought together science nerds, weed aficionados, and businesspeople, and eventually introduced thousands of people to Mary Jane. The eclectic mix of stakeholders helped create a booming industry that spread across Canada, the US, and other parts of the world. I quickly learned of the vast network that was helping to funnel billions of dollars into our economy, creating a trickle-down effect that everybody across the province got to feed on. Sales of new cars went up, and new houses, malls, and retail stores were built. BC was getting fat off cannabis, though it was a sticky game to be a part of. Even the politicians understood the importance of letting the revenue continue to flow, yet they, and the RCMP, had to appease its big brother to the south who wasn't happy seeing an unregulated export get through his borders, at least without a cut of the profit. BC had become a haven for the ordinary Joe to make large amounts of money in a short period of time.

The industry saw a massive influx of new growers during the mid- to late 1990s, and I was one of them. Kip and I entered a partnership. He supplied the equipment, and I took on the responsibility of being the garden caretaker. Organized crime had controlled a large share of the industry for quite some time, with new factions getting involved. No longer was it solely the Hell's Angels who dominated the headlines, as new groups were moving in to quickly shore up a good chunk of the market. The Red Scorpions, United Nations, Independent Soldiers, and myriad Asian gangs were becoming big power brokers, not only in the weed industry but in all types of drugs, prostitution, and money laundering.

I justified breaking the law and growing marijuana because I believed, and still do, that it's my sovereign right to do so. Of course, the money appealed to all of us, but my hope was for the industry to provide another outlet for the cultural-social revolution I strongly believed in. I believed the law needed to be changed, but most of my grower friends didn't share my desire to make marijuana legal. They didn't share my vision to generate tax revenue from this industry to be spent on health and education for our children.

It was impractical for the Canadian government to continue turning a blind eye, even though they desperately wanted to. No longer were hydroponic companies being coy about what their products could do for the cannabis grower; now they marketed them directly to the huge illegal industry. Companies like Advanced Nutrients blatantly advertised their products as being formulated specifically for cannabis. The US Drug Enforcement Administration was acutely aware of the billions of dollars being siphoned out of their country. Knowing it was highly unlikely they could stop it, they set plans to direct its course.

The drug laws should have been overhauled years ago, more so in the US than in Canada, as they were not written with the public's best interests in mind. Rather, they were put in place to serve the interests of long-established businesses that manipulate government and tax-spon-sored police forces to hold a monopoly on the drug trade and, more impor-tantly, control the vote. It is no longer a secret, although it is still not highly publicized, that these big pharmaceutical and illicit drug cartels had built a finely tuned machine that stretched its tentacles to connect every aspect of the world's social and economic fabric.

For years the Mexican drug wars have been ravaging the lives of mil-lions of people in that country, with the Mexican government supporting the policies that Nixon, Reagan, and Bush imposed on the American peo-ple. Mexican presidents Vicente Fox and Felipe Calderón made it public policy to go after only certain drug cartels, targeting specific groups but allowing others to continue operating their business unhindered. *Why?* Quite simply, it helped consolidate most of the power and control of the drug trade under one organization. To a degree, the same thing had been happening in Canada. Certain organizations were allowed more flexibility to operate, often working as informants with Canadian intelligence to help bring down foreign nationals who had gained a stronghold in the black-market trade, including some who had infiltrated the upper echelons of our government.

The revenue that was being generated from cannabis in BC was stag-gering. Most growers I knew, but certainly not all, were using their profits for themselves, giving little back to their community. I saw the need for regulation and a degree of control by our government so that some of the revenue generated from the pot industry could go toward health, educa-tion, and social programs. Many of my friends and colleagues working in the industry respected my social idealism but insisted that giving control to the government was the worst thing possible. There was reasonable concern that the biggest players would get a stranglehold on the industry and lock out the smaller players who helped build it in the first place. I supported the legalization of marijuana so that those who wanted to continue to grow and sell could do so undisturbed by our government. At the same time, production and distribution by big business could provide a quality product that was taxed, sending money into general revenues.

I find it ironic that I have been arrested twice on marijuana-related charges, and yet I was the one quietly endorsing the government to make this industry legitimate. While I had built and operated smaller gardens, some people I knew were building forty thousand-square-foot indoor marijuana farms, and profiting significantly from their endeavour. Many of these highly organized growers were left alone because they didn't flaunt what they did. They understood the need for secrecy if they wanted the gravy train to continue. But not all grow operations concealed what they were doing adequately. An incident in early 1998 involved a BC Hydro crew who alerted a guy I knew — the owner of a three hundred-light garden located in the Greater Vancouver area that produced half a million in cash every year — that his indoor garden was causing power spikes in the grid, affecting other commercial buildings and retail stores in the vicinity. The workers from BC Hydro left a note that said, "Come on, guys, a little more incognito!" with a smiley face beneath the words.

This is where the world of black and white begins to grey. Some crews were left to operate unencumbered because they were connected. In short, our intelligence apparatus works closely with people involved in organized crime to effectively combat other elements they regard as a greater threat to national security. This is nothing new. Cooperation between organized crime and government dates back to the days of Caesar, and probably even longer. The RCMP would target individuals like me because it showed our neighbours to the south that the Canadian government had an interest in shutting down the illegal trade. However, it was clear they did not. Upholding the status quo is a game played with smoke and mirrors, and small-level guys like me were often hung out to dry because it served someone else's agenda.

I took great delight in the entire process of cultivating this amazing plant. Taking a seed and growing it until it flowers is good for the soul. Smoking and eating cannabis provide numerous health benefits, and the growing of God's sacred plant is therapeutic as well. The stigma that had wrapped itself around cannabis needed to be addressed. Educating the public and changing the laws could be the first step toward a worldwide cultural revolution.

CHAPTER 29

KEEP THE FAITH

Those who can see beyond the shadows and lies of their culture will never be understood, let alone believed by the masses.

— Plato

November 13th, 2010

I fly from Victoria, BC, into Seattle, Washington, clear customs, and move on to catch a connecting flight for Chicago. I have always wanted to go to Chicago, just not in these circumstances. History is on my mind. I think about the Myami Tribe's name for the Chicago region more broadly, Shikaakwa. I think about the lives of the First Peoples of this region, and how their lives changed forever after European colonization. I consider the Haymarket Affair in May of 1886 and the infamous Memorial Day Massacre fifty years later. Rich in history, Chicago is considered the birthplace of the American labour movement and the movement for the eight-hour workday. I wonder if this was why Barack Obama made this city his home base. My thoughts spin inside me, turning to frustration. I had achieved little in terms of helping to affect the course of the nameless revolution that has been brewing for generations.

I land in Pittsburgh late into the evening and catch the transit to take me to the bus depot. My bus to Philipsburg doesn't leave until 8:45 am, and I'm left with a long stretch with little to do. I've brought little money with me and no credit cards, so a good night's sleep in a hotel is not an option. Fortunately, the bus depot is open, which provides me with a warm place to rest. I attempt to get some sleep, but all the chairs have permanent armrests, making lying down impossible.

The once-proud steel town looks like many other US cities with segments now in decay. Of course, your perspective is defined by where you are standing. Your income and position in the hierarchal society help determine your view. There is still big money to be made in these cities. People who have the means and the desire to capitalize on what is available to them can afford to isolate themselves from the growing number of hungry, disparaged lost souls. Like most major capitalist cities across the western world, Seattle, Pittsburgh, and Chicago house their own gladiator arenas, just as Rome had the Coliseum. Tonight, the hometown Pittsburgh Steelers hosted the visiting New England Patriots. The football game finished just as my bus pulled in, and now people are walking the streets, trying, I assume, to make their way to their cars or catch transit. I assume many of the loud and raucous are infused with spirits. I am humbled by the distance that exists between us. I am on my way to prison, and they're on their way home to their comfy beds.

Are these people distracted from seeing what is happening around them? While they drink and watch their favourite players perform on the field, other more obscure warriors fight it out in other arenas. I wonder how many of these people know of Aung San Suu Kyi, the Burmese Social-Democratic politician and president of the National League for Democracy in Myanmar, who has been under house arrest for twenty years since winning the 1990 general election with 81 percent of the seats in Parliament? She was released from prison today. I too feel like a political prisoner but know my exploits for smuggling weed would be front and centre in the minds of those who read the headlines. The underlying common denominator that ties me to people like Suu Kyi will get buried under gossip and misconceptions.

I pull the Christmas letter back out of my pocket and reread it before dozing off. I awake to fluorescent lights flickering above my head and sirens wailing in the nearby concrete jungle. I'm floating between sleep and consciousness, thinking back to years past when I prayed to be shown my path. After awaking to my truth, identifying who I am and where I come from, I was able to see where I needed to go. *Receive thy sight; thy faith hath saved thee. I must hold the faith and continue with what I set out to do. You can do this, Corky.*

CHAPTER 30

SURRENDER

"In detachment lies the wisdom of uncertainty...in the wisdom of uncertainty lies the freedom from our past, from the known, which is the prison of past conditioning. And in our willingness to step into the unknown, the field of all possibilities, we surrender ourselves to the creative mind that orchestrates the dance of the universe."

— Deepak Chopra

November 14ᵗʰ, 2010

The bus ride to Philipsburg is a pleasant diversion after the rough night I spent in the bus depot. The bus lets me off in the downtown core of the rural community next to the local grocery market. I hadn't eaten anything of nutritional value since the day before, so I entered the market to purchase a small yogurt and a banana. Walking as a free man, picking items off the shelf and taking money out of my pocket to purchase them, feels surreal. I am hyper aware that this is my last taste of freedom for months.

After exiting the supermarket, I walk a few blocks east, then step into a gas station to ask the cashier if he can point me in the direction of Moshannon Valley Correctional Center. He looks at me inquisitively.

"If you head about one mile east and then take a right onto Graham Station Road, it's about a mile up the hill."

I thank him and walk out the door, making my vestigial two-mile trek outside the city gates and up the hill to Calvary, carrying my burden with head held high.

As I crest the hill, the large MVCC complex comes into sight. The road leading to it is connected to a large rectangular track that encircles the entire unit. Inside the perimeter are two rows of chain-link fence, roughly forty feet apart, each reaching at least fourteen feet high and topped with a large coil of razor wire. Inside the second row of fencing are six large buildings and an open area comprising two running tracks and two sports fields. As I walk down the final four hundred-yard stretch, I take in the terrain around me, filing in my memory the best place to run to if I am ever in need of escaping.

A white security truck pulls up beside me.

"Are you lost?" the security officer asks.

"I'm here to self-surrender."

He looks confused. "You're here to self-surrender?"

"Yes, I am," I say assuredly.

He radios Command and asks what he is to do with me.

"Ok, walk beside me as we drive up to the top."

At the top of the road, he points me to the main entrance of the administration building. "Just go in through those doors, and they'll be ready for you."

I picture four friendly admin staff standing inside the doors, holding balloons and a sign that says "Welcome, Daryl!" but I surprise the staff of MVCC, as nobody has walked into their facility on a self-surrender before.

It doesn't take long to process me. I give up my clothes and belongings in exchange for the prison garb. A guard walks me from the administration building through the courtyard connecting the four main housing units. I am assigned Unit A, the building on my left, and will be penned up with men from all over the world. The guard tells me that each housing unit, A, B, C, and D, has six separate pods that each contain up to sixty-four men at a time, and they're currently full. Each pod is connected to one other pod by a door that opens from 8:00 am till 11:00 pm to allow people to move "freely" and interact with their neighbours throughout the day. At the centre of the building, there is a circular hallway that forms a perimeter around the guards' security bubble, giving them a direct line of sight and access into pods one through six.

As I make my way into pod three, I anticipate some hooting and hollering like I received when I first arrived at SeaTac Prison, but no one pays much attention. The guard points past the common seating area to the back of the room.

"You're bunk seventeen."

I quickly scan the open room, taking note of the thirty-two bunk beds. I walk through the front room and past the people sitting at tables, either watching one of the three TVs or playing a board game with their fellow compatriots. There are multiple conversations taking place. I'm certain most of what I hear is in Spanish. The door that gives access to pod four is on the west side of the room. The only place for privacy is the six showers and four toilet stalls on the east side of the room. Not quite what I had in mind, but I will make the best of it.

I get right to work putting the second set of clothes they gave me in the plastic bin that tucks in beneath the bottom bunk. The few remaining items, such as soap, toothbrush, and toothpaste, go into the top locker adjacent to where I would be lying my head at night. There's a paper-thin mattress, which I roll out over the steel frame, along with two ratty sheets, a pillow, and a pillow case. As I am making my bed, a tall Caucasian man, he must be around six feet four, in his mid-twenties walks up to me and introduces himself. He has been instructed to welcome the newly arrived

Canadian and provide me with assistance. He hits me with a barrage of questions, giving me little time to reply between each one. My initial impression is that he is paranoid or struggles with severe ADHD, as he continues to look around the room, diverting his attention from me to others, as we talk.

He gives me another toothbrush and offers me a novel to read. I thank him, trying to wrap up this meet and greet, but he continues to ramble on about the dos and don'ts while I'm in Moshannon. I listen impassively until I hear something that makes the hairs on the back of my neck stand up.

"...and it's important you know to stick with your own in here."

"Pardon?" I say, certain I understood what he is implying but wanting to give him the benefit of the doubt.

"We stick with Canadians and few others in here. We don't mix with the other crowds," he says while looking around at the people of Hispanic descent, making sure no one is listening to him.

I finish placing my pillow in its case, laying it on the bed before facing him. I maintain my composure, making sure not to reveal my agitation. "Tell you what, I will associate with whomever the fuck I want to associate with. Ok?"

His body straightens, and he takes a small step back from me, a look of shock on his face. A fake smile attempts to conceal his disappointment as he walks away. "Sure, man, suit yourself."

CHAPTER 31

INSPECTION

"Do not let your fire go out, spark by irreplaceable spark in the hopeless swamps of the not-quite, the not-yet, and the not-at-all. Do not let the hero in your soul perish in lonely frustration for the life you deserved and have never been able to reach. The world you desire can be won. It exists.. it is real.. it is possible.. it's yours."

— *Ayn Rand, Atlas Shrugged*

December 9th, 2010

I was assigned a job in the cafeteria cleaning tables a week after my arrival. Apparently, every new inmate gets stuck with table cleaning. Everyone detests it because it puts you in direct servitude to the other prisoners. During the first week, I receive my first bit of mail. Candace sends me some pictures of the kids, along with a picture from one of my bodybuilding contests and one of me running in the 2008 Iron Man. I tape them inside my locker to remind me of the dedication it takes to achieve success. I also receive the first of many letters from my mom, who sends at least two per week, updating me on the happenings back home.

I'm standoffish with the other inmates, spending my time doing intense training and meditating. I intentionally create an aura of mystique that garners interest from the prisoners who have some pull within these walls. But it was only after my first interaction with the prison guards that their interest turned to respect, elevating my status. Locker inspections are part of the daily routine, and while I lie on my bunk reading Ayn Rand's *Atlas Shrugged*, one of the guards approaches me.

"Fontana, I'm inspecting your belongings."

Without taking my eyes from the book, I said, "Sure thing."

A couple of minutes goes by, and I look up to see he is staring at the pictures taped inside my locker.

"Fontana, who is this freak you have pinned up in your locker? That's not *you*? Is it?"

"Yeah, that was me, another lifetime ago."

The guard stands there for a few seconds. "How much did you weigh back then? What could you squat? How much could you bench press? What supplements did you use?"

The guards rarely talk with the prisoners, and when they did, it wasn't long conversations. The guys who shared my pod were intrigued, wondering what sort of trouble I had gotten myself into. Within minutes of his departure, two guys came over to ask what all the fuss had been about. I am conscious of protecting my casual demeanour, telling them the guard has taken an interest in the pictures taped in my locker. One of the guys, Escamilla, asks if he could have a peak. I oblige.

"Holy fuck, Fontana! You were a beast, man!" Escamilla says.

I repeat to them what I said to the guard: "It was another life, gents."

Our conversation is cut short by the guard's return. He's accompanied by three others, all big boys, who obviously lift weights. This time around, the guard is polite and asks for permission to show his co-workers the picture from sixteen years ago.

"Of course," I say, sitting up and putting my book down before swinging my feet to let them hang over the side of my bed. The five of us talk for another ten minutes before they take their leave. I casually look from my left to my right and notice all eyes are on me.

The following week, Jones, the guard who inspected my locker, put in a good word for me, getting me an early transfer from table duty and putting me in charge of the kitchen's stock room. A position that can make you good money on the inside.

CHAPTER 32

WE THE CHILDREN

"The planting of a tree, especially one of the long-living hardwood trees, is a gift which you can make to posterity at almost no cost and with almost no trouble, and if the tree takes root it will far outlive the visible effect of any of your other actions, good or evil."

— *George Orwell*

August 1998

"You should have seen Mariah yesterday at the park. She can climb the stairs to the top and slide down on her own. She's fearless. The only problem is, when she gets to the bottom, she turns around and tries to climb back up, paying no attention to the other kids who want to come down. I think she takes after you," I said to Candace.

"Yeah, right, Cork, I don't think so."

We were spending a gorgeous summer day at home catching up on chores. I finished cleaning the downstairs of the house and came upstairs, through the kitchen and outside onto the deck to meet her on the porch where she was hanging laundry on the clothesline. We had made some changes in our lives in the last few months, and we were getting along better than ever.

I felt the warmth of the afternoon sun on my legs, and decided to lie down by her feet and close my eyes until she finished hanging the rest of the basket. I was lying there, feeling happy, at peace. I remember taking in a long, slow breath, and as I released it, I was transported to a place that resembled a giant cathedral with at least twenty massive marble pillars. Packets of information streamed all around me, in every direction, on soft rays of light.

Boom! My fifth epiphany. A thunderbolt hammers into me, jolting me straight up into a sitting position. I started talking so fast that Candace asked me to slow down.

"What's going on in that head of yours?" she asked.

I described the vision I saw and the three words that kept flashing in my mind as I was experiencing it. "Photo thetic imagery."

"What do you think it means?" she asks.

"I think I need a couple of hours to write down my thoughts, but for now, simply said... what I saw is the key to life eternal."

That same afternoon, I wrote a paper called "We the Children, the Inheritors of Your Legacy" and sketched out a drawing of an ankh that encompassed the eye of God looking through the plain of the Unknown and back onto the observer. Beside the sketch — an image that Candace and I later had tattooed onto the back of our necks — I wrote the three English words that describe the ankh, the symbol I interpret to be the master key: Photo-Thetic Imagery

I had no recollection hearing of photo-thetic imagery before, though I was certain it represented an important piece of my puzzle. The key symbol pre-dating antiquity found throughout ancient Egypt made my place within our Universe relevant. Whatever the mind could conceive, it had the power to achieve. We are all God looking unto ourselves, playing in a vast field: "The Playground."

I was forthcoming with my friends and family, telling them I believed that one day there will be a planetary spiritual revolution. "People of different ethnic backgrounds and religions will come together, desiring the same fundamental rights and freedoms afforded the aristocrats. The corporate oligarchy that works to manipulate, bending the truth as they see fit and supporting a system that continues to enslave millions of people, must be faced down. There is a hero inside every one of us, but the hero must stand if they hope to ever claim freedom." I passionately expressed my sentiments wherever I went: at house parties with friends, new and old, in the ferry cafeteria, at the gym — anywhere and everywhere. My six-foot rule meant anyone coming within six feet of me stood a good chance of hearing my ideological take. The angst and frustration that had once gripped me tightly were no longer weighing me down. The foreboding that had once been so strong was replaced by foresight.

CHAPTER 33

HEALING

"The wound is the place where the Light enters you."

— Rumi

Spring 1999

A fter six years of living in the city, Candace and I decided to leave Vancouver, and started to look around for other places to live. There were a few choice locations we had considered moving to but opted to move back to the community we had grown up in, as it provided most of what we were looking for: easy access to the ocean, rivers, and lakes, and a multitude of mountains and hiking trails. The Cowichan Valley offered affordable land where we could grow our food and let our children run free. It didn't hurt either that we had a solid network of friends and family there.

Cowichan was culturally diverse, but it was not immune to the racial tension that lurks in most colonialist countries. The same ignorance that existed in the 1970s still lingered in the late 1990s, and I committed myself to tackling it if I made Cowichan my home again. I had many supportive friends who offered their services to help me build community, suggesting they camp out on our property over the summer months to help build the wellness retreat I dreamed of. But I strongly resisted the idea. "Commune" and "preacher" were two words that got stuck in my mind. I had an image of David Koresh's community in Waco, believing any positive attributes exercised by these people were surely demonized and held out to the world as being more than what it was.

The institutions that control the headlines, finances, government, and education are not to be trifled with. I neither feared them nor respected them, but I was cautious of them. I encouraged my friends and family to do more for themselves so they could do more for others, but outside of that, I had no clear strategy on how to substantially make any tangible difference in terms of serving out justice and trying to establish a true democracy.

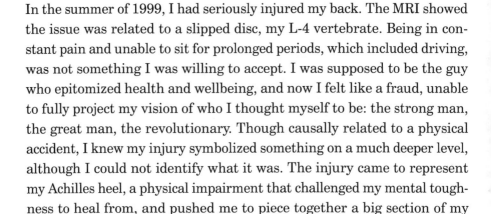

In the summer of 1999, I had seriously injured my back. The MRI showed the issue was related to a slipped disc, my L-4 vertebrate. Being in constant pain and unable to sit for prolonged periods, which included driving, was not something I was willing to accept. I was supposed to be the guy who epitomized health and wellbeing, and now I felt like a fraud, unable to fully project my vision of who I thought myself to be: the strong man, the great man, the revolutionary. Though causally related to a physical accident, I knew my injury symbolized something on a much deeper level, although I could not identify what it was. The injury came to represent my Achilles heel, a physical impairment that challenged my mental toughness to heal from, and pushed me to piece together a big section of my spiritual jigsaw puzzle.

I persevered, and finally had a breakthrough. On the recommendation of a fellow trainer, I found some excellent therapists. The first was Scottish-born Alex McKechnie, regarded as one of the best athletic therapists in the world. Alex introduced me to cutting-edge training modalities that revolutionized my approach to fitness. The second was Sheel Tangri. Sheel epitomized the man who walked smoothly with one foot in the East and one foot in the West. He was born in Mumbai, India, and raised in Canada. Sheel became the catalyst that made many of the physical and mental protocols, including the work I was doing with Alex, bond like a strong resin that glued my body back together. What transpired was the merging of my mental and physical aspects, culminating in another psychological breakthrough. I only had two ninety-minute sessions with Sheel in which he asked me an assortment of questions while he conducted strength testing on my body. It was a form of treatment I liken to Gestalt therapy mixed with chiropractic and a mix of other modalities, as Sheel was well versed in a spectrum of holistic teachings. He asked me a broad range of questions while I lay on his therapy table, my right arm extended and raised out in front of me. Every time he asked me a question, he would simultaneously push down on my arm. If my arm held, it showed I had strength in that cognitive area. If my arm gave way, it was a sign of weakness that he would probe further. I had heard of this type of therapy but had never experienced it. Of course, I was skeptical, lying there thinking I was probably wasting a lot of money on some quack, as every question he asked me came with him pushing down on my arm and it not moving. But then he questioned me about trust, and I had no strength to resist him. Now I was interested! Sheel explained I had a blockage relating to past events. I took what he said in stride and finished up my first session, not aware of any difference in how I felt.

I had my follow-up session the next day. This time he didn't perform the strength testing; instead, he did some hands-on physical work, which included massage and chiropractic adjustments. At the end of the session, I paid him his fee and then extended my hand to shake his. He stepped past my hand, wrapped his arms around me, and gave me a firm, loving hug. I was taken off guard, surely tense at first, but after the first couple of seconds, I let myself go, hugging him back, fully trusting he was coming from a place of sincerity. Five minutes later, sitting in my car outside of his office, I burst into tears for the first time in years. There was a breaking of tension I didn't know existed, followed by a sensation of something washing over me like freezing, cold water, which had me sitting up and sucking in deep breaths as if they were to be my last. Less than a minute later, I took notice of how still and calm I was. Something had lifted, leaving me unabashedly aware of my emotional nakedness and not caring, but soaking in the freedom that it represented.

Awakening did not mean my learning was over; rather, it felt as if it was just beginning. The shape and flavour of my revolution, how I perceived it, was continuously working itself out inside of me, broadening my perspective of the world I was living in and my place within it. This added feeling of liberation drove me to make big changes in my training practice. I wanted to help others, to make as much impact on their lives as Sheel had on mine. The issue I had with my back was not 100 percent cured, but it rarely gave me problems, and my overall physical conditioning increased twofold. I was now able to help others who were experiencing the same issues.

That injury pushed me to open myself up into higher states of awareness, but it wasn't until many years later that I learned that physical pain is most often a manifestation of emotional and mental issues or blocks. When I looked up what obstructions were specific to feeling pain and having a disability in the lower back, I read that fear of losing your freedom when others need your help is one of the primary ones. Freedom is sacred. You often fear for your survival. The back provides the greatest support for the physical body. Therefore, a back problem might indicate that you aren't receiving enough support.

During what turned out to be my last episode of being laid up on the couch, a good friend from high school phoned me. Jason had recently asked Jesus, his Lord Saviour, to set him free, and with a fire lit under his ass, he turned to preach the gospels. I related to his enthusiasm, though

I believed he was too tightly wrapped in the religious dogma that accompanies the teachings of those who have a skewed version of the truth. Yet, whose version of the truth isn't skewed? Jason was concerned for the wellbeing of his friends, believing Satan would trap them if they didn't change their ways. I knew he meant well, but I also thought that a man who knows Jesus so intimately shouldn't be so quick to cast judgment.

"The God I know is all-encompassing and fears nothing. God resides both inside and outside of me and is inclusive of everything, including Satan. Therefore, I embrace Satan, not as an idol or power to follow, rather as part of the Universe that I love unconditionally," I said. There was silence on the other end of the line. It wasn't my intent to shock him, but it seemed I had developed a propensity for whipping my words and laying them down onto others when what they said contradicted my philosophical beliefs. I never told him what I had only shared with Candace: when I would go into deep meditation, and twice while using magic mushrooms, I would see Lucifer the Angel.

I had been certain I was on the right path, that my truth was the same truth spoken by the Masters of our past. I was still feeling the powerful effects of waking fully to our universal consciousness, believing the love I felt for everything and everyone would serve to protect me from that which gripped so many others in fear. Had I been rash? Did I tempt fate by willingly embracing the dark aspect of a Force I was perhaps not yet equipped to understand? The red carpet had been rolled out with a bright neon sign above it, flashing the words "Welcome, Satan."

CHAPTER 34

THE LAND OF OZ

"The main thing you got to remember is that everything in the world is a hustle."

— Alex Haley, The Autobiography of Malcolm X

June 1999

I flew south to see my friend Tyson in LA on a Friday night. Tyson arranged for a car to pick me up and drive me to where he and his wife, Allison, were spending the evening. We drove north on the 405 before switching to La Cienega Blvd, driving past Beverly Hills and the Sunset Strip and into Hollywood Hills. The driver pulled into a driveway belonging to one of the many magnificent homes that adorned the area. Before I could make it to the door, Tyson stepped out of the house to welcome me.

"Yo, brother, you made it," he said, moving forward to give me the traditional one-handed, one-arm, bro-shake-half-hug.

I walked into his friend's home. Ron, Allison's friend, was a well-known music producer. He was feeling pumped about the work he had just done with one of his new young artists, who had just hit the top of the charts. Ron, his girlfriend Stephanie, and Allison were sitting in a room toward the back of the house, chilling with drinks in hand. As soon as introductions were made, Tyson asked me to share with the group some of the things we had talked about when he was last in Vancouver.

"I don't know what in particular you are referring to," I said, smiling and feeling a little uncomfortable with all eyes now on me.

Tyson said, "C'mon, man, you know, the shit we were talking about."

I laughed, realizing what he was referring to. "Ok, I get it. I suppose you want me to share my convictions and personal philosophy with these fine folks. Thanks for putting me on the spot."

Everybody laughed, and I felt my anxious feelings dissipate. As I began recounting in abbreviated form the key moments of my life, Ron lit the joint he had just finished rolling, taking a couple of long puffs of the sweet-smelling herb before moving to pass it around.

"This bud probably comes from your home province," he said, which made me chuckle. I was witnessing up close how much our sought-after product was getting into the hands of the Hollywood establishment, and I was there sitting in among them, sharing the events that led to my spiritual awakening and the launching of my grandiose quest to bring more goodness into the world. These people met me when I was at my peak of love and enthusiasm and only seeing the best in others. They probably thought I was endearing and sweet, most definitely naïve. That trip was an eye-opener. Tyson and Allison opened their home and introduced me to their world. Allison worked as a music producer. She was the VP for Warner Bros., R&B division, and a baller who gave Tyson instant credibility. Tyson was the Hollywood star dog trainer long before the Dog Whisperer made his television debut. He found his niche working with dogs and their human masters, building a reputation for dishing out the same type of tough love I was known for dishing out to humans.

Tyson encouraged me to build my training business in LA, telling me there was a market that would pay big money for my services. "People are thirsty to soak up what you've got to say, bro."

The opportunity to grow my business and connect with people who were part of an influential network should have been seen as a gift. I knew this could serve the mission I was on, but the truth was, I wasn't ready to commit full-time to working in that environment, as I doubted my ability to stay grounded and not lose myself in the World of Oz. I had enough self-awareness to recognize how impressionable I was. Though I passed on this opportunity, I promised to continue visiting. My trips usually corresponded with a big birthday celebration or an Oscar party. Most people I met were kind. People whose names and faces have graced the covers of magazines and who are idolized by people the world over turned out to be just regular people like most of my good friends back home. There were a handful of solid cats, people with whom I would have spent more time if Tyson didn't always have somewhere else to go. I wish the times connecting with Tom Morello and Adam Jones weren't so few, as they exemplified the qualities in the human spirit I admired most.

The first time I met Adam, his wife asked me to join them at a rally in downtown LA to support the Zapatistas, the revolutionary leftist political and militant group based out of Chiapas, Mexico. In 1994, this group of mostly Indigenous people declared war "against the Mexican state" and military, paramilitary, and corporate incursions into Chiapas. I told Tyson, "I want to go with them. You know this is my kind of thing."

Tyson thought otherwise. "You don't need to be drawing that kind of attention to yourself, bro."

CHAPTER 35

CONCEPTION

"It's not in the book or in the writer that readers discern the truth of what they read; they see it in themselves, if the light of truth has penetrated their minds."

— Augustine of Hippo

November 11ᵗʰ, 2000

I travelled from Vancouver to meet Candace in Victoria, the provincial capital. She was at The Forge Night Club, one of Victoria's best venues for live music. I was able to find parking a couple of blocks away. The night was clear, but the temperature was cooler than normal for early November. Maybe leaving my jacket behind hadn't been such a smart move. As I cut across Broughton making my way to Douglas Street, I looked ahead and saw a group of people standing on the corner.

A middle-aged man I had seen a few times in years past was talking with two men and two women. I easily recognized the man because he was dragging his large wooden cross with him, something he had been doing for years. The Forge was right across the street, and though I had been looking forward to seeing my wife, something made me stop and listen in on the conversation. His audience were in their early twenties. I quickly scanned their faces, locking eyes with one of them as I did. "Good evening!" I said with a smile. "I hope I'm not intruding."

The man with the cross looked at me kindly. "Welcome, brother. I am the Man at Arms. It's my responsibility to share the Word with those who have the ear to hear."

"Please continue," I said.

It was obvious to anyone who spent five minutes listening to him that he cared tremendously about others. He was an eclectic mix of Gnostic and maybe a few different branches of Protestantism: Methodist, Evangelical, maybe Lutheran, I wasn't sure. He opened with the Biblical story of Adam and Eve, then quickly moved through tales of Gilgamesh to Noah and the Deluge that wiped out a good chunk of human civilization. He was just getting warmed up when he started talking about the coming Apocalypse, preaching from the Book of Revelation: "Blessed is the one who reads aloud the words of this prophecy and blessed are those who hear and obey what is written in it because the time is near."

I felt the impulse to engage. "Thank you for devoting your time to the service of others because, as you know, there are millions of people who are in the dark." I looked to my left, where the four smartly dressed young people were standing. "I'm most certainly not referring to you fine people." They were all smiling and seemed to be enjoying themselves. They were certainly listening intently, especially the taller of the two men, who kept nodding his head, as if in agreement with what he was hearing. One of the women, the one who made first eye contact with me, was making no effort to hide how intently she was looking at me. I turned back to my right.

"You are right, brother, something is coming, but I believe we have more power to direct the course than what John prophesized. I believe much of what was written in the Bible, specifically the New Testament, was altered over the centuries to serve special interests. Now, I'm not saying the four horsemen of the Apocalypse won't be riding in, but I have questions, just as I question most of what we're told to believe."

Once I started, I couldn't stop myself from hijacking this guy's soapbox, but he didn't seem to mind. "People would have us believe Jesus, who was Jewish, never married or had children of his own, yet we are told he lived till his thirties... please. He was a Jew working to radically change long-held traditions, welcoming gentiles to join them, which meant going directly against the Pharisees. The guy painted a huge target on his back."

The taller man in the group added, "And they crucified him for it."

I questioned, "Did he really die on the cross? Maybe. Regardless, his bloodline, the Holy Grail, is most likely alive and strong today."

"Yes, I also think this likely," said Man at Arms.

"But does it matter?" I asked.

The tall young man added, "For a lot of people, it would mean a great deal."

"I think you're right. I also think if Jesus were here today, he would be pissed at how much bullshit has been attached to his name. First and foremost, he was a mortal man. No different than any one of us here. He fought to awaken people to the true nature of God." I was now in full-blown preaching mode, something many of my friends had come to know well. "You reference Revelation and the end of the days, and I get these images of people from the Church selling fear, warning about those who belong to the synagogue of Satan, who warn against the liars pretending to be Jews. There is some truth in this, yet my concern is that all Jews get lumped into the same group, as we have seen happen in the past."

Man at Arms looked a little unsettled. "If we don't wake up, I will come like a thief..."

"... 'and you will not know the hour when I will come upon you.' Yeah, more truth, but always blanketed with a layer of fear. If you don't do this, I will disavow you. I will smite you down. I understand the desire to grab people and shake them awake, but I'd like to do it without having to scare the bejeezus out of them."

Man at Arms didn't mince his words. "People are blind and will not be motivated to change unless they fear the wrath of what lies ahead."

"Fear has run its course. We need to do more to inspire," I countered.

"How do you inspire people who are not awake?" The woman with the intense stare asked, looking as though she already knew the answer to her question.

"With more love," I cocked a big grin, knowing I was being truthful in a smart-ass kind of way. "Isn't that what Jesus would say?"

Man at Arms didn't miss a beat. "'Therefore repent! Otherwise, I will come to you shortly and wage war against them with the sword of my mouth.'"

"I have no doubt Jesus was a warrior, and if needed, would have swung a sword. Same as Muhammad. They predicated their mission on educating the public using esoteric knowledge and scientific understanding. They worked to uncover the truth, not bury it further. I think we should be doing the same."

The staring woman asked, "Do you think people are given the education they need to help them discern this truth?"

"That depends on where in the world you were born, to whom you were born, and what you were born. Our system is far from being fair. It neglects to provide for children who, if not for their situation, could grow up to become some of our finest engineers, doctors, and leaders."

"Difficult to do when you have people in positions of power who oppose each other," she states.

"True. We have the means to provide for all, but our politics keep us divided. We battle instead of helping one another."

There was a moment of silence, then Man at Arms spoke again, trying to keep his discourse on track. "'I am coming soon. Hold fast to what you have so that no one will take your crown. The one who overcomes I will make a pillar in the temple of My God, and he will never again leave it. Upon him, I will write the name of My God and the name of the city of My God.'"

"Ahh... you're referring to Zion," I beamed, thinking of the mountains I had summited.

"Yes, the Holy City, the New Jerusalem?" Man at Arms replied.

"Some would say the creation of Israel fifty-five years ago is the precursor to this taking place. Either the Lord is intervening by divine intervention, or there are a good number of people who are working to manifest this story into reality."

"'The fifth seal has been opened,'" Man at Arms warns. "'The souls of those who have been slain for the word of God are in waiting. What follows next...'"

The young woman stepped in perfectly. "'...is the opening of the sixth seal. There will be a great earthquake, the sun will blacken, and the moon will turn blood red. The stars in the sky will look as if they're falling to Earth like unripe figs dropping from a tree shaken by a great wind." She was flawless with her delivery, staring straight at me as she spoke. "The kings of the Earth, the nobles, the commanders, the rich, the mighty, every slave and free man will hide in the caves and among the rocks of the mountains. They ask the mountains and the rocks, Hide us from the face of the One seated on the throne, and from the wrath of the Lamb, for the great day of their wrath has come, and who can withstand it?"

No one said a word. Her friends were looking at her in awe. It was a good time for me to say good night. "You've given me much to think about, but now I must bid you farewell as my wife will be wondering where I am." At that moment, I sensed I had lived through this revelation before. Not exactly, but facing a similar challenge, a test of the ages.

I left the group, making my way across Douglas Street, conscious of how plugged in I was. I felt near indestructible, immortal. If there was any truth to the messiah returning, I knew what I felt was the same as..., yet, my understanding, my knowing, reminded me we are all one. We are the Lord.

I found Candace dancing with her friends. One of my best days ever was capped off with an amazing night and connecting beautifully with my wife. Candace is convinced this was the night of Kahlil's conception.

CHAPTER 36

THE GAME

"I do not always know what I want, but I do know what I don't want."
— *Stanley Kubrick*

June 2001

C andace's first trip to LA with me coincided with a party Tyson and Ali were having at their home in Hollywood Hills. Their house was warm and inviting, with vaulted ceilings, curved archways and doors, and large windows that looked out to the lush jungle valley below. They furnished and decorated their home with pieces from Africa and India, a style that depicted a lavish Indian ashram. Incense was always burning in front of a large Buddha, which made napping on one of their many comfortable couches even more enjoyable. Swami, Tyson's massive American pit bull terrier, would always come and lie down beside me — or on me.

Ali had hired a tarot card reader, a henna artist, two chefs, two bartenders, and a host of servers for the party. While Candace sat back to get her eight-and-a-half-month pregnant belly covered in henna, I mingled with the guests, listening in on gossip, some of which helped reinforce what I already believed: *A lot of time and energy could be better spent elsewhere.*

I decided to make my way back to Candace, first stopping at the bar to grab us both a drink. Standing off to the side, I could overhear a man and two women talking politics, specifically about the new administration. I heard one of the women blurt, "They're up to no good! Always are." They appeared to be well versed and up to date with what was going on in the world, so I politely edged my way into the conversation. The women were attractive, every detail of their appearance having been tended to. They both wore summer dresses that hugged their curves without overtly revealing all. The guy, whose name I later found out was Leo, was a couple of inches taller than me, probably around six feet. His golden tanned skin, enhanced by the Sioux blood that I discovered ran through his veins, matched his shoulder-length light brown hair. His sandals, knee-length shorts, and short sleeve white button-up shirt made me assume he was a surfer.

"Sounds like another cash grab to help feed the insatiable appetite of the rich," I said, in reference to Leo's expounding upon the Bush administration's decision to auction off millions of acres of protected lands throughout the United States. All three turned to look my way, smiling at me in return. When Bush had announced he was running for the presidency, it hammered home what sat at the heart of my conversation with Adriel two years earlier, which triggered me to invest countless hours in watching the world's dominating political establishment play out their agenda in the run-up to the 2000 presidential election. There were strings I couldn't yet see pulling on the socio-political fabric, affecting every single person I knew, and I wanted in on the game. "They're eliminating regulations that protect the environment to make more money."

"Yes, they are," Leo said. "But are they doing it, just to make more money? I don't think so. It's a ruse."

One of the women said, "Why else would they risk damage to the environment if not for being greedy fucks!" I could tell she was feeling no pain with her drink in hand.

Before Leo could answer, I threw in, "Maybe for security?"

"Precisely!" Leo said, nodding toward me in agreement. "But is the push for security signalling something still to come?"

I had just met a kindred spirit, a person who was posing the same questions I wanted answers to.

A pretty Latina in her mid-twenties stepped in with a tray of glasses full of Petron Silver tequila, my favourite.

"I think it's best my clothes stay on tonight. At least until I get home and into bed with my husband," said the other woman in our group.

The rest of us smiled at her remark, all of us reaching for the Petron. I said, "I rarely say no to Petron, but I think I'm safe, as my clothes have yet to come off in public."

"That's a shame," said the first woman.

I blushed and choked for something smart to say back, but before I could, Leo stepped in and saved me.

Raising his glass, he said, "To vigilance and perseverance, that we may all see a future without war and prejudice."

We clinked our glasses together before slamming the double shot back. I felt instant warmth hit my belly and then spread out to the rest of my body, as is always the case when I drink good tequila. The woman who had not taken the shot excused herself, and her feisty friend decided to join her, making sure to give me a wink before turning around to catch up with her pal, leaving just me and my new friend.

"Do you smoke ganja?" he asked me casually.

"Occasionally."

"I'm heading outside to light up. You're welcome to join."

"Yeah, thanks. I'm going to check in with my wife first, and then I'll come find you." As I made my way back to Candace I reflected on the last two years: the amount of time I committed to studying geopolitics, the relationships made, building my business, raising a daughter, and the strengthening of my marriage. I felt truly blessed.

Candace was leaning back in a big comfy chair as the artist worked on her beautiful belly, half of it now covered in henna. As I moved to give her non-alcoholic fruit-punch, I paused in admiration. She was glowing, partly because of the warm Cali air, but mainly because of carrying Kahlil.

She smiled when she saw me. "About thirty minutes to go."

"Are you having fun?" I inquired, leaning over to kiss her on top of her head.

As I made my way to find Leo, I thought again about how good things were in my life. The world out "there" was chaotic, but within my little circle, I was doing alright. I met Leo on the veranda of the second floor where he had been waiting for me. He held a perfectly rolled joint in his hand, lighting it as soon as I stepped out beside him.

"Sorry I took so long," I said, "I was having a sweet moment with my wife."

"Ahhh… you don't want to rush something so precious. Besides, I'm off the clock tonight," he said, passing me the newly lit doobie. "Things are going to get crazy, I know it." He looked out into the valley, with a mild look of distaste on his face.

"What are you referring to?" I asked.

"I hear things."

He seemed apprehensive about sharing his thoughts, but since I was already feeling the effects of the green, I unabashedly pushed for more. "Are you going to deliver the goods, or are we going to continue talking shit?"

He chuckled, took another pull from the potent herb, and asked, looking at me half-serious, "And whom, may I ask, am I talking with?"

For the next thirty minutes, Leo and I discussed family, our education, work, and the current state of world affairs. He was a mix of Sioux, Lakota, Dakota, French, Irish, and Scots, and proud to be 100 percent American. He grew up wanting to serve his country as his father had. The call of duty wasn't something he could easily dismiss, but he was plagued with conflicting beliefs that made his path a difficult one. He left the military after ten years, five of which he spent in special forces, to turn his attention full-time to instructing martial arts and yoga. His outlook was similar to my own. We both had parents who are polar-opposites, and we both spent the first twenty-five years of our lives working to reconcile the differences between them. His big waking moment happened for him very much the same way it did for me. He awoke one morning after having a dream that seemed more real to him than his actual waking reality. He began reconnecting with his Native American roots, prompting his decision to leave the military. Many people who knew him were as surprised about his departure from that life as my friends and family were about my departure from my sport. A year out of the forces, Leo followed his heart to San Diego, having fallen in love with a woman who complemented him in every way. He worked as a martial arts instructor, yogi and stunt man.

Leo and I managed to connect for a workout before I flew back to Victoria. Neither of us tried concealing we wanted to put each other to the test. We decided on a full-body workout that consisted of many power movements, plyometrics and core stability. We fed off each other, pushing harder and harder with neither of us willing to quit. At the end of an exhausting ninety-minute session, he took me through half an hour of deep-cycle yoga, finishing it off with fifteen minutes of meditation.

Every square inch of our bodies was wet with perspiration, making it appear as if we had showered with our clothes on. We cleaned ourselves up then grabbed a smoothie at a café around the corner.

"If you want to work together... I'm game."

I pictured a Zen-style training centre. "We could open a studio and make a killing."

He laughed. "I don't do this work to make a killing. I do it to give back."

I agreed with his sentiments, explaining I too enjoyed helping people succeed, often discounting my fees or working pro bono with people who wanted to train with me but couldn't afford to. "But we still need to make money to live."

Leo's eyes narrowed, and a cheeky smile emerged. "If you want to make real money, why don't you send me some BC bud?"

"Are you serious?" I asked, knowing he was.

He looked at me inquisitively for a few seconds before answering, "Corky, I think I read people pretty well. I'd say you're a man who can be trusted."

Ooh, there was that word again. *Trust.*

"I have contacts here in LA and out East who can move large quantities of premium green. If you have the right contacts, and I'm assuming you do, we could make a lot of money together."

"Leo, let's say you are right to assume I have contacts who could help make this happen. I'm not sure if I'm willing to involve myself in something that could land me in a whole lot of trouble."

"You look to be a guy who does what he thinks is right, not what he's told to do. Based on what you've told me, and I'm in agreement with you on this, marijuana should be legalized and available to everybody, whether it's for medicinal purposes or simply because we want to get fucking high!"

"Yeah, I agree, but deciding to put yourself on the front line..."

"Sometimes people need to stand up and do what serves the greater good, even if that means getting punished for it. For me, this is also political. I have a moral obligation to stand for what is right, and it's a ballsy business, bro. I can do as much good with the wealth I make from selling God's precious herb as I can from the work I do with my clients. And you know what, I fucking enjoy doing both."

He spoke with vigour and conviction, making what he said more appealing.

"It's tempting. I have some things to consider. My wife is expecting our second child within the next month. I'll think about it."

Leo didn't push the topic further, letting me know he was just a phone call away. I left him and drove back to the house where I knew Candace,

Tyson, and Ali would be waiting for me. I asked Tyson about Leo, and Tyson simply said, "The guy's solid. But if anything is ever to go down between you two, you better make sure to take him out before he takes you."

Tyson's statement left me puzzled, as I couldn't foresee any reason why I would ever be at odds with this new brother. "Why would I ever have to worry about taking him out?" I asked.

"You probably wouldn't. Just saying."

Growing and selling cannabis in BC came with risk, but getting involved in cross-border transportation was a whole other game. I had a good thing going, and I didn't want to screw it up.

CHAPTER 37

ORTHOGENESIS

"If a man has not discovered something that he will die for, he isn't fit to live."

— *Martin Luther King Jr*

February 2011

I experienced a death and rebirthing in my mid-twenties. Letting go and surrendering myself to the all-encompassing truth was simultaneously the most difficult and the most liberating thing I ever aspired to do. I wanted to experience that heightened awareness again but realized it will take a considerable amount of time for it to come back. I have a lot of healing to do first. My daily meditation practice gets easier as the days go on, although it takes me two months to drown out the noise around me. As I go deeper into meditation, my daily journaling gets easier; sometimes I spend hours philosophizing and writing down my thoughts and ideas.

Slowly, but surely, the neurons in my brain begin to fire again, transmitting the important electrical signals which communicate to the rest of my body. Can a person achieve enlightenment and then lose it? Someone who considers themselves enlightened could very well be entranced. You can intellectualize something all you want, but it does not mean you are what you think you are. To be enlightened means having no form of attachment, only a knowing.

People who desire to connect with others — whether it's through a church, mosque, the media, radio, TV, books, or any other medium — have some form of attachment. The people vying for our attention are trying to connect and ultimately sell us their version of their truth. I say "version" because no matter how hard someone works to articulate what they "think" they "know," something will always, even minutely, get lost in translation. Yet, people who share a set of goals can achieve a shared sense of enlightenment, tying their individualistic need to survive to their desire for evolutionary progress as a species. When I am enlightened, I have attained realization and am in a state of bliss. All my earthly desires evaporate, and I float in a place between this world and death.

When we are enlightened, we no longer have an attachment to Maya, the illusory world. We experience oneness with the divine, the creator, that many call God. This God does not play favourites and does not care who wins or loses.

As one reflection of God, I can be defined by what I am attached to. I am attached to my desire to help the children of this planet. I am attached to my wife, family, and friends. I am very much attached to you, regardless of the colour of your skin, whether you are rich or poor… It does not matter.

I am an emotionally sensitive person. This is both a blessing and a curse. Sometimes it seems I don't care, but most of the time I care too fucking much, and it hurts.

Martin Luther King Jr. was someone who inspired me and helped me define my path. Although his assassination was four years before my birth, he significantly influenced my life's path. I vowed I would not go the way of the martyr. I wanted to have my cake and eat it too. And there crept in the foolishness. I remember what I once knew. Although my path in this life is meant to be fluid, so too am I to live true to my purpose. The passion for my mission should cut straight through like a sword with no hesitation and no remorse. So, even though I agree with the saying "live by the sword, die by the sword," I wish to clarify that my sword is one of love — albeit razor-sharp and unyielding.

It is not the end goal but the journey we have embarked upon that is often thought to be the meaning of life. If we focus too intently on our past or our future, it will hamper our appreciation for the moment we are in now, and we may find ourselves teetering, losing our balance. But giving yourself completely to the now is the same as turning off your capacity to navigate our ethereal space-time conscious network, forgoing our ability to tune using Photo-Thetic Imagery.

CHAPTER 38

BUILDING A PLAYGROUND

"No man can reveal to you aught but that which already lies half asleep in the dawning of your knowledge.The teacher who walks in the shadow of the temple, among his followers, gives not of his wisdom but rather of his faith and his lovingness.If he is indeed wise he does not bid you enter the house of his wisdom, but rather leads you to the threshold of your own mind."

— *Khalil Gibran, The Prophet*

Summer 2001

We bought acreage on the outskirts of Duncan, next to the vibrant Cowichan River, in late 2000. This property was our home base for a decade. We worked hard and made sure to play hard, whether it was competing in adventure races or playing for our local sports teams. Following our visit to Cali, I spent the rest of the summer building my next garden. The remainder of my time was split between training and finishing off the business plan for the future health centre. I knew I could best serve people by expanding on what I was already good at. Adriel had asked me what I was passionate about. I loved to train, and coaching others came with ease. Until now I had been working out of other people's gyms and studios, sometimes out of people's homes, but I wanted my own establishment, a place that was dedicated as much to spiritual evolution as much as it was to physical and mental fitness. I envisioned building a sports training centre that would be a collaboration between me and other like-minded individuals who were just as passionate about enhancing the quality of life for every person in their community as I was.

My plan was grand. I cut no corners, including everything I thought a Zen health centre should include. I wanted to have the best of the best, with everything you would find in top-level gyms, plus enough plants to transform it into a jungle. I designed a juice bar that would serve freshly squeezed fruit and pressed vegetables, along with craft-infused spirits. Yes, alcohol. I wanted my health centre to reflect who I was, a person who strove to live a balanced life. I included in this plan an atrium in the middle of the centre. A room with lots of natural light, and silent filters and ventilation, so those who wished to puff could do so in an environ-ment that supported it. At twenty-eight years of age, I was on my way to becoming an Imagineer. The only problem was that I sometimes got too ahead of myself.

By mid-August, days before the delivery of Kahlil, my business plan was finished, complete with graphs and pie charts. I began showing it to friends, looking for some help to polish it, and possibly names of people who might be interested in investing. A well-thought-out game plan is key to achieving success, but how was I to devise a game plan that included everything I wanted to do? How was I to make a revolution happen? What did that revolution even look like? How was I to raise healthy, strong, smart kids while starting a new business and continuing with my studies, all the while trying to fly under the radar?

CHAPTER 39

PEARL HARBOR II

"If we stop fighting, terrorism will spread all over the world."
— *Ahmad Shah Massoud*

September 11ᵗʰ, 2001

F inding someone willing to invest their money in the type of business
venture that statistically fails more frequently than it succeeds
was near impossible. I conceded temporary defeat and resigned
myself to the notion that if I was going to open a health centre, I would
most likely have to do it with our own money, which meant working and
saving for another three to four years.

But three weeks after the arrival of Kahlil, I received a call from my
friend Ocean.

"I think I've found you your investor."

She was vague about who her friend was but said he had money to invest and was looking for new business opportunities. I let Ocean know that I would be coming to the mainland the next day and would appreciate meeting her friend if he was free.

I chowed down my salad on the ferry ride to Vancouver, while skimming through the newspaper, always looking for stories that seemed a little out of the ordinary. In the world news section, a name jumped out at me: Ahmad Shah Massoud, the leader of the Northern Alliance in Afghanistan, and a man Leo had referred to in conversation during my visit eight weeks earlier. Massoud, the Lion of Panjshir, had been assassinated the day before by two individuals, who a spokesman for the Northern Alliance had said were connected to Osama bin Laden and Pakistan's intelligence agency.

Leo had told me the night of Tyson's birthday bash that something big was about to happen. There was a lot of chatter in his circles. He talked about an Afghan warlord named Massoud, saying, "This guy just addressed the European Parliament, with support from the French and Belgian governments. In his speech, he warned that his intelligence agents had gained knowledge about an imminent large-scale terrorist attack within the United States. The Lion, for many Afghanis, is another Che Guevara, a hero to the people. Massoud opposes the Taliban and their hardline fundamentalist interpretation of the Quran. He has no love for al-Qaeda either."

Goosebumps appeared on my arms. I put the paper down and looked out the large window. The ferry was exiting Active Pass, making its way out into open water. Leo had also told me, "The noose is tightening." At the time I wasn't sure who or what he was referencing, but the picture was becoming much clearer now. Israeli Prime Minister Ariel Sharon had taken a hardline stance against the Palestinians, resulting in a series of bombing attacks by radical groups. Surprise! In retaliation, Israel struck back with a strong hand. They bombed Palestinian security offices, invaded Palestinian-ruled cities, and ordered the killing of senior Palestinian leaders. I reflected on the meaning behind the old saying "The road to Rome wasn't paved in a day." It has taken thousands of years of fighting one another, building together, adapting, evolving, and striving to create the world we now have. Sequencing the human genome, landing on the moon, and creating the internet were heralded as momentous achievements. *Could we have made these milestones without war, bloodshed, and brutality?*

The forty-five-minute drive to my garden-house in Burnaby gives me time to work on reconciling my differences with the dominant ruling establishment. I understand that progress, security, and safety demand hardship, sacrifice, and the acceptance of collateral damage, but sitting through dinner listening to Lou Dobbs interview Donald Rumsfeld on CNN literally made me choke on my chicken. There are US$2.6 trillion missing from the Pentagon.

I went to bed that night trying to block out all that is wrong with the world, giving my attention to the visualizing of my ideal fitness training centre.

The following morning, I woke up feeling groggy. Unusual, considering I didn't drink, eat sugar, or smoke weed the night before. I chalked it up to needing a good workout, something I had planned on doing after I tended the garden. When I entered my brightly lit room, there were a hundred happy, green plant children greeting me. The room oozed success, freedom, peace, and tranquility. I worked for a little more than an hour that morning before going upstairs to make breakfast. I heard the TV was on in the living room, so I bypassed the kitchen and made my way to say good morning to my buddy, Wade. He was sitting on the couch watching what appeared to be breaking news.

"Hey, man, what's going on?" I said, curious as to why he was still at the house as he had said he was going to Whistler for the week to do some mountain biking. Wade was a good friend who helped take care of the "kids" when I was away. He had a garden of his own in North Van, so he would bounce back and forth between our places.

"You're not going to believe this. Terrorists hijacked a bunch of planes, then flew them into the World Trade Center buildings and another one into the Pentagon," he said, barely moving his eyes from the TV as he spoke to me.

"What?" The minutes passed, and I hadn't moved from where I was standing. I watched the TV, listening to the reporter relaying what was happening. The noose was tightening.

"Those Americans are going to dish out a whole lot of whoop-ass when they find out who did this," Wade said.

I looked at him, my eyes wide, and I could feel how heavily I was breathing. My blood was starting to boil. "This is bullshit!" I couldn't contain my anger.

I admit that, at the time, my knowledge of US military defence was limited, but I knew enough to see that what had transpired would have involved help from people on the inside. Later we were to learn the full extent of what that looked like. People all over the world believed World War III was about to happen. But all I could see was our inheritance of a war that had been going on for hundreds of years. My stomach felt queasy. I felt the dark, dirty game of corrupt politics and back-room deals were sucking in the masses in greater numbers than ever before. I wanted to reach out to those who believed everything they were being fed and shake them as hard as I could.

I cancelled the rest of my week, asked Ocean to reschedule my meeting with her investor friend, and asked Wade to hold the fort as I wanted to get back to the Island to be with my family. For the next four days, I shut out the world. I hiked up to Zion every morning, watched movies with Candace, played with Mariah, and gently rocked Kahlil in my arms. The overwhelming feeling of despair gradually subsided, and I centred myself on what I could control, not on what I couldn't.

CHAPTER 40

CAPITALISM 101

"When I sell liquor, it's called bootlegging; when my patrons serve it on Lake Shore Drive, it's called hospitality."

— *Al Capone*

September 19ᵗʰ, 2001

The week following 9/11, Candace, Mariah, and Kahlil made the return trip to Vancouver with me. Our friends wanted to meet our new addition, and I was eager to meet with Ocean and her friend. We met at a little sandwich shop in North Vancouver. Candace knew Ocean had once liked me more than just a friend, so the meeting could have been awkward. But Mariah and Kahlil hogged the limelight, which worked for all of us. Then in came RJ, Ocean's friend. He was dressed in what I came to know was his usual business attire: denim jeans, black cowboy boots, and full-sleeve denim button shirt with a black leather vest over top. He sported a thick goatee that matched his curly dark hair, which hung down to just above his shoulders.

Once the introductions were made, I explained my concept for The Playground Health Centre, giving him a copy of my business plan. He was interested in what I presented but said he would need time to look over my numbers. A lot was being left unsaid, something he confirmed when we next met, one week later.

RJ hadn't expected my wife and children to accompany me for that meeting, acknowledging it had taken him aback. "Who brings their wife and kids to a business meeting?" he asked me.

"I didn't know a casual Saturday afternoon meeting should be so formal," I responded.

He had been slow to respond to accept my hug at the end of our first meeting, something he later told me nearly shorted his circuits. Nobody, except for his closest of friends, had ever hugged him, and after I did — he admitted months later — it triggered a chain of questions for him.

For the next three months I spent more time with him than any other individual outside my immediate family. Our philosophy and approach to life were similar, except he made money the centre of his focus and I focused on service to others. He told me that he didn't usually let people into his world as quickly as he was doing with me. RJ was a heavy, an enforcer, the man called to do jobs that required a lot of nerve. Like Kip, my brother Scott, and my new friend Leo, RJ carried an intensity that emanated from his acceptance that he is a lion living in a concrete jungle. He can either kill or be killed. We would often debate the governing principles that ruled our lives and what moral code one should adhere to. I had been upfront with RJ about my desire to be a force for good in a world that was too often shrouded in darkness. He hardened me as much as I softened him.

"I think there are times you can show more patience," I said at one point after hearing him tell me why he broke a man's hands before throwing him into the deep end of a swimming pool. RJ had been sent to collect

$100K from a guy who had embezzled from his business associate. When I asked him why he was collecting $100K when it was only $50K that had been taken, he told me, "It's called a stupid tax."

The money he was going to invest for the building of The Playground never materialized, but the opportunity to make millions through other avenues was soon made available. After spending the next six months building a semblance of trust between us — enough for him to introduce me to the crew who worked for him and the man he worked for — I decided to tell him about my connection in LA.

"There's no question you've got a lot going on, Daryl, and what we're talking about is a serious undertaking. I can get you upwards of a thousand pounds a month. According to you, your people can handle it. The question is, do you have it in you to pull this off?"

I laughed. "Yeah, I know I've got it in me. Just not clear if it serves me."

RJ worked just as hard to convince me of my need to create wealth as I did to convince him to spread his wealth and help others. His, Kip's, and Leo's shared desire to build an empire displayed an obvious correlation with the motivations of the people I considered the Titans, the people whose table I wanted to sit at, people who were all business 99 percent of the time. They could be ruthless and cunning, and would not think twice about ending someone who crossed them.

"Daryl, you're your own boss, and you move to the beat of your own drum. Surely you wouldn't want to pass up an opportunity that could put millions of dollars into your pocket. You can then do whatever you want with it, making sure nobody can fuck you over and assume control of your vision."

RJ's words rang with the same tone that Leo's had months earlier. Why not stand fully behind something I believed in? With so much unchecked pillaging and murder taking place across the globe, I felt justified breaking some of the "Imperial" rules. Did the money entice me? Of course, it did. But I wasn't buying in just yet.

"Tell you what, I will go and pay my friend a visit, and you arrange to set up a meeting with your handler. If you feel, out of the kindness of your heart, like giving me money for my cause, then I will accept it, but under no circumstances whatsoever will I take ownership of this."

RJ had come to know me well in the short period we had spent together, but this was something he hadn't anticipated.

"Daryl, this is business. If you want to do this, you've got to accept that you have a large part to play in it, which means you will get compensated. Not because I want to support you for being a good guy but because this is how we operate. Some may admire your non-amenable qualities, but they cause others to worry." The look on my face told him I wasn't buying what he was selling. "Listen, if you want to operate like a Church, so be it. You're one stubborn individual. I'll be sure to make my donations."

The following week I flew to LA. My arrival was considerably different this time around, as my mind had made the shift from going with the flow, kicking back chill-style, to getting serious and making things happen. I took in a deep breath and exhaled just as the plane touched down on the tarmac, already ten steps ahead, focused on the task at hand. First on my to-do list was buying two burner-throw-away phones from a local 7-Eleven. I used one phone for calling RJ's contact in LA, and the other to talk with Leo. I continued to use my own phone for regular use. RJ impressed upon me how essential it was not to leave a trail and to be aware that people might be following me. Next on my list was calling Leo and arranging a place and time to meet.

I had been looking forward to seeing Leo again. He knew things I didn't, and I wanted to discuss face to face the invasion of Afghanistan and the build-up to war with Iraq. I was hungry for answers. Leo helped fill in many of the gaps in my knowledge, neatly tying together the last two hundred years, explaining there was a powerful syndicate that had been involved in nearly every major political assassination from Lincoln to Massoud.

"I know shit runs deep, but you're insinuating these people have full dominion over us," I said.

Leo looked amused. "We're owned, brother. You've got a few rogue states trying to hold on to what they've got, with Spectre going for the jugular. The events of 9/11 were pre-orchestrated years in advance, man. The Wolfowitz Doctrine spelled this out years ago. The targeting of the Twin Towers and the payroll-auditing offices in the Pentagon enabled the killing of two birds with one stone: two trillion dollars Rumsfeld said were missing from the Pentagon, money that couldn't be accounted for. Auditors were working to find where the money disappeared to, but unfortunately they were killed and the documents destroyed when the Pentagon was hit by a jet airliner? Yeah, right! This was another false flag event staged to siphon trillions of dollars out of the pockets of millions while asserting global dominance."

Though I had already come to believe 9/11 was an inside job, my mind was still reeling from everything he laid out for me. "Another false flag? Like the Gulf of Tonkin or the Reichstag fire?" I said.

"Like Pearl fucking Harbor, bro!"

"Whoa, whoa, whoa…" putting my hands up in front of me. "Pearl Harbor was real, man."

"Yeah, it was fucking real." Leo was working himself up. "A lot of innocent people died that day so the power brokers could get the US into the war. Up until that point, 90 percent of the population opposed getting into WWII, and FDR promised he wouldn't send our boys. It's a sham, man."

The vein in his neck was bulging, and his skin was flushed, the blood pumping harder than it did the day we did our workout together. "Chiang Kai-shek took a fucking bribe and set up shop in Taiwan so Mao could control China, creating the illusion of a threat that wasn't real."

"Slow down, bro, you're going to give yourself a jammer." I could only make sense of half of what he was saying, not knowing how much truth there was to any of it, but seeing he was convinced. In fact, he was acting like he was possessed.

Leo took in a deep breath and slowly exhaled, calming himself down as he did. "Sorry. I'm fucking fed up with the lies and manipulation, the massive cover-ups, the exploiting of innocent lives everywhere." Tears welled up in his eyes, and I reached out, placing my hand on his shoulder, squeezing it firmly. He looked out across the water from where we were sitting in Malibu. "The New World Order is here, and those who run it don't give a shit about you or me. The question is, what do you do with what you know?"

"Jesus, Leo. What can we do? I'm worried if we speak up, we'll just get put down."

"These people are going to use 9/11 to subvert the American Constitution. Orwell's *1984* is upon us, brother. I recommend you buy as much gold and silver as you can. Buy lots of guns and learn how to farm. That's what many are doing across this country and I reckon in yours too."

We eventually turned our attention to the details of our more imminent business at hand, agreeing to send a small, one-hundred-pound shipment for the first run to make sure everything ran smoothly. I would facilitate the first run, meeting the handlers for both crews separately, directing them where to go. Leo's driver rented a storage container and gave me the passcode, which I would later pass to RJ's delivery guy, who would make the drop. I would receive a call within the hour confirming the product was on the money. Leo's crew would move the grass, and payment would be shipped the following week. I was on my way to becoming a modern-day bootlegger, providing a service to those who were within their right to access it. I liked thinking I was cutting into the profits of the pharmaceutical companies, seeing marijuana as a cleaner substitution for the many prescription opiates being pushed by the medical establishment.

CHAPTER 41

DARK SIDE

"Do actions agree with words? There's your measure of reliability. Never confine yourself to the words."

> — *Frank Herbert, Chapterhouse: Dune*

March — April 2002

Within forty-eight hours of my return from LA, our test shipment went ahead. Five days later, the money was already back in Canada. It went so smoothly that I found myself wondering if it was too good to be true. The decision to send a bigger load was made, and five hundred pounds were shipped the following week. Three days later, I received two calls, one from the handler who worked directly for RJ and one from Leo.

"We have a serious problem. Need to see you right away." Leo said.

"I've got a lot going on right now. I can probably make it there by the end of next week."

"No good, man, this needs to be taken care of ASAP!"

"Yeah, fine, I'll be there within forty-eight hours"

I knew something was going to happen that would suck me in deeper than I wanted to go. I had been clear with both sides that I wanted nothing to do with the daily operations. I tried phoning RJ every couple of hours for the next two days but he never got back to me. I asked the handler to try contacting him too, and even reached out to RJ's boss, a man I had met only once. I couldn't reach him either. Something didn't feel right. Both RJ and his boss were always reachable, twenty-four hours a day. I rearranged my schedule and flew back to LA to sort out the issue at hand.

Candace and I were not financially well off. We did ok, but flying down to LA meant missing work, which meant the loss of dollars we couldn't afford to lose. The day before I left, Candace and I talked about the opportunity LA presented and how it fit into the life we were trying to create. I left the next morning with a heavy heart, not wanting to leave my family and not looking forward to mediating over a shipment worth seven figures in US dollars.

I had entered the fighting arena with my eyes wide shut, naively thinking I could spread the gospel of love to others, conducting business supported by altruistic ideals. I learned quickly that love for others rarely holds centre court in the game of business.

I arrived late at LAX, rented a car, and picked up another phone before making my way to Leo's. What he shared with me was a little unnerving.

"Two-fifths of the product you guys shipped us is shit, bro. We're supposed to be getting Grade A trips, not Grade B bunk."

Grade B marijuana was regarded as low quality. Grade A was considered higher quality and easier to sell. In those days, Grade A could be broken down into four more categories: a single, a double, a triple, and a quad. These categories all represented the best premium cannabis you could get. A single A would need to meet some basic criteria: good smell (pungent, spicy, savoury), nice appearance (well-manicured, an abundance of crystals, no chemical or light burns from fertilizers and grow lights) and smoked smoothly (cured properly with days spent drying, ideal temperature, humidity levels, absence of light, and flushing the plant of all chemicals). For an A to be considered double, triple, and the always coveted quad, the product not only needed to be good in all areas, but also needed to stand out. A double could have all the basics covered, but perhaps there it had a little bit more sugar (crystal) every chronic smoker salivated over. Some people preferred a strong smell over appearance. The true connoisseur and intelligent buyer would always take a random bud from the half-pound sample bag, lightly squeezing and smelling it before holding it under his portable lighted microscope. The microscope highlighted every characteristic, clearly identifying whether the product was adequate on appearance alone. Once the product had passed this test, the buyer would snap one of the smaller nodes or nuggets from the stalk of the bud, placing it into a portable grinder and shredding it into a ready-to-use product. These were the days before portable vaporizers were on the market, so more often than not, the buyer would roll the ganja into a joint and give it a final test. If the joint lit well and burned smoothly with good taste and there was no trace of chemicals, the deal was made.

I pressed Leo on what he had just told me, for if it was true, then someone along the line was trying to pull a fast one. Leo was patient with my questions, but I could tell he felt slighted at having to answer them. I told him I would talk with the handler the following day and try to get to the bottom of it all.

I met up with RJ's guy, Kyle, at a coffee shop the next day, pressing him for every detail about this shipment he could remember.

"Daryl, I inspected the product before dropping it off and can confirm some of it wasn't on par."

"Did someone make a switch during transport?"

"Maybe, I don't know," Kyle said. He wasn't looking good, worried that this mess-up would somehow become his to clean up. He still hadn't been able to get a hold of RJ or his boss.

"Don't you think it's kind of weird that you can't reach either of them?" I asked.

"Yes. If either one is away, the other is always there to take care of things," Kyle said. The longer poor quality cannabis sits in storage, the more likely it is the quality will degrade further, especially if, as Leo had mentioned, it has traces of mold.

"Listen, all I can do is suggest what I'd do. If it were me, I would wait a couple more days to hear back from RJ. If you don't hear back, then you're going to have to negotiate a reduction in price so they can unload it right away," I said. "My hands are tied. I am doing more here than I ever agreed to, and quite honestly, will be cutting ties altogether once this is done."

~

I received the expected call from RJ one week after I returned home and agreed to meet with him. He greeted me at the front door of his house and invited me inside. It was obvious he was off, a little on edge. He always had an edge, but this edge closely resembled the one he displayed the first time we met.

"I would appreciate it if you accompanied me to Keith's place. He'd like to speak with you as to what went down." *Oh great.* Keith was RJ's boss; someone I didn't wish to spend any of my time with.

I followed RJ into the kitchen where he started packing his food for the day. I was hesitant about agreeing to go because, quite frankly, I didn't owe Keith my time. As if he could read my mind, RJ turned to me and said, "It would mean a lot to me if you came."

Damn it! He pulled the "friend in need" card.

I had spent a big chunk of the past eight months getting to know RJ, and I had come to trust him, perhaps not fully, but enough to believe I was safe. We made a couple of stops on the way to Keith's place. The first was to ditch his BMW for a 1964 convertible Impala, which supposedly belonged to a friend who supplied antique cars and furniture to

Vancouver's film industry. The second stop was to take the Impala through a car wash just outside of the city. He said he wanted to drive with the top down since it was such a nice day. *Picking up a vehicle that couldn't be traced to him and wiping it clean of all prints. Hmmm.*

We drove for ninety minutes outside the city, arriving at Keith's farmhouse mid-afternoon. We got out of the car and walked toward the house. Keith walked out from around the corner to greet us. His wife was with him. Having a woman there made me feel a little more at ease, but truth be told, she looked to be a little spacey, behaving as if she was taking some barbiturate, her eyes slightly glossed over, and she wore a smile that didn't match her energy. Keith said he had worked hard that morning and could use a soak in his hot tub.

"Care to join me?"

I looked over at RJ and asked if he was going to get in, but he declined. I wasn't keen myself but didn't want to insult the man. "Sure, why not."

I eased myself into the 104 degree Fahrenheit water, facing Keith. RJ sat on the edge of the tub directly to my right. There I was, sitting in a hot tub with one of the biggest players in the criminal underworld. Keith was the top dog in his empire, and those who worked with him were never in any doubt that they worked *for* him. He owned many houses throughout the Lower Mainland, all outfitted with forty-light grow operations, some as large as one-hundred-light ops. Every indoor garden was expected to pull a minimum of one pound of cured product for every one-thousand-watt bulb. If you had a forty-light garden, you could expect to harvest around forty pounds of product every eight to ten weeks. RJ told me Keith owned close to eighty houses which he utilized explicitly for his marijuana business. So, 3,200 pounds every ten weeks, that's approximately sixteen thousand pounds every year. The going rate in the US back in those days was around US$3,500 per pound. Gross revenue for a player this size was roughly US$56 million. There were fees for the transport across the border ($500/pound), for the farmers who grow it (let's say $750/pound), for equipment upgrades and materials ($250/pound), and for wages for the crew for running the operation ($500/pound). Keith's total expenditures came out to around CDN$2,000/pound. The Canadian dollar usually hovered around 75 US cents. After Keith exchanged his money and accounted for the usual hiccups, he would have netted upwards of US $10 million a year. This revenue excluded profits made from his other business dealings, which I cared to know nothing about. Keith was a millionaire many times over. The assets in his real estate portfolio alone would have set him up to retire comfortably.

I had been in the water no more than five seconds when Keith stretched out his arms to the side, resting them on the edge of the tub before focusing his attention on me. I knew why I was there. To answer questions about why I would have suggested to Kyle that he reduce the price on one-third of his shipment.

"Let's get down to business. You understand everybody's got their role, which comes with a set of responsibilities, and if people don't take care of their responsibilities, everyone in the organization takes a hit. And there's a hit of $125,000 that needs to be addressed."

I realized how difficult that moment must have been for RJ. Over the years he had climbed through the ranks, abiding by an honour code that had him stand solidly by Keith through thick and thin. What Keith wanted, RJ did for him. I explained myself, my actions, and those of their boy Kyle, defending him as much as I did myself and putting the full responsibility of what went wrong onto the two of them.

"Somewhere along the line, at least two-fifths of your Grade A marijuana turned into Grade B bud."

Keith's face contorted and his body squirmed in the tub, revealing his distaste for what I said. He was past the point of being annoyed. He kept looking over at RJ and then back to me while challenging everything I said. I looked Keith in the eye and said very calmly, "I mean no disrespect whatsoever. I helped the best way I could. You weren't around, and neither was RJ. You passed your responsibility on to Kyle, who wasn't prepared to handle this fiasco. No instructions had been given on what to do with a situation like this." Keith's nostrils started flaring in and out. He removed his arms from the side of the tub, placing his hands on his thighs, pushing himself up taller. I wondered if he wanted RJ to pull out his pistol and point it at the side of my head. I could feel the conflict raging inside them both. RJ's loyalty to his master versus the love and respect he held for me.

We sat there for a breath or two before Keith snorted, "Don't expect to be compensated for this job."

My smile wasn't meant to put him off. "I never attached any expectations, other than conducting myself in an upfront and honest way. You do what you feel is right."

Keith shipped bunk weed, thinking he could strong-arm us into accepting it.

I left that meeting questioning whether I could continue a working relationship with RJ, and decided on the ferry ride back home that night that I was out. I felt ill-equipped to navigate the shark-infested waters, turning predators who feast against shepherds who are fodder. I was an idealist who still had much to learn. I would connect the crew from LA with the one in Vancouver and step out for good.

A couple of months after that meeting, RJ told me he left his master's side. One month after that, he was baptized. I was fortunate to have worked closely with individuals like RJ and Leo. They saw every interaction as a hustle, a means to progress further in the game. They trusted me more than most others because I was straightforward with my hustle. I was honest about how I thought the game should be played, though my naivety and refusal to conform and whore myself out was surely seen as a weakness.

I made it home from my meeting with RJ and Keith late that night. Tut and Jacquie, my two loyal dogs, greeted me at the front steps, happy to see me. I tiptoed through the house, peaking in on Mariah and Kahlil, before deciding to sleep on the couch in our sun-room, so as not to disturb Candace. The anxiety I had been feeling completely subsided, assuring me my decision to step out of the game was the right one. I went to sleep feeling at peace.

I awoke slowly out of my slumber, feeling the warmth of the early morning sun, its rays shining through the open blinds down on my face.

Candace entered the room and nudged me gently, waiting for me to fully open my eyes. She was standing over me with tears in her eyes and a pregnancy test in her hand.

"I was excited to get my body back," she whimpered.

Kahlil was now eight months old and had recently ceased his daily bouts of crying, giving Candace some much-needed relief. There was no mistaking her anguish, and even though I comforted her, telling her I would support her in whatever decision she wanted to make, I could see and feel nothing else except a miracle. I could hear a voice in my head saying with some urgency, "Hey, guys, wait for me!" I felt the wisdom of the Universe at that moment and the sense this little one understood it.

Candace took the day to search her feelings. The shock and initial disappointment she felt had dissipated by dinner, and by bedtime, she told me, "There's only one way forward."

CHAPTER 42

KEEPING A PROMISE

*"Pain, anguish and suffering in human life are always in proportion
to the strength with which a man is endowed."*
— *Alexandre Dumas, The Man in the Iron Mask*

January 21ˢᵗ, 2011

I am lying on my bunk reading a book I picked up out of the library
this morning when one of the guards enters our pod.

"Mail call," the guard yells out. "Alcantara, Escamilla, Fontana…"

I received a half-page letter from Candace that included a poem written by my darling daughter, Mariah, three months before her fourteenth

birthday. My pleasure in receiving a letter from one of my children was quickly replaced with despair.

They just don't understand all I've been through without you.

I used to feel invincible. Now tell me, why'd you have to go?

Seems like every day gets worse. Why'd you put me in this curse?

Comin' home each day, waiting for you to say, just say something.

I miss your voice, that lovely noise.

How about that smile? I could see it from a mile.

Then I'd smile cause I was the one that put it on your face.

It was such a beautiful thing, and I'd always want to sing:

She will be loved, she will be loved.

And she was, just like you'd say, but now I'm losing my way.

Look what you've done, this is no fun.

I'm furious and very curious.

You promised, didn't you? Me, who? Yes, you!

Looked me in the eyes; why am I not surprised?

Cause you had all my trust and kicked it around like dust.

I sit in my room, wishing on the moon.

The shooting stars don't seem to help.

But they did last time. Somebody give me a sign.

I've figured something out, and there's no doubt.

I don't want to stop.

What do I do when I don't want to give up on you?

Maybe nothing, but my heart's crushing.

Will you come back? Feels like you're poking me with a tack.

This hurts so bad. Are you glad?

Candace said the poem was about a boy, but the underlying message is glaringly obvious. I lie motionless on my bed, with tears running silently down my cheeks. I am failing to guide my daughter in this hyper-critical world. I have no desire to get up from my bunk and decide to skip dinner. Eventually, I fall asleep with my clothes on and the letter clasped in my hand, held against my heart. I wake at 2:00 am, pull myself out of bed, and quietly sit down at one of the tables in the cell with pen and paper in hand and a determination to set things right.

I am disappointed with my inability to turn the switch off and to sleep peacefully without a care in the world. I remember the days when I could sit myself down anywhere and doze for a quick fifteen minutes, waking up feeling energized. When I laid myself down for bed at night, I would inhale one long, deep breath, exhale, and I would be out within seconds, satisfied I had done all the things that were required of me. I was in tune; I was at peace.

Now, how can I afford to rest when there is so much wrong with the world, with my own life? How can I sleep peacefully knowing my children are hurting? I must keep the promise I made upon Mariah's arrival.

Prison Thoughts — January 2011

I have been foolish for suppressing my inner voice, my truth. I went into hiding and buried my head in the sand. Like so many others, I was afraid to be ridiculed, scorned, and cut down. Where did the fear carry me too? Exactly to this place I've been trying to avoid.

Prison Thoughts — February 2011

Defiant! I feel the flicker of the flame that whispers passion, giving me needed strength and a clearer vision of what lies in front of me. What happens to sheep if left unattended? They will get slaughtered. What is the objective of tending to your herd? Maintaining a healthy and happy food supply. For what do I watch out? The wolf in sheep's clothing.

I became so entrenched with wanting a certain outcome that I allowed my attachment to blind me. I fell into the very state that I was trying to shake people out of. I was asleep! The apologies have been made. There is nothing to be sorry for anymore. If I am sorry, then I negate who and what I am. I am also negating who and what you are. Do I continue to run the risk of keeping my mouth shut, fearing people in power may not like what I have to say? Will there be retribution? Mine or theirs? We must take responsibility to effect positive change in and among our lives and the lives of others. The wisdom of God — our collective consciousness — sees the beauty in its ability to separate and experience "life" as one of many. The individual interactions between us should be viewed for exactly what they are, a harmonized state of being. However, many people do not perceive their living reality as a special part of the whole. They are disconnected from the source.

As I finish writing and close my journal my attention turns to Bob Marley. I begin singing the song, 'Get up, Stand Up', which automatically brings a smile to my face. Bob believed there is an evil that prevents people from knowing the truth and through his revolutionary songs tried to awaken people to their inner power by expressing love through music. I wish to tell the other half of the story.

Prison Thoughts — March 2011

Along with the extra sleep I am now getting, my dreams are coming on strong.

I awoke this morning to a dream where I had entered the bike storage room of an apartment building and found three young children: a girl, age seven, tending to an infant around nine months old, and a boy who was around five years old.

I asked them, "What are you doing in there?" The girl explained, "When my mom is smoking, we are not supposed to be in the apartment because the smoke is not good to breathe in." I asked if I could hold the baby, and she handed him to me. The feeling I had was overwhelming. My want to protect the young is so powerful that it often elicits strong emotions. I asked the children to come with me to see their mother. We walked into the apartment, surprising the woman who wasn't expecting guests. She looked to be drug-induced. I sent the children into another room while I remained holding the infant in my arms. I sat in a chair while she remained standing. There was no need for words. I could see the pain and suffering in her eyes and her wanting to be saved from the torture she was enduring. I beckoned her to come and sit on my knee as would a parent to a child so that I could hold her, protect her, and give her the chance to surrender completely. She began to cry.

At first, I made the connection that these children represented my kids, and the woman was my wife, but as the day wore on, I understood my dream to be my two older brothers, and the nine-month-old babe was me. My mom, a smoker, was represented by the mother in my dream, both of whom had been worn down by life's trials and tribulations. My desire to help my mom was so strong, I continued as I grew up to feel the need to heal and save others, including my wife. The innocent babe, the one I wished to protect so badly, was my desire to save myself.

This dream triggered memories of when I used to lay my hands on the parts of Candace's body that were hurting. When she was menstruating, I would place my hand on her lower abdomen and low back and breathe with her. I would visualize a pale bluish cool light flow through my hands and push out the orangey-reddish hot pain emanating from her. It was something we never talked about with others, and for whatever reason, I stopped doing it as the years rolled on. *Why did I stop? Why did I disconnect?*

I awake from another powerful dream, one that saw the return of a creature that had visited me twice before, years ago. I was driving my car to our family home when suddenly the road began to narrow, shrinking until it was a dirt trail. I was no longer driving my car. I was now running. From out of a tree, twenty-two feet in front of me, a black panther jumped down to the forest floor, forcing me to an immediate stop. I could feel my fear rise with each step the big cat slowly took toward me. But there was something unusual about this feline that I hadn't picked up on during our two previous meetings. The slowness of its movement indicated the cat was tired. It reminded me of my favourite teddy bear from when I was a kid, after it had endured six years of being dragged through every one of my adventures. This cat appeared to be just as worn. Was it labouring to breathe? Perhaps it is hungry, looking at me as its next meal. Shit! I quickly scanned my surroundings, looking for a stick or rock to use as a weapon but could not find anything suitable other than a soccer ball lying next to my feet. Strange, it was just lying there on the ground, waiting for me to pick it up. I decided to throw it into the bushes, hoping to distract it. The cat turned to chase after it and I proceeded to run in the opposite direction, knowing it would soon be chasing me down. My frantic escape had me sprinting straight ahead through the dense rain forest of the Pacific Northwest, which began to open with every stride. There was a quarter the length of a football field to go, but instead of hitting an end zone, I saw the edge of a cliff that dropped a hundred metres to the ground below. I only had seconds before the cat would be on me. There was no time to think. Acting on pure instinct, relying on faith that I would be protected, I launched myself forward, flying through the air, traversing a distance that would have surely killed me had I been outside the matrix. The forest floor transformed in mid-flight, becoming an open landscape of light earthy-brown hills and mounds, rocks, and dirt. In every direction, I could see heavy machinery, bulldozers, excavators, trucks, and concrete buildings that closely matched the colour of the landscape. I landed in the middle of what appeared to be a massive fortified industrial complex, spanning at least one thousand hectares. I'm not sure what this complex was, but my thoughts zeroed in on military-corporate-construction, sensing something "they" didn't want the public to know about.

When I dreamed of the black panther in the past I always awoke with the feeling the majestic cat is trying to tell me something. While walking to the gym that morning, I share my dream with Fernie, one of my ultra-fit training partners from Colombia.

"You need to speak with Memo. He can interpret this dream for you."

I'm exhausted by the time Fernie and I complete our second workout. I contemplate skipping Memo's yoga session, but before I can excuse myself, Memo walks over to me and places his hand on my arm.

"You need be here. Stay," Memo says in his broken English. "What on your mind?"

I looked to Fernie, who shrugs his shoulders. I tell Memo about my dream, allowing Fernie time to translate into Spanish.

"The black panther represents power, grace, and beauty. It might be here to remind you that if you wish to move forward, you must act with wisdom." Memo looks at me thoughtfully as Fernie struggles to find the right words. "Be careful of how others are trying to use you. If a panther is stalking you in your dreams, it might mean you have enemies who are spreading negative energy toward you."

I could hear my inner alarm bells ringing, lending support to my suspicion that my being stuck in an American prison didn't come about simply because I made a bad decision. "The Sacred Mother will send this powerful spirit to watch over those with great courage, acting as a strong protective presence around you," says Fernie.

I took what Memo said with me to bed that evening, contemplating how to protect myself from the poison of others.

I found myself standing at the side of the same river that held me twenty years earlier. I can feel the dark force churning inside my chest. I know it's real. I look over to the other side of the river, knowing the flag I was meant to capture is still there. I inhale deeply and dive into the water, smothering myself in ignorance, losing my connection to my perceived reality.

I have been underwater so long I can no longer tell up from down. I need air. I surface to take a breath, realizing I am now in the middle of a soothing warm ocean. The pre-dawn greyness blends water and sky into one, making it difficult to discern the two apart.

After paddling for an hour in the same spot, I decide to forgo the advice given months earlier by a dear friend who had never seen me so beaten down: "Sink or swim, bro, sink or swim."

A sense of calm washes over me, and I stop paddling. I float on my back, staring up into the abyss, experiencing for the millionth time being wrapped inside our great mother's womb. My soul swims effortlessly through this primordial fluid.

With full acceptance, surrendering myself to what I am, the prescient universe births itself.

I awake feeling grounded.

What keeps people trapped within their self-imposed prison? A lack of understanding. Ignorance is that which slumbers in the dark. The absence of light is the absence of truth. Living without truth is to live in fear. To live in the dark keeps you in fear of disrupting the status quo, to take a stand, to expose yourself to the brilliance of the light. Yet, we all know the importance of donning sunglasses and wearing protective clothing when venturing out at high noon on a midsummer day.

There are those of us who are blind to the illusion of their perceived reality, living with limited vision, silently trotting along, being spoon-fed GMOs, pesticides, flu shots, CNN, FOX, the War on Terror, all kinds of fear. They fulfill their civic duty by reposting the top trending Facebook political excerpts, which are routed to them based on their internet activity and a slew of algorithms. Others can read between the lines and are caring, empathetic, and intelligent, with enough know-how to tune out the propaganda, all the while serving their community to the best of their ability.

The truth is that I love life and everything and everyone in it. But, I'm not satisfied. I not only want more, I *need* it. I must have it. Simply look inside of yourself, and you will find it. I get it. The Universe is a realm of infinite possibilities, but the possibilities are just potentials. Things we feel and see internally are the breeding ground for everything that eventually forms into our living reality.

DARYL FONTANA

Why is the song "Everybody Wants to Rule the World" playing in my head?

CHAPTER 43

GOD'S WELL

"Maybe you who condemn me are in greater fear than I who am condemned."

— *Giordano Bruno*

August — September 2002

I was invited to my friend Jag's house for dinner one evening. Jag and I became good friends following high school, having met at the gym. His parents had immigrated to Canada from India in the late 1960s, joining the large Sikh population living in the Cowichan region. Though his mother couldn't speak English and I couldn't speak Punjabi, she and I had a close relationship. I respected the family's traditions, and she believed I was a good influence on her son.

Tonight's dinner was my first time meeting Jag's new love, Sage. Sage and Jag had met at work and soon began an affair, which quickly ended Jag's marriage that his parents had arranged. I had asked Jag multiple times before he got married, "Are you 100 percent sure this is what you want?" It was one of a handful of times I was angry with him. Being the intermediary between Jag and his family during this period was not easy. Sage made rice pilaf, grilled salmon, and mixed seasonal vegetables. She also served copious amounts of red wine. By the time we had polished off the second bottle, I felt quite relaxed. The evening's conversation started light: work, family, and hobbies. Halfway through the third bottle our conversation turned to world affairs.

After five years, I was winding down from the natural high that accompanies a spiritual awakening, but my passion for affecting positive change in the world was still bubbling at the surface. Like many of my good friends, Jag shared my desire to have influence in the world. He wanted to be more than a nine-to-five man.

"The world is fucked! I say do what you can for yourself and those around you. Let other people take care of their own," said Sage.

I detected a bit of a chip on her shoulder, and something I could see in Jag's eyes told me something was not sitting well with him.

"I don't profess to have the solutions to the world's problems, but I do believe we are capable of doing much more for ourselves and everyone else we know. Personally, I wish to contribute to the conversation as well as learn from people like yourself, believing a substantial portion of the population today is disillusioned with the world. The ones that aren't are either blind to what goes on outside their bubble, don't give a damn about anyone other than themselves, or have managed to find the Holy Grail — seeking nothing, liberated from the illusory bonds that grip the masses," I retorted.

Sage sat silently, refortifying her defences from the inside, and then went on the attack. She posed the regular questions, which were par for the course, but she made one accusation that shook me harder than I thought possible. In fact, her words brought my preaching days to an abrupt end.

"It sounds like you're starting a cult!"

Her share of the downed wine helped to heat the tone in her voice, reflecting an attitude that looked to fight rather than to solve. High-profile cult leaders of the last forty years flashed through my mind: David Koresh, Jim Jones, Shoko Asahara, Marshall Applewhite... I didn't want to control anyone, I simply wanted to empower people, and in turn, they could do the same for others. I had thought that if we could all work together for the common good, then the world would drastically change. I had no aspirations to be a cult leader, but I knew beyond any doubt that I could easily be made to look like one.

For the next month following that dinner, I reflected on the slain socio-political leaders I had come to admire. I had no illusions of being in their league, and I did not care to join them if it meant a shortened life and a failed revolution. I had seen enough in my short life to figure out that if I wanted to break the chains, I would have to play the long game. I needed a stronger foundation, one that I could not be pushed from, one that wouldn't crack.

When I made my 30th birthday wish (September 25, 2002), I had a deep connection to God's well. I was certain I would get what I asked for, believing when it came time to plug back in, the universe would help to make it happen. But I had no idea how painful it was going to be.

CHAPTER 44

DARK CLOUD DESCENDS

"Intense, unexpected suffering passes more quickly than suffering that is apparently bearable; the latter goes on for years and, without our noticing, eats away at our souls, until, one day, we are no longer able to free ourselves from the bitterness and it stays with us for the rest of our lives."

— *Paulo Coelho, The Alchemist*

2006 — 2009

My health club had been up and running for about a year when I heard that my friend Lonny had been arrested in an elaborate sting operation. My first thought was about his children and how this would impact them.

I immediately reached out to offer him support. I left him a message but didn't hear back from him until he surprised me with a visit to The Playground the following evening. For a half hour Lonny poured out a good chunk of what had happened, telling me the cops were pressing hard for him to roll on one of his colleagues, something he said he wouldn't do. I felt horrible for what he was going through, as I had always considered him a decent man with well-meaning intentions. He was more brother to me than friend.

Over the next three days, I had two RCMP officers sign up at The Playground. Two days after that, a third officer, Graham Rowling, the same officer I would later ask Agent Shannon to get a hold of following my 2010 arrest and who worked undercover for the drug and crime squad, hired me to train him.

The business was growing strong but my health was declining. I was burning out. In February of 2007, I was diagnosed with full-blown vertigo. My doctor ordered me to bed for a week, saying, "Corky, if you refuse to listen to me, I will call the authorities and have them commit you to a bed in the hospital."

I felt an outpouring of appreciation towards her. I was nine years old when I became one of her very first patients in Cowichan. She knew how hard I pushed. "Thanks, Lynn!" I said, giving her a smile.

Candace and I argued about my desire to step away from the daily operations of the business. She insisted that most people who went to the gym did so to see me and feared if I stepped back, the business would not continue. I allowed that fear to corrupt what I believed in my heart was the right thing to do, something I resented her for years afterwards. I continued working full-time at The Playground, losing ground as I did: my finances, my health, and my relationship with my wife all declined. The world that had been shining bright began to dull.

My desire to build community was an altruistic endeavour, and my heart was in the right place, but ironically, I strayed from the things that had served me so well. My efforts to achieve the things I coached my clients on — daily meditation, hikes in nature, and adequate amounts of sleep — sent me to the very place I was working hard to pull others out of.

I had been working a rare Friday evening shift behind the front desk, making use of my time to finish a couple of programs and do some fact-checking on the internet. I was listening to past speeches of US presidents from the Presidential Archives when Jeroen approached the front desk counter.

"What are you listening to?" he asked.

Jeroen had always taken a keen interest in what I did with my time, and I cared enough about what he thought to always tell him. Though we had become close, I had always held back about how impassioned I was about global issues, as I did with most friends I made post-2005. But on this day, I decided to reveal what secretly held my interest. "I am listening to a speech Kennedy gave shortly before his assassination, the speech that may well have gotten him killed."

"Why are you listening to that?" he asked, with a hint of condescension.

"Because if you want to navigate the world today, you need to know where we came from."

"What does he say that could possibly help you steer your course?"

Gut instinct kept me from immediately responding. Jeroen was one of my more affluent friends, someone who had become as much a mentor as a client. We had welcomed each other into our respective inner circles, but still, there was always a discernible space between us. This man had become my counsel in all matters concerning my business, and I trusted him implicitly, even though he represented the Man, the patriarchal society I had sworn to reform.

He once said, "Corky, you have everything it takes to move light years ahead of me, though your refusal to conform will surely hold you back."

I understood his position and always found it difficult to respond without fully revealing my true aspirations. "We differ on what our definition of success is, though I admit, I still have a lot to learn. Like figuring out how to effectively manage my business." I was hoping to steer the conversation away from what I felt would become a debate.

"I agree," he said. "There's at least one person you should fire right now, but you don't because you think they'll eventually get with your program."

"Yeah, maybe you're right," I admitted.

He intentionally deepened his voice, perhaps hoping to lighten the mood. "Cork... you must join the dark side."

I didn't miss the irony in his referencing the storyline I had internalized thirty years earlier. I didn't go as deep philosophically with Jeroen as I did with some of my other friends. It was a conscious choice, as I knew that once I started, I would have a difficult time holding back.

I was irritated, having taken exception to Jeroen's critique of how I was applying my time.

"This was the speech in which Kennedy called out the secret groups which operate in the shadows, the network that runs the entire show."

He shot me a look of surprise. "Corky, I thought the president ran the show."

"I know you don't believe that."

"Don't I? How do you know that this recording isn't a fake?"

I laughed. "Because I pulled it from the Presidential Archives." My contempt for his questions was blatant.

He paused, his face serious, having discarded the mask to which I had grown accustomed. "Maybe some things are meant to be kept secret." He snatched his keys from behind the counter and walked out the door.

CHAPTER 45

CENTER POINT

"Let evil swiftly befall those who have wrongly condemned us."
— Jacques de Molay

Prison Thoughts — April 2011

Arrogance could be the number one Giant Killer. Think about such battles as George Foreman versus Muhammad Ali, David against Goliath, the Spanish Armada of 1588 going against the English, the Knights Templar facing off against King Philip IV and Pope Clement V. The crushing defeats of Foreman, Goliath, the Spanish Armada, and the Knights Templar are stories that become legend. I am still awed by how brilliant Ali was at using his strategy to outwear, outthink, and outlast his much bigger, stronger, and more powerful opponent. I'm still amazed that English became the dominant language and the world's greatest empire because the Spanish Armada was caught in a freak storm that decimated its fleet. Was the Templar Order arrogant or just naïve? Regardless, they affirmed their suspicions that their enemies were real. Were these events born out of divine intervention? Many people would argue that all of life is.

I can say with a modest amount of certainty that the fight I was waging and the thumping I am taking has a lot to do with my own arrogance. Crushing defeats can do one of three things: they can destroy you, turn you into a victim, or transform you into something far greater than what you were.

I am sitting in the library right now surrounded by people talking loudly. The library's rules are that we must be respectful of others, keep talking to a minimum, and be as quiet as we can. This raised some interesting questions for me: Do I interject and politely ask these people to refrain from their disruptive rudeness? Do I try to work through it, or do I leave? When and where do you take on the battles that are worth fighting? Do we choose to fight only when we know we can win, or do we fight when we know that our cause for doing so is just, regardless of whether we think we are likely to win or lose?

One of the guys who spent a lot of time in the library told me that inmates who had degrees or relatable work experience could assist in running new programs at the prison. The education programs, if you can call them that, offer no diplomas or certificates, nothing of substance that can be used in the real world. But there were tangible options like learning Spanish, guitar, basic economics, and real estate laws from the other inmates. If I could get a program approved to instruct two classes per week, it would get me out of my duties guarding the kitchen store room. Teaching two shifts a week on something I liked would be a better use of my time than working three shifts a week in the kitchen.

I spent a couple of days working on a program before presenting it to the educational coordinator for his review, and I got approved!

My program is called Center Point. I make a flyer and put it up on the education department bulletin board along with a sign-up sheet. Four people signed up for the classes, which was four more than I expected.

In my first session, I opened with these words:

"I came in here today knowing full well I was going to have a tough time containing my emotions. Whenever I engage and speak to what I am most passionate about, I tend to choke up. I think my emotional release is due to my belief people would see something they didn't like, that they would take what I had to say, and scoff at it, rebuff it. I was also worried people might actually listen, really listen to what I had to say, and that I would be silenced for demanding social reforms. This course will cover how to define your purpose and get to the root of "Why." We are going to look closely at our desires, what drives us, our collective history, attaining realization, including seeing our bodies as temples. We will strengthen our physical and emotional foundation and utilize our breath. We will work to let go of anger and resentment and strive to be the righteous warrior."

One of the four men who attend my classes usually remains quiet, even though I encourage participation throughout the course. David is the only Caucasian and at least thirty years older than the other three.

I was surprised when he first showed up and enquired about the material I had prepared, as he was known to keep to himself, spending time with only one other person, walking the track, and passing the time in deep discussion, as so many of us did. At the beginning of the first class, he told me he could only attend once a week, and I said that would be fine.

Months earlier, one of the guys I sit with in the library pointed David out to me. "See that guy over there?" Daniel asked. "He used to be an economic hit man, with ties to the CIA and Vladimir Putin."

I had made it my policy not to pay attention to the gossip but will admit my interest was roused when a fellow Canadian showed me court documents his sister had found on the internet, presenting David as a powerful and influential man. He must have crossed someone equally powerful, because guys like him usually avoid doing time in shit holes like MVCC.

It's the end of our last class, and David stays behind to talk with me, which he has never done before. "You did a superb job teaching this class, unusual as it was."

"Well, thank you, David." I hoped he would elaborate on what made my topic so unusual and that he would divulge his reason for attending.

"I was intrigued when I saw your class description posted on the wall but hadn't considered checking it out until I discovered it was you that was running it."

My curiosity spiked. "I admit, I'm surprised. However," I said quickly, "I have wondered daily since our first class what prompted you to come check it out."

He looked at me intently for a moment before speaking. "Daryl, my whole life I have taken an interest in the people around me; anyone who can play a role in helping to facilitate what I do. What I do is not important; what you do is. I have spent most of my life negotiating and waging war for others. Not because it was the right thing to do, but because I was good at it, and it paid me very well. I have had time to reflect on the past forty years of my life, and though I regret little, I can tell you that if I were to do it all over again, I would do some things differently. A person, if they are fortunate, will be able to look back on what they have accomplished and be able to see a legacy of which they are proud. I have directly influenced the lives of millions of people, and as I stand here before you today, I cannot tell you — because I really don't know — whether there is a legacy I can be proud of."

His use of the word legacy makes me think about my paper "We the Children, the Inheritors of Your Legacy."

"I want to share what I know with good people, well-intended people, who have the ability to influence others. Perhaps, millions of others." His words flow smoothly, and his convincing sincerity pulls me in a little closer.

"David, do you believe I can influence millions?" There is a tinge of doubt coating my words, the smirk on my face betrays my disbelief, but deep down, I want it to be true.

"Does it matter what I believe, Daryl? Does it matter what anybody other than you believes? You are your own man, and you will do whatever you think is the right thing to do. Take what you shared with us in these classes and own it like you asked us to own it. You have all the tools to be successful. How you go about it is entirely up to you."

This was the counsel I had been longing for. "Where were you the first six months of my stay?"

For the next two hours I conceptualize and write out a one-year game plan, which includes the projected ten-year end goal. I feel jubilant as I calculate the last of my expenses, which account for the kids, mortgage, and fifty thousand dollars allotted to start-up business expenses.

My feelings of excitement about getting home and starting work again are intruded upon when Thomas, a young Canadian from the Montreal area, discloses some gossip he knew I would want to hear. "Someone is talking shit about you."

"What exactly is being said?" I ask. He squirms a little bit, knowing he has opened a can of worms and there was no way to put them back.

"Well, I overheard Daniel saying that Arlo had said you were a snitch." My eyes open wide, focusing hard on Thomas. Arlo is one of only a handful of guys I spend time with. We play a lot of cribbage together and hijack a TV whenever the Vancouver Canucks are televised on an American station.

"Tell me everything you heard, and make sure not to leave out any details." My gut tells me what I am hearing is true. Arlo had previously made accusations against people he suspected of being "rats," but I never paid much attention, believing his deep resentment about what happened to him skewed his ability to see clearly. His time spent behind bars is due in large part to someone he trusted talking with the DEA. According to the US government, Arlo is a big fish with ties to international drug smuggling. From what I knew, the Feds did him dirty and he was still very bitter.

I couldn't confront him with what Thomas told me until I could verify it. I seek out two Canadians who are on friendly terms with Arlo and me. They hesitate before answering my questions, hoping they can avoid making a bad situation worse, but they end up confirming what Thomas had said. I am left with little recourse but to confront Arlo and to do it with as few people around.

~⌒

The weather is chilly and overcast, so the yard is empty except for me. I keep busy reading my book, hoping Arlo and his two companions will stick to their usual routine, walking laps around the track. Like clock-work, they turn the corner at Unit B and enter through the gates and onto the track. I am sitting on the bench half way up the track, giving ample time for the butterflies to stir in my stomach as the three of them make their way to the fifty-metre mark. As they walk by, they look over to where I sit, nodding their heads to acknowledge me. I reciprocate the casual greeting and then return my attention to my book. I decide to let them walk one full lap before I join them. As they turn the last corner, I feel the butterflies flutter again, and I move to get up, but my legs are shackled to the bench. They pass by me again while I keep my head down. I am frustrated by my inability to engage them. I went through all the scenarios of what could happen by confronting the three of them alone. I reaffirm my position that what I am doing is right.

I need to engage him in front of his crew, so there is no possibility of any misunderstanding. As they make their approach for lap three, I close my book and get up, walking onto the track. "Do you guys mind if I join you?" I ask, making sure to start the conversation with a dual message: first, I will be cordial and respectful, and second, I am going to walk with them whether they like it or not.

"Uh, sure," Arlo said.

"I'm going to cut right to the chase." I tell them what I heard the day before and that I verified it with two others. "I'm not sure how much truth there is to this, but I figured you guys could shine some light on it." I can see by the look in their eyes and the straightening of their spine that they are taken aback by what I said.

"There's no truth to what you heard, Daryl. Sounds like someone might be getting their story mixed up," says Arlo.

"Perhaps, but if there is any truth to it, I'd like to take the time to resolve it."

"Hey, man, aren't you going to be released from here soon?" says Persian Mike, who is one of Arlo's close confidants.

"Yeah, that's right," I say, knowing the direction he is going in.

"Well, do you think it's advisable to jeopardize that release date over some bullshit?" he adds.

"Trust me, I appreciate what you're saying, but this kind of talk has to be dealt with when it arises. Listen, I don't owe you an explanation, but I will tell you this. I packed a measly twenty-seven pounds of marijuana across the border. Stupidest thing I have ever done, and I wound up getting caught the first and only time I ever did it. The guy who led our packing crew left us high and dry. The details aren't important, but I will say the right people were protected. I told the Feds that as far as I knew, it was this guy's gear and his operation. If that means I'm a snitch in somebody's book, well, I don't know what else to say."

"Yeah, that's cool, man. I get that," Mike says.

I nod my head in acknowledgement, smiling as I did, "Ok, great, glad I could get that off my chest." I leave the three of them to continue walking on their own as I make my way back to my pod, relieved that it has gone as well as it did.

During my last two weeks in MVCC, I met up with David a few more times. He asks me many questions about my business and the five years leading up to my arrest. I told him the opening of my health centre was new ground for me. I had always been the rebel in hiding, anti-establishment, wanting to be like Batman, though I had never planned to follow in the fictional character's footsteps, serving time in a prison with hardened men.

"I created The Playground to be a space where I could covertly connect with people who had the power to influence, but I held back from talking about the things that mattered most to me. I believed igniting a worldwide revolution could only be done after I had built a strong network of established people. It was a good plan, but I got lost in the game."

"Where do you go from here?" David asks.

"Good question." I'm still uncertain of the answer. "Years ago I made a commitment to those closest to me that I would spend my life bettering the lives of others, most importantly the lives of children. That will never change."

"What, if anything, could hold you back from realizing your dreams?"

"Losing the desire."

David gave me a lot to think about. He is an interesting man, yet I know little about him other than what I have heard from others and the little bits he would bring to our conversations. I tell myself that the next time we meet, I will ask him to explain how he thinks the system operates and who runs the show.

The week before my scheduled departure, David and I meet in the yard after lunch, having arranged to walk the track. I don't waste any time getting to the heart of what I want to know.

"What has the banking cartel's great Ponzi scheme accomplished? What have we been left with? People are enraged at the greed of the moneyed elite, Wall Street, and the rest of them, believing they have been hoodwinked and cheated out of the wealth that should rightfully be theirs."

"You say 'people,' but aren't you referring to yourself as feeling this way? Are you representative of the people?"

"Millions of people have paid an exorbitant amount of money in taxes that gets doled out to the military, which in truth gets funnelled directly into the accounts of big companies like Lockheed Martin and Boeing. How does this not equate to stealing from the citizens of this country?"

"But what wealth are we talking of? Do you know where money originates?"

"I understand the basics. I know world currency is based on the US dollar, which, years ago, got rid of the gold standard."

"Right. But it is much simpler than that. Money is based on an idea, supported by the strength and security, and a wee bit of faith in a system that allows for greater energy expenditure."

"How so?" I ask.

"You would be correct to say money is made from thin air. It is derived from energy potentials and forecasts of those potentials. The conversion of 'potential' energy, human, solar, gravitational, and the list goes on, into monetary units we can measure is in the quadrillions, perhaps more."

"Ok, I think I'm following. Based on what you're saying, we have more than enough money, or the potential to have enough money, to go around for everyone?"

"Yes, but the reason some people don't have enough money isn't that there isn't enough to go around. It's because our social, economic, and political systems would collapse if it was distributed among everyone."

I understood the truth in what he said. "Ultimately, what you're saying is that our monetary system is set up as a way to control?"

"Absolutely. And our current paradigm could not exist any other way. We created the means by which we can convince the public to dream bigger, using a system that has helped build a world inconceivable a hundred years ago. Many people, including myself, have acquired a lot of wealth, and the standard of living across the globe has improved for most others too."

"Come on, David, you know not everyone gets the same opportunities. The quality of life in some parts of the world has gone up, but colonialism, the expansion of empire has displaced and killed millions in the process."

"Quite often, when given the responsibility to govern and lead others, you are faced with decisions that no matter what choice you make, will, in some way, be wrong. Some people will get hurt, and there will be pain, there will be hardship, there will be loss. Trust me. I know this all too well."

"I grew up believing that I was in bondage, a slave like most everyone else. I have been looking to those who rule to get them to change their ways and give us something better than we have."

"Look at where we have come from, Daryl. Look how far we have come in such a brief period."

"Where have we made it to? Why would I believe we have advanced when people from all over, many of them children, are sacrificed and left to rot? What would you have me call this, a progressive world?"

"To move ahead requires struggle and hardship. Yet, what you say resonates more with me now than it ever has," says David.

"Who's the top dog pulling all the strings?" I think back to my conversation years earlier with Adriel.

"You want to know who runs the world? Be careful of what you ask for, you may not like what you find out."

I sit on my bed thinking about my upcoming release, making notes in my journal about what I must do once I return home. I am going to be a free man. *A free man to do what?* Was I ready to go back and take on what I had left behind?

Having a hefty mortgage, a father in his late eighties, and no immediate job to go to upon my return means having a clean slate is far from a reality. Candace has bought another house and already moved into it. I have my home, my kids, and my health; I'm planning to put my head down and work hard for a year, focusing on re-establishing myself within my community and earning back the trust and respect I once had. *But was I going to be a free man?*

My ego supports the theory of quantum mechanics, wanting the Universe to be one of chance, but my heart resonates with Einstein's belief that God does not play with dice. We, as observers, directly influence and determine the outcome of our lives through our own personal perspective on the world in which we live. However, that world, in its natural state, has a set of characteristics that influence and most often govern the perspective of the observer. We work in unison with the Universe, and when it sends us messages, we must pay attention.

CHAPTER 46

WORD FROM THE BIRD

"Remorse for what is done is useless."

— Philo

June 14th, 2011

I arrive at the Niagara Falls Border Crossing and walk inside the Canadian Customs building, entering with a clean record because what happens out of the country does not automatically transfer over to a Canadian criminal record.

It feels odd that after exiting the transport van at the border and having my cuffs removed, I am now on my own with nobody watching over me. At least, I think no one is watching over me. Once inside the building, I wait for the customs supervisor to connect me with Candace over the phone.

"I've booked you a flight out of Hamilton to Vancouver tomorrow morning. You're going to have to take a bus to Hamilton and stay there for the night. I've booked you a room at Howard Johnson Hotel on the main strip. The next morning there is a flight to Vancouver. Arrive by 9:00 am and check in with Air Canada." she states flatly.

"Thank you, I really appreciate it." We both said bye and I hung up the phone. Thank goodness I still had money from when I entered Moshannon. It wasn't much but it was enough to cover my two hour bus ticket.

The senior customs officer returns to his office a few minutes later, telling me he has arranged for a taxi to take me to the local Greyhound bus station which he has paid for. He walks me to the front of the building before stopping me with his outstretched hand. I took his hand, and he gripped it firmly.

"Good luck," he says. I feel certain of his sincerity as he holds my hand for a moment longer than I would expect.

The time passes quickly, and before I know it, I am boarding a bus to Hamilton. I say hello to the bus driver before walking halfway down the aisle, taking a seat next to the window. Most of the seats are empty, with ten to twelve people spread throughout the front portion of the bus. With my destination being a little more than two hours away, I decide to lean my head up against the window and close my eyes. I feel a sense of calm wash over me and I begin to doze off to the purring sound of the bus's engine.

I am asleep for no more than a few minutes when I awaken to the bus pulling over and stopping to allow a man to board. The man removes his sunglasses and takes a quick look down the two rows of seats before stepping ahead to pay his fare. He is tall, at least six feet two. At first glance, I think he is in his late thirties, early forties. He is broad through the shoulders and looks very fit, as his physique is noticeable through his semi-tight hoodie. He proceeds to walk down the aisle, stopping at my seat, then sits himself down beside me.

My first thought is to say, "Seriously, there are how many seats available?" but I catch myself just before the words can escape my lips. My Spidey Sense is tingling. I want to spring up and hang from the ceiling of the bus, but I feel glued to my seat, and all I can do is sit still and act calmly while my stomach tries climbing out my throat.

"How are you doing today?" I say, with the nicest smile I can muster.

He removes his ball cap before turning to me, saying, "It's been a wonderful day, don't you think? I had been hoping to get a run in today, and everything lined up just perfectly."

He is older than I first thought, closer to fifty, but a well-aged fifty. His tanned skin helped to accentuate his strong jaw. I can now see he has a full head of brown hair. His eyes are a piercing light blue but soft around the sides, making me think there is a whole other universe inside those windows.

"I had been waiting all morning on word from the bird about the time and place I was going to be able to connect with you. Phone rings, I get confirmation, and here I am." He is looking ahead to the front of the bus while he talks to me, not making eye contact.

"Pardon?" I am stunned. No, scratch that, more like shell-shocked. My ears are ringing, and I begin to lose focus, feeling as if I am going to throw up, but then my adrenaline kicks in, and I settle into myself. He anticipates my heightened sense of awareness, shifting his head slightly to look at me through the corner of his eye as he continues to talk.

"What are you planning to do with yourself?

"Who wants to know?" I say with the least amount of resentment and hostility I can manage, surmising I am there to listen and not to ask questions.

"Daryl, this conversation can never, ever be discussed." He speaks kindly but with authority. "What's important for you to know is there is more at stake regarding what you do and how you go about doing it."

"I'm sorry, but who are you?"

"I belong to an organization of well-intentioned people who would like to help see you through to the other side."

"Right." The slight sarcastic tone in my voice and the cocking of one eyebrow did little to show I am in the market to buy what he is selling. *Someone is trying to help me out. Where was this help a year ago?*

"You're apprehensive. It's to be expected."

"Yes I am, but I assure you have my full and undivided attention."

I can see a slight grin form on his face. "What are you planning to do once you get home? I'm sure you want to see your loved ones, but you must have something else planned for yourself, besides the obvious?"

"Are you asking if I'm planning on doing something illegal? Because I'm not." I begin reviewing all the conversations I've had during the last six months at Moshannon. I never engaged with anybody in talk that was of an illicit nature. *Did my new friend David contact this man without telling me? Who all knew the day and time I was making my return to Canada? Did a friend set this up, and if so, why? Is this guy a government agent, and if so, which branch?*

"I did not seek you out to pass judgment or to tell you how foolish you were in agreeing to be a pack mule. Though I will say, there are far better ways to get attention and speak your mind without adding the unnecessary conflict and turmoil."

"Listen!" I say with a forced strength. "What I did was foolish, I know that, but how about the people in power who use these laws for their own self-serving agendas?"

No longer am I fumbling for the right words; they come out on their own volition.

He remains poised. "First, I am not your enemy. Second, I sympathize with you. Third, you are misguided."

"Misguided? Yeah, perhaps, but there is obviously something I am doing right to have gotten your attention." His reaction tells me I've struck a chord.

"Yes, there is something about you, Daryl."

"Why the interest?"

He turns and cocks his head, so he is now staring straight at me, looking like he is trying to penetrate my mind. "You have a keen sense of purpose to help people. You make leaders of others but struggle to make the quality leader you see in yourself."

"How do you assume to know who I am or what it is that drives me?"

"Everybody has a file. Mind you, some are a little thicker than others, and yours has more than enough information to give a fourth-year psychology student what they need to ascertain what your driving force is." He quickly rehashes a condensed account of my life, concluding with, "From the outside looking in, you appear to be a badass Boy Scout who stumbles his way through life. But not everybody sees you this way."

"How do you know all of this?"

"You can learn a lot from looking at a person's tax filings and debit card purchases, but your profile provides so much more, as your network of friends and associates automatically puts you under the watchful eye of your government."

Full stop.

"And where do you fall into place? With all that you know about me, I would have to say that you work for the government."

"No. We have had our eye on you longer than they have."

My mind wants to go in multiple directions but I stay on track. "What's your organization?"

"That is something I am unable to share with you today, but if we are fortunate enough to meet again, I will gladly tell you more. For now, you must listen, as our time is short. Your arrest and subsequent downfall last year did not come about simply because you made a poor decision and got caught. You had been set up to fail."

"How so?" I feel like I am in free fall.

"In 2005, you popped up from out of nowhere. Now, the authorities had known about you for years, but you weren't someone they considered important."

"Besides opening The Playground that year, what else did I do that was of any significance?"

"How can someone who appears to see through the veil not know it wasn't what you did, it was how you did it?"

I can't fathom what he is referring to, and I feel foolish for it, but then my first visit to LA twelve years earlier flashes back to me. "Just talk," Tyson had said, in wanting me to espouse my view of the world.

"Yes. Most of your marketing material referred to the uplifting of people's spirits and the igniting of the 'Revolution' from within. You surely knew you were going to get people's attention."

"Yeah, I was trying to. Are you saying I was flagged because of this?"

"You were playing with words that make some people nervous, plus you have a history of breaking rules. It wasn't clear if you were merely a charlatan interested in grabbing a slice of the pie or if you were something more dangerous."

"I wasn't interested in anybody's pie! Dangerous?!"

"You're on a mission, Daryl. Your words. You were looking to build community before moving on to tackle bigger issues."

"You said these people set me up to fail?"

"No, I did not. I said you had been set up to fail. You definitely had your detractors, people who would have happily sabotaged your efforts to bring about the type of change you wanted, but they alone would have been hard-pressed to bring you down."

"I don't follow you. How was I set up?"

"Ultimately, it was by your own doing, but you did have some help along the way."

"How?" I am starting to lose my patience.

"You went from being a person of interest to all eyes on you after the arrest of one of your past associates. The authorities believed you were a key player in an organized crime syndicate."

"You've got to be kidding me." But I knew he wasn't. It was like a flood gate had opened and the missing pieces to my puzzle began dropping into place.

"Your friend knew you were no longer involved in the business, but they didn't. You were a plausible scapegoat as you had ties to that world."

My mind rewinds through the past five years. "This makes so much sense. I am so angry."

"At whom?"

"Myself, of course."

"It was clear to most that you are who you said you were, and continuing the investigation into you was unwarranted. But someone in upper management saw things differently. They argued you were a slick operator, someone who could shut things down and hide for as long as needed. So, the investigation continued right up until you were arrested."

I now understand why Officer Shannon asked, "How do you think we found you?" the night they picked us up from the mountain. They had been watching me the entire time.

"Life isn't always what it seems, and what just happened to you doesn't define you. As for my being here with you right now, it was put into play years ago, as much by your own doing as it was ours."

"You said you can't tell me who you work with."

"For now."

"Could you have at least given me a heads-up I was being watched?"

"We never believed you to be in any danger. You had a few associates who participated in shady business dealings but nothing that involved you, so we never deemed it necessary to warn you. Regardless, we are mandated not to interfere in your affairs. My being here and talking with you is a significant risk to our organization. The conflict that arose within our circle on how to best collaborate with you was a heated debate. It was decided, contrary to my objection, that contacting you was worth the risk."

My stomach still reels, though not as badly. My memory flashes back twenty years to when I was standing at the side of the river, screaming at myself to wake up. My eyes closed tightly, and when I opened them, I was certain I would wake up sitting alone, with my head against the bus window.

But no, he was still there, still sitting calmly.

"Will they still be watching me when I return home?"

"You are still of interest. Be mindful of who you talk to as there are informants everywhere, at all levels, who make it their business to sell your secrets to others."

"Like you?" I instantly regret saying this, as I could tell my words put him off.

"No, not at all. I understand the importance of what I do. I know the end game."

"The end game?" I ask.

"That point in time when millions of stories will coalesce, our individual paths will converge to make one superhighway, leading us to a future you have been dreaming about since you were a small boy."

"What the fuck!" Nothing in my life had prepared me for this moment. "You asked me what I'm going to do. Honestly, I don't know."

"I'm trying to help you clarify what your truth is. Those who decide to live entirely in the realm of black and white find it much easier to structure and govern their lives because there is little confusion between what is right and what is wrong. Your refusal to conform and follow the direction of others is shared by countless people around the world, but those who are vocal and as charismatic as you may find themselves with their back against a wall and a cigarette in their mouth."

"Fear is powerfully effective at keeping people in the dark."

"Yes, it is," he says.

"I have allowed fear to hold me back from speaking out more in the past, yet it sounds like, according to you, I may have spoken too much. Sounds like I need to conform or face another beating."

"One thing is for certain: you tend to assume more than you should. I never implied that you spoke too much, nor have I suggested that you try to conform. What I have tried to convey to you is that not everything is the way you see it. You know this, but you still throw caution to the wind by taking risks and investing your time in things that do not serve you."

"And why should I believe you care?"

"I can't tell you what to think but I would suggest you reflect on why I would make an effort to see you."

I am still unsure as to what his motives are. He is obviously a man of importance. He has an intensity that matched many of the players I had spent time with in the past and a brilliance I have only ever encountered a few times in my life. "Because you believe me to be a good man?"

"Daryl, make a plan and execute it with precision."

"I will do my best." I say, not knowing what more there is to say.

He stands up and extends his hand for me to shake it. I take hold of it, saying, "Hopefully, the next time we meet, it will be under different circumstances."

"I hope for that as well. Daryl, think hard on why it is best not to share our conversation with anyone. If you wish to keep us safe, me, my organization, you and your loved ones, you must not breathe a word to anyone."

"I understand."

"Excellent. I trust you do."

"Can you at least give me your name?"

He pauses, then smiles. "You can call me Philo," he says as he raises himself up and asks the driver to let him off the bus. He jogs off in the direction from which we had travelled.

How many experiences have I had in my life when I called into question whether they were real or not? Had I just imagined that conversation? I reached over to touch the back of his seat where he had just been sitting to feel the warmth his body would have surely left behind; still there. I start to replay every piece of our conversation. *What am I to do with this?* He genuinely seemed concerned for me but never gave me any real directive. *Why would someone take this much interest in me?* Was he trying to steer me away from something or *to* something? Who could I tell about what happened? Who would believe me? Candace had always been my main confidant, but those days are gone. It would be wise to follow his instructions and never breathe a word of what just transpired. I sit back and wait out the final hour of my bus ride, contemplating everything he said.

CHAPTER 47

DISSOLUTION

"All men make mistakes, but a good man yields when he knows his course is wrong and repairs the evil. The only crime is pride."
— *Sophocles, Antigone*

June 15th, 2011

As I sit in my seat waiting for the plane to take off, I can feel genuine excitement bubble inside of me, the first I felt in years. I want nothing more than to see my family. The plane's engines begin to roar, and I feel the surging of an energy force I have long been without. The wheels leave the tarmac, and we are in the air. As we soar through the pillowy clouds, I finally rejoice, knowing I am going home.

The flight home is loaded with emotion: anticipation about seeing my children, the shock and awe from yesterday's conversation on the bus with Philo, and mixed feelings around wanting to save my marriage. The fact that Candace made the decision to move out two months prior to me coming home felt like an act of betrayal, but I understood why she did it. It was a culmination of so many things that went wrong, decisions I made that were in the best interest of our family but ended by blowing up in my face and causing a lot of collateral damage. I know she is relying on the counsel of others to help guide her through this period. I know deep down she still loves me. The dissolving of a twenty-year relationship did not fit my vision. I want the fairy tale for her as much as I do for myself, for us. Winning her back and regaining her trust will require a lot of work; it will take time. I can do that. *I want that!* But how do I secretly work toward the end game without involving her? I'm certain she will resist any more forays into the fantastical. *I must try.* I will devote one year to doing everything I can to make amends and make things right.

The twenty-five year goal I set prior to Mariah's birth ends in 2022. I had created a timetable based on a loosely developed plan that would unite the working class and create a world republic, but in truth, the years have been spent struggling to find my place in a dream envisioned by others. The path I have chosen will certainly continue to test me if I stay its course. If I quit, life will become easier to navigate, but I know my inaction will eat at me and will regret not going all-in. I want my wife in my life, but I don't want to give up on the dream. There is so much at stake.

My emotions continue to come in waves, feeling as if they will erupt and spill out as I fly into Vancouver, a few hours before the Stanley Cup riot started to rip through the city. *What a homecoming.* My good friend Dev picks me up from the airport. It's nice to be able to chill with a friendly face before catching the ferry home later that night.

Like countless times in the past, Candace is on the other side, waiting to drive me home, only this time I will be entering our house alone. I am anxious to see her. *Do I pick her up in my arms and give her a huge hug?* When I walk out of the terminal and see her standing there, she looks as cold and removed as the last time I saw her. My heart drops into my stomach and any courage that had been building disintegrated, leaving me to give a soft hello and an even weaker hug. I fail to be the strong man who can't be cowed by his wife's detachment.

The first couple of months back pose many challenges. I don't have the luxury to sit back and ease into daily life, because funds are limited and the bills are coming in.

I have been given a lot to think about and there are few people with whom I can share my thoughts, especially now that I have to consider who in my circle is a potential informant. Who am I to trust and how do I possibly validate everybody I know?

My home training studio is a decent size, providing me with the required space to work with multiple clients simultaneously, but my home is too far out of town to service the market I coveted. At the behest of close friends and family, I take the plunge and lease a larger space closer to town. I am surrounded by people I consider my angels, people who have attained hero status, people who were there every step of the way. My parents help me on the home front, making extra meals and assisting with the kids when I need it. The one week on, one week off arrangement sharing the kids isn't ideal but is conducive to getting my business back on track.

As I work toward opening the new studio, a few things line up that gave me a big boost, replacing more strands of the neural network that had been so badly fried. It had been a long time since I had sat in the company of men, talking honestly and laughing uncontrollably. One of my best friends is getting married, and I get to join his stag celebration, a two-night August-weekend in Whistler. We eat mushrooms and hike Blackcomb Mountain, laughing and playing as teenage boys would. Every element of this weekend provides me with the release I need, reminding me the black cat needs time and space to roam.

I return home with a renewed sense of purpose, excited to open the new training studio and reacquaint myself with the cannabis industry. Over eight years, I learned what it took to become a good grower. I took as much pride in cultivating the herb as I did in cultivating my own body. I believed my background in health and fitness combined with my years spent in the cannabis industry could one day be branded and successfully marketed.

Cannabis could be used as a vehicle to help usher in a grassroots revolution, providing me with clean-green funding and the perfect stage to stand on alongside the rest of society's misfits, lawbreakers, reformers, and legalization advocates. I reckoned I had around five years to create and perfect three cannabis strains to combine with a series of health food bars. I knew eyes were still on me, that my every move had to be executed with the utmost care. If the authorities wanted to slow me down, I had to make sure not to make it easy for them.

~

September sees the start of a new school year for the kids, affording me the time during the day to get the studio finished and research, plan, and build a health and cannabis business. I have ten years left to bring my life project to fruition, and my children are at the centre of it.

The opening of the new training studio, Core-Qi Fitness, coincided with a visit from a dear friend whom I hadn't seen since before I left for prison. She knows me. She knows I will risk a lot to move the revolution. "Nancy, what do I do? Do I bite my tongue, fearing a backlash against myself and those I love, or do I say, 'Fuck it!' and roll the dice?"

"Your friends don't want to see you going back to prison, but I support you in following your heart."

What would Philo say? Probably something smart like, "God does not play dice."

Right up until the end of 2011, I worked hard every day to re-establish both my training business and my good name. I also moved ahead with my plan to create a cannabis company based on a revolutionary brand. After months of deliberation, my neighbour Dan decides agree to build a cannabis garden. Dan applies for and receives his legal growing licence from Health Canada, and makes use of a buried shipping container that lay hidden underneath his workshop.

I had plenty of time to think about the conversation I had had with Philo. Besides the undercover officers, how many paid informants did I interact with in any given day? Who was legit, and who had been concealing a secret agenda?

I haven't wavered from believing that every person has the sovereign right to grow, eat, and smoke marijuana. Even though it is still illegal in 2011, I am not blind to the direction the industry is heading; it will be legalized soon, and those who find themselves in the right place at the right time are going to manoeuvre themselves into a position that will connect the pioneering growers with mainstream society, getting the stamp of approval from the Canadian government.

I didn't tell Dan about Philo but let him know I suspected something was up.

"My paranoid concerns are somewhat justified," I tell him. "I feel there's a push back and sense I've been targeted."

"If you have this 'sense' that eyes are watching you, maybe it's best not to have any involvement in the garden at all."

"I know my intentions, and I know the quality product we can produce." I am firm in my stance.

"*I* know your intentions, Cork, but do they? And if they do know, does it give them cause for concern, or do they let you play the game?"

I took a moment before responding, "I don't know with any certainty. If they come for me, for being involved in a small-time, Health Canada licensed operation, this far out in the countryside, we will know something is up. And if they come at me this time around, I'll come back swinging."

I am convinced the authorities have no special interest in what I am doing. Why should I give Philo room to roam through my psyche, creating doubt and increasing my paranoia? Surely the events of the past two years were down to chance and bad luck?

Philo had advised, "When the time comes for you to make your stand, you have to know what to do, and how to do it. You must plan and execute with precision."

Revolution! Revolution! Long live the revolution! My sense of pride swells, certain if there is a side to be on, it is the side I subscribed to. However, for the immediate future, speaking out needed to wait. The kids are not old enough to stand solidly on their own, to make sense of what I am doing. They would surely be battered by the storm that would come my way. They are still impressionable. Knowing the level of ignorance of people within my village, some of whom were their teachers, friends, and a relative or two. I can't take the chance of having their minds distorted by fallacies. I could not afford to be taken from them again, not at this stage of their life. *Just a little bit longer.*

CHAPTER 48

CLIMBING BACK

December 2011

T he kids are doing well in both school and their various sports. Dan and I are finding the time we need to set up the garden, and I have secured a solid footing back in the fitness-coaching market, which includes building the first stage of an obstacle course on my property. It fits naturally with what I do: not so secretly training young warriors who can aid the cause. I have always maintained, and encouraged those I work with to believe, that we train to fight so we never have to fight. When we work to master a discipline, embracing it as an art form, we become what we focus on. Your warrior spirit naturally shines through for others to see, and if approached with the right understanding, you can channel that energy in a way that signals you are a person who should be treated with all manner of respect.

I am steadily making progress, establishing a platform to reconnect me with youth who I see making the revolution happen. The paper I wrote for John Dixon's philosophy class reminds me that my children's generation will usher in the New Republic. Things are looking up.

However, I have occasional bouts of depression whenever the kids are with Candace. Not spending Christmas together as a family was just as hard as spending the previous Christmas alone in prison. Feeling down, I decide to take advice from a couple of friends who urge me to try online dating.

"Cork, you don't have to spend your days alone. Go out and have some fun. Doesn't have to be anything serious, and who knows, maybe it will make Candace reconsider her position," my good friend Dev says.

Do I want Candace to reconsider her position? She told me she doesn't love me anymore. My love for her hasn't changed but I still question whether it best we be together.

CHAPTER 49

PHILO

"Why would the gods send a warning if we can't heed it and change what's to come?"

— *George R.R. Martin*

April 23rd, 2012

L ife is moving fast! I've been dating a woman, which has caught me by surprise as much as it has everyone else around me. Work is going great and my kids are healthy and seem to be happy. I have a day to myself and decide to hike behind my place. It has been a couple of weeks since I last hiked. Staying away from "Church" never bodes well for my psyche. My fitness training is going well; I am the strongest I have felt in years, but instead of pushing hard in the gym that day, I choose to use the time to connect with nature.

I leisurely hike to the top cliff that I always make my way to, sitting on one special rock, reminiscent of the one Bob Marley would sit on in Nine Mile. Like Bob, I call my place Mt. Zion. I have a clear view of the Cowichan Valley below and the mountain on the other side, with my home sitting dead centre between the two. From this point, you can look up and down the river for kilometres, although most of the water is obscured from view as the trees quite often grow close to the shores.

Sitting quietly with my eyes closed to the sun, I hear footsteps behind me and a man clearing his throat.

As I turn my body around to see who it is, Philo greets me. "Hello, Daryl. I bet you didn't think you would be seeing me today."

My initial apprehension is short-lived, as nothing seems to surprise me anymore. I stand up to face him, extending my hand toward him for a formal greeting. "To what do I owe the pleasure?" I ask.

"You're being watched again."

"Well, I admit I may be a little slow sometimes, but you standing here beside me is proof of what you say."

"We watch you from a distance, and others watch you up close. While we have your best interests at heart, others do not."

"What do these 'others' wish to do with me?"

"Shut you down and make an example of you."

I can feel my temper begin to flare, not at Philo, but at the suggestion that someone could find me of any interest. "I'm not hurting anybody. I'm working my ass off while trying to stick to the plan."

He gives me a questioning look. "Have you done your best sticking to the plan?" waving his hand at me not to speak. "Would you consider yourself a straight arrow, avoiding temptation in all forms that hinder your progress?" He steps over to the spot I had just been sitting on and sits down himself, watching three hawks fly effortlessly in the wind currents that move up and down through the valley. "I can see why you come to this place. Rich with life."

I know of only two things I have involved myself with that others might see as an issue. "Do you speak of my new love relationship, or are you referring to my involvement with my friend's medicinal grow show?"

"I speak of both transgressions."

"Transgressions?" I feel like I've been shot in the back. "That's kind of harsh, isn't it?"

"I didn't come here to pass judgment, though you may want to consider what your friends and family think."

"Which is what?"

"You are acting brash, without due care. Enough so that you may find yourself in the same situation you were two years ago."

"You mean getting arrested again?"

"Yes."

"I tried to lay out the best course of action. I thought you said my government is no longer interested in me."

"I said, they weren't *as* interested. I told you to be wary of who you let into your inner circle, and I also told you to be smart with your choices."

"I'm not following."

"Let's take the new love you have in your life."

"What does she have to do with me being watched?"

"I can see why you decided to settle so quickly, but I wonder, don't you think you are neglecting to consider other people's feelings by taking a new woman so soon?"

"C'mon," I said abjectly. "Whose feelings?"

"Your children's, your friends, some who think you should have worked harder on making amends with your wife, or at the very least have given it ample time to have settled smoothly."

"How can you possibly know the thoughts of my friends and their expectations of me?" I don't try hiding how irritated I am.

"Daryl, I've been at this game for a long time. It is my responsibility to watch people and make sure I know as much about them as they do themselves."

"And you know all that by looking at my tax filings and tracking my credit card purchases?"

"Plus, every email, text message, and picture that you take..."

"You've hacked into my accounts?"

"I wouldn't be good at my job if I was not thorough."

"You have no right!"

"Listen!" I could see he was frustrated. "You left your front door wide open. I'm not concerned with what's in your file; it's whether you're keeping your file under lock and key. And you're not! People can easily steal and sell your information, use what they find to manipulate, incriminate, and set you up to look like a terrorist, a pedophile, whatever suits their need."

"What the hell!"

"Come on, Daryl, are you playing for keeps? Because I know they are."

"Who are *they*? Better yet, why don't you explain how you know the thoughts of those who know me? Unless you're going to the trouble of watching them too."

"No, but enough attention is given to those who create problems for you, though you don't need any help with that."

I want to defend myself but know it is pointless. "You asked me on the bus to think on why you would have gone to the trouble to seek me out, and I still don't know with any certainty. Why should I believe you are here to help me?"

"When we last met, I said I would share more details about why we took an interest in you, though I never thought it would be so soon." Philo shifts his feet out in front of him and leans back, holding himself with his arms. He takes in a long breath and slowly lets it out before he resumes talking. "We stumbled upon you by chance."

"I would think I would remember."

"You crossed paths with close associates of mine in such a manner it was thought to be non-coincidental, and yet, we are certain it was not planned. You piqued our interest. Enough to prompt a thorough background check, including a search of your family history."

"And what did you find? Why now, why the mystery?" I ask, frustrated.

"Years ago, a motion was made to give you every opportunity to join our ranks. I advised against it."

"Hmmm," I'm not impressed. "Why the concern?"

"When we first looked into you…" he says.

"Which was when?"

"Soon after the second contact, late 2000. We knew little about you, other than the conversations you had with two of our members, along with what we pulled from the database." The tightening around his eyes tells me he is thinking about what to say and how to say it. "I thought you were unpredictable. I still do. However, I softened my position after you showed you possessed the qualities you were being touted for."

"I must be dreaming."

"Which is what you have preached to others for the last fifteen years."

"To dream?"

"Dream, desire, and dedicate is one of your mantras, is it not?"

"Yes."

"You believe everyone has the power to manifest their dreams. Are you still convinced this is true?"

"Within reason. I may be more cynical now than I was. I believe every person alive is special but not equal. Some of us are born with healthy genetics, allowing for quick learning and speedy recovery. And there are the millions who are born into poverty-stricken, war-torn provinces that makes a person's ability to manifest the same dreams I can conjure less attainable."

Reminding myself of the gross inequality that permeated all facets of the global political-social system darkens my mood. I don't want to discuss philosophy, my ideals, or what others think I am supposed to be doing or not doing. "Are you going to tell me who it is I met?"

"No, I can't, but maybe, if you can accomplish one or two of your goals, you will get the opportunity one day."

"I don't understand. If I was being recommended, why the holdup?"

"There is a process to follow, with much to consider. I requested to be the lead and keep an eye on you. Only making direct contact if we deemed it appropriate."

"Which you did following my release from prison."

"We initiated contact immediately following your arrest."

"When?"

"You must recall the meeting with Michel a few weeks after your arrest."

"Michel? The guy who did the numerology, who told me that all I had to do was meditate?"

"After we heard of what you had done and where you were, the decision was made to get to you right away."

"Michel told me his visa had just expired, and when he had gone through a routine traffic stop, he was sent to the immigration centre. He was going back to France to get his paperwork in order before returning to his wife and children back in the US."

"Yes, I know the story, some of it is true, but all of it was necessary to get in touch with you. We wanted to make sure you were ok."

"But why?" I growl, frustrated at all the secrecy. I want answers! I want to be included. I want to know. "Who do you think I am?"

"You are right when you said everyone is special, but not equal. You are special to us, and in time, if all works out, you will know all. For right now, neither you nor your family or those who champion you are served by revealing everything in its entirety. I am here only to remind you of the role you can play."

"Yeah," I said hesitantly. "If I am destined to do something of importance, then surely I will wind up doing it in due time, all on my own. And if I don't, we will know the time and energy spent on me was a waste."

"That's the thing, Daryl. We don't know if we should assist you. One thing that concerns me is your lack of patience and displays of frustration."

I look away, biting my tongue and shaking my head in disagreement, but knowing what he says is true. "I don't understand. You come to me with nothing concrete. Nothing I can use."

"You have placed a target on your back, once again, walking yourself onto the firing range. What more do you need to know?"

"Firing range? Are you suggesting someone is considering using a bullet on me?"

"It may not be you who has a finger on the trigger, but you have a hold of the handle."

I look at him. The strength and vitality in his arms and legs reveal an even more impressive physique than I noticed the first time meeting him. This person is credible.

"The way you talk, what you've said, are you an Angel or a Watcher?"

"That's a fair assessment. The answer lies somewhere between truth and fallacy."

"Are you Biblical?"

"Further back." He smiles.

We sit there quietly for a couple of minutes, watching the hawks glide effortlessly on the wind currents from a few hundred feet down below the rock face, giving me the chance to digest his words. There are so many things I want to ask him, but I also want to respectfully address only the concerns he raised.

"I may have disappointed some people by getting into a relationship so soon. I understand why, but this woman is 100 percent supportive of me and my endeavours." Philo doesn't look convinced, and I don't feel compelled to try and convince him. "As for the garden, how can I be attached to something I am not directly involved with?"

"Daryl, they're coming for you."

We continue to sit without speaking while looking onto the valley below. "I have done no wrong. If people want to try and take me down, so be it. I will fight back with everything I've got."

There is disappointment in his eyes. "I think you're taking yourself down."

"And why would I wish to take myself down?" I'm half asking, not sure if I want to hear what he would say.

He looks at me inquisitively, and in that moment, I wish to be inside his mind, to know all that he knows. "What is the main theme of your story?"

"I wish to make a positive contribution, leaving this place in better shape than when I first got here."

"Then do it."

"Do what exactly?"

"Your aptitude to pull people in as easily as you do, coupled with your desire to effect massive social change, has marked you."

"And this all started after they began their investigation on me in 2006?"

"Within months of them starting their investigation they were able to piece together the underlying motive behind your business."

"I have no underlying motive other than to connect with my community and help people be the best versions of themselves."

"You don't believe that to be true, and from their perspective, with you being indicted as a key player in a network that connects to prominent people with a lot of influence…"

"This movie keeps getting better."

"And better yet still, you were labelled a PDT."

"What's a PDT?" I ask.

"A potential domestic terrorist."

I'm stunned, and Philo knows it.

"Your actions and conversations make people nervous. If given the chance, will you disrupt the status quo?"

"It has never been my wish to disrupt, only to encourage."

"Do you think your government will sit idly by as promoters of dissent and rebellion run free? It's better to nip something in the bud before it gets the chance to flower." He looks at me intently, helping me acknowledge the truth in what he is saying.

"I'm nothing close to being a terrorist. They must see this."

"As I said, in *their* book, you're merely a potential. Like me, those who get to know you over time eventually see you for who you are. They know your intentions are noble, but you are still a concern."

"Enough to go after me for a small marijuana garden?"

"You cannot be afforded any space to foment public opinion. It's best to keep you side-tracked and off-balance, something you don't have a problem taking care of on your own. You make this far too easy for them."

"What am I to do? I have children. They never asked for any of this. I can't…"

Philo cut in. "Instead of coming out carte blanche, you stall on the sidelines thinking yourself cloaked and hidden, never fully engaged, always waiting. You do everything you can to avoid the spotlight, yet you get it anyways, but for all the wrong reasons. Like it or not, your children cannot be sheltered from what you are. You are robbing them by holding back."

"Holding back from what? Spell it out for me."

"How long do you think you can continue denying expression in its purest form? When are you going to step in? What battles are worth fighting, win or lose?"

"How about someone from your organization steps out from the shadows and calls into question what you see wrong with the world?" I asked with obvious annoyance.

"We already risk much. To step out fully would be suicide. But we can help others, such as yourself. We would like to see you seize upon your birthright."

"You say birthright like it matters."

"It matters to me. It matters to many others. But it matters not unless you believe it does."

"Tell me what to do, and I'll do it."

"It doesn't work like that. You must choose." He sweeps his hand out in front of him, pointing from east to west. "All of this is yours, and the answers you seek are right there in front of you."

I am aware of how relaxed he is. He seems to be genuinely concerned. "I'll figure this out," I say, as he rises to his feet.

"Make a believer of me, Corky." His use of my nickname was a first, piquing my curiosity as to why he used it instead of Daryl. He turns and begins walking back the way he came, leaving me standing there by myself.

I remained on Zion, sitting back on my meditation rock to contemplate what lay before me. The tension I have been working to release since leaving prison ten months earlier is building back up on my shoulders. *Have I been down this road before?* My arrest in 2010 had been a wake-up call, making me realize my ability to push hard was hindering me as much as it was helping. Philo is making me reassess how I am using my time. Should I end my relationship with my new girlfriend? Should I walk away from growing weed once and for all? As I hike down the mountain, I feel justified in my belief that I am doing no wrong. I would continue as I was.

CHAPTER 50

EVERY MACHINE HAS
A CONTROL PANEL

"As long as the general population is passive, apathetic, and diverted to consumerism or hatred of the vulnerable, then the powerful can do as they please, and those who survive will be left to contemplate the outcome."

— Noam Chomsky, Who Rules the World?

May — June, 2012

I am paid a visit by a friend who wants to let me know they had been given some unsettling news. His trusted source says the Green Team, the police unit responsible for taking down illegal grow operations, is watching me. I tell him I already know.

"I appreciate your concern, but I'm hands-off. It would be a far reach for the authorities to try and tie me to anything."

"Ok, Cork, this is legit. Sounds pretty serious."

A few days later, another friend stops by the training studio to tell me I am under surveillance. Three different sources came to me within three weeks of each other to let me know I am being watched. I should feel grateful I am receiving confidential information, but it only makes me angry. I let my friend know I heard the same report a few days earlier and will be sticking to my guns.

"Corky!" she protested. "I'm worried about you."

"I do appreciate your concern, but this is now a matter of principle. Here are some facts: my neighbour applied for a marijuana licence from Health Canada and was approved. I helped build his grow room and agreed to supply electric power to his shop. I'm not trying to hide anything because I'm not doing anything that should matter to anybody. If the RCMP come knocking at my door, then we will know for sure someone has it in for me."

I am defiant, perceiving an old paradigm as relevant in my new world. *Why am I looking to martyr myself?* Martyr for what? For cannabis legalization or world revolution? Where is my energy best directed?

I hiked back to Zion to take my place on the meditation rock. Would Philo show his face once more to lend his support? No, I don't think I'll be seeing him again for a while. I made clear my intentions. Bring it on, G, bring it on.

June 27th, 2012

Most Wednesday mornings, I work. I'm normally out of the house by 5:15 am, but I am sleeping in today, as I had switched this morning's class to Thursday morning so I could accompany Drédyn on a school field trip. I hear my dog Jackie barking and look out the bedroom window. There are close to twenty RCMP officers making a perimeter around the house.

The doorbell rings, and I quickly put on my clothes to go greet them. As I make my way to the front door to unlock it, the officer standing there motions me to turn around and head to the back door, where another three officers are waiting. I thought I was ready for this. Some low blows are coming my way, and I'll be made to pay a heavy price.

EPILOGUE

My apologies if you feel I have left you hanging, but I do have my reasons as to why I ended the book where I did. I had mentioned that on the day of my thirtieth birthday, I prayed to God ~ Universe to give me every experience, no matter how challenging, that would provide me with the necessary tools to achieve my end goal. You read what followed from 2002 until 2012. The ten years since has been filled with just as many adventures, trials, and tribulations; some people wanted to see me fail and others continued to light my way. I received what I asked for, although I gave up so much in the process, details of which I plan to share in my follow-up book, *Coming Clean*.

You may have worked out that the title of this book, *Dark Water Fountain*, was derived from both my mother's and father's surnames, Douglas-Fontana, and comprises the first forty years of my life. It's worth mentioning I cut more than three hundred pages, omitting side stories and mentions of valued friendships in order to follow a template that will help me reach the largest audience possible.

Agreeing to mule cannabis across the border, although stupid, is not what I regret the most. I was operating from a place in which a dark cloud had descended upon me, and my ability to think rationally had left the building. Was I set up? As of this day of writing, I cannot tell you with certainty, though it is a likely possibility.

Jumping into a relationship so soon after separating from my wife was a decision that haunted me for years, a decision that likely fanned the flames of someone who was upset with me, bringing the RCMP to my doorstep when they might have otherwise stayed clear. I should have heeded the warnings that I was under investigation again, but I could not believe the RCMP would go to the lengths they did for something I considered trivial. The repercussions included the Ministry of Children and Family Development (MCFD) —trying to take my children from me, a move orchestrated to make me hurt, and one that drove an even bigger wedge between Candace and I. The fallout from this recent arrest caused more upheaval than I thought possible, dramatically altering the path I had laid out for myself and binding me to people I would have otherwise cut from my life.

I would certainly take a few things back if I could, but I can't. Instead, I remain grateful for the lessons learned, the opportunities, and the experience I gained from veering off the path I had mapped out.

Having said that, what seemed at the time like a veering may well have been what was needed to get me to where I wanted to go. I had been blown off course and needed to readjust my sails, believing that when the time came for me to make my last tack, it would be swift and in line with the control panel.

I would like to tell you with complete confidence that the dream I have nurtured since I was a child will manifest in its entirety, but one thing life has taught me is how far from being infallible I am.

— *Dream, Desire, and Dedicate for Life*

ACKNOWLEDGMENTS

I wish to give thanks to my friends and family who remained steadfast by my side when people living in glass houses were throwing rocks; I never would have made it without your support. You were the glue that held me together when I felt like I was breaking apart.

Paying homage to the pioneers, warriors, rockstars and heroes who lit my path is a must, as these icons had the greatest impact on my worldly outlook, for which I will be forever grateful.

Kahlil Gibran, Eleanor Roosevelt, Albert Einstein, Hannah Arendt, Aldous Huxley, John and Robert Kennedy, Martin Luther King Jr., Muhammad Ali, Doris Lessing, Frank Herbert, Stanley Kubrick, Bob Marley, Roger Waters, and so many bright and questing minds that space does not allow me to list.

This story would never have come to fruition without the pillars to which this book sits upon:

My mother planted the seeds; sharing her love of history, science, and esoteric knowledge, opening my mind to a conscious Universe that is engineered through imagination.

My father knew what he meant to me, but I don't think he knew how much I was going to hurt after he passed away. Not being there by his side is one of the few regrets I have, but in an odd way, that guilt helped spurn me to make a stand and start the book.

I was blessed to have spent twenty years with my best friend and the mother to my children. Candace provided me with fertile ground for those seeds to root and spread out, supporting me, always, as I pursued my dreams.

It was no accident that the arrival of Mariah, my first born, coincided with my awakening. Her birth and the births of her two younger brothers, Kahlil and Drédyn, brought a tidal wave of clarity, feeding the roots, and inspiring me to become the best version of myself. There has been no joy greater than the joy I've experienced being your father.

What I grew into was robust but largely unkempt. A huge amount of gratitude and thanks goes to Laura, my editor, for extending her patience while we painfully cut large segments of the story. Our worldly chats while hiking and discussions over coffee at the Garage helped to flesh out and make clear what I was driving towards. Memories I will forever cherish.

— *Daryl Fontana*

Manufactured by Amazon.ca
Bolton, ON

26114505R00180